Moodle 1.9 for Teaching Special Education Children (5-10 Year Olds)
Beginner's Guide

Create courses and therapies for children with special educational needs using Moodle for effective e-learning

Vanesa S. Olsen

BIRMINGHAM - MUMBAI

Moodle 1.9 for Teaching Special Education Children (5-10 Year Olds)
Beginner's Guide

First published: July 2010

Production Reference: 1020710

Published by Packt Publishing Ltd.
32 Lincoln Road
Olton
Birmingham, B27 6PA, UK.

ISBN 978-1-849510-94-3

www.packtpub.com

Cover Image by Vinayak Chittar (vinayak.chittar@gmail.com)

Credits

Author
Vanesa S. Olsen

Reviewer
Mary Cooch

Acquisition Editor
Sarah Cullington

Development Editor
Mehul Shetty

Technical Editor
Aaron Rosario

Indexer
Hemangini Bari

Editorial Team Leader
Akshara Aware

Project Team Leader
Priya Mukherji

Project Coordinator
Zainab Bagasrawala

Proofreader
Chris Smith

Production Coordinator
Melwyn D'sa

Cover Work
Melwyn D'sa

About the Author

Vanesa S. Olsen is a Speech Therapist. She has been working for more than five years at therapeutic centers, schools, and hospitals. She has been applying modern technologies in treatments for language disorders and learning disabilities, and in helping schools to keep their students in the least restrictive environment. Specifically, she has been working with Moodle as an e-Learning platform, Alice, and other tools, combined with the use of Web 2.0 and general-purpose modern hardware such as gamepads, pen sketches, touch screens, netbooks, and joysticks. She enjoys helping children and teenagers to improve their skills.

She lives with her husband, Gaston, and their little son Kevin. When she is not working, she devotes her time to her family and hobbies. She enjoys modeling in cold porcelain, swimming, and researching new technologies and techniques to apply in her treatments.

You can contact her at vanesaolsen@gmail.com and at olsenvanesa@live.com.

Acknowledgement

While writing this book, I was fortunate enough to work with an excellent team at Packt Publishing Ltd, whose contributions vastly improved the presentation of this book. Sarah Cullington helped me to transform the idea in the final book and to shape this Beginner's Guide. Zainab Bagasrawala helped me to follow an organized schedule. Mehul Shetty provided many sensible suggestions regarding the text, the format, and the flow. The reader will notice his great work. Aaron Rosario made sure that all the exercises were accurate and added great value to the final drafts.

I would like to thank my reviewer, Mary Cooch (`http://www.moodleblog.org`), for her thorough reviews and insightful comments. I was able to incorporate some of the knowledge and wisdom she has gained in her many years of experience with Moodle, Hot Potatoes, and Virtual Learning Environments. The exercises and the pictures include Mary's great feedback.

Special thanks go to my husband, Gaston Hillar, who a few years ago, suggested that I use new technologies in therapeutic environments, and motivated me to work on this new project. Moreover, I would like to thank my sister-in-law, Silvina Hillar, who also helped with her teaching expertise; my son Kevin and my nephew Nicolas, who enrich my life with their affection; my friends, and my father-in-law.

About the Reviewer

Mary Cooch (known online as the **Moodlefairy**) is a teacher, VLE trainer specializing in Moodle, and the author of Packt's *Moodle 1.9 For Teaching 7-14 Year Olds* and *Moodle 2.0 First Look*. She is based at Our Lady's Catholic High School, Preston Lancashire, UK and can be contacted for training and consultancy on mco@olchs.lancs.sch.uk.

To my family at home, and to Mark at school; thanks for your support.

I would like to dedicate this book to my son Kevin

Table of Contents

Preface

This book will help the reader to build interactive and rich online content oriented towards the needs of Special Education Children using different techniques and open source tools. It teaches you how to create exercises as if you were playing with children at the school, the zoo, the beach, the supermarket, a birthday party, an aquarium, a farm, a shopping center, a circus, and at home. You will be able to work with drawings, music, sounds, videos, photographs, and text, and you will combine all these pieces into memorable experiences for children that need to find extra motivation in order to improve their learning skills.

Besides, it will teach you how to take advantage of general purpose, non-expensive hardware such as gamepads, joysticks, digital pens, multi-touch screens, netbooks, and touchpads. The usage of some of these hardware devices combined with visually rich activities usually offers children extra motivation to focus on solving the exercises.

What this book covers

Chapter 1, *Matching Pictures*—In this chapter, we create rich activities with 2D and 3D clipart using Inkscape to manipulate many different picture formats. We use JMatch and JQuiz to create visual exercises and then upload and run them in the Moodle server. We also take advantage of free 2D clipart, 3D models, and comic strip generation tools, as well as work with general-purpose hardware, in order to create activities that are even more engaging for children with special education needs.

Chapter 2, *Working with Abstraction and Sequencing Disabilities*—In this chapter, we create many visually rich activities combining text and pictures. We use JCloze, an upload a single file activity, and Moodle's Quiz to create visual exercises that can provide further motivation for children with special education needs.

Chapter 3, *Associating Images with Words*—In this chapter, we create many visually rich activities combining images, sounds, scenes, layers, elements, words, and pictures. We will work with many web pages that offer images and sounds, interactive assignments, and Inkscape, in order to create attractive exercises in Moodle.

Chapter 4, *Developing Sorting Activities, Mixing Shapes and Pictures*—In this chapter, we develop many visually rich sorting activities that involve combining geometric shapes with pictures and text. We take advantage of JMix's capabilities to work with HTML code in order to add pictures that can be dragged and dropped by the student. We also work with many applications to create pictures that represent a jumbled temporal sequence.

Chapter 5, *Creating Exercises for Improving Short-term Memory*—In this chapter, we create many visually rich activities that combine animations, effects, text, pictures, and sounds. We work with many tools to create realistic activities that can improve the student's short-term memory management.

Chapter 6, *Reducing Attention Deficit Disorder Using Great Concentration Exercises*—In this chapter, we create visually rich puzzles that combine digital photos, virtual pieces, letters, and words. We create a jigsaw and a word search puzzle, and work with many tools to create realistic activities that can reduce the student's Attention Deficit Disorder and improve their long-term memory management.

Chapter 7, *Playing with Mathematical Operations*—In this chapter, we play with mathematics that combine scenes with pictures of animals, images of apples, and symbols, allowing students to practice simple mathematical operations by working with visually rich activities.

Chapter 8, *Mental Operations with Language*—In this chapter, we create a visual exercise by using different images, allowing students to arrange them according to a particular sequence. This way, students can perform mental operations by working with visually rich activities.

Chapter 9, *Writing Guided Sentences and Paragraphs*—In this chapter, we prepare exercises to motivate children to write guided sentences and paragraphs. We create a list of words related to a scene and combine it with questions to motivate the students to describe spatial relationships. We also discuss the use of Audacity and NanoGong assignments to allow students to record their voice with the answers and to upload an audio file with their sentences.

Chapter 10, *Running Cognitive Evaluation Tests*—In this chapter, we prepare exercises that test the students comprehension of simple and complex instructions, evaluating many simple cognitive aspects. We create a simple activity with instructions that contain text and pictures, test the possibilities offered by a webcam in such exercises, create questionnaires related to simple everyday situations, and add audio resources to allow students to hear each question and record their answers.

What you need for this book

Some of the important prerequisites for the exercises mentioned in this book are as follows:

- ◆ Moodle 1.9.x (Moodle 1.9.5 or later, not Moodle 2.0)
- ◆ Microsoft Word
- ◆ Inkscape 0.47
- ◆ JClic for Moodle
- ◆ GIMP
- ◆ Edraw Max 5.1
- ◆ Wondershare PPT to Video 6

Who this book is for

If you are an SEN teacher or SEN therapist with minimal knowledge of Moodle who is willing to exploit Web 2.0 possibilities using Moodle 1.9 as the background platform, this is the book for you.

Conventions

In this book, you will find several headings appearing frequently.

To give clear instructions of how to complete a procedure or task, we use:

Time for action – heading

1. Action 1
2. Action 2
3. Action 3

Instructions often need some extra explanation so that they make sense, so they are followed with:

What just happened?

This heading explains the working of tasks or instructions that you have just completed.

You will also find some other learning aids in the book, including:

Pop quiz – heading

These are short multiple choice questions intended to help you test your own understanding.

Have a go hero – heading

These set practical challenges and give you ideas for experimenting with what you have learned.

You will also find a number of styles of text that distinguish between different kinds of information. Here are some examples of these styles, and an explanation of their meaning.

Code in text are shown as follows: "We can include other contexts through the use of the `include` directive."

A block of code is set as follows:

```
<h2 style="color:blue">
<em>There is a big blackboard and a big eraser</em>
</h2>
```

When we wish to draw your attention to a particular part of a code block, the relevant lines or items are set in bold:

```
<h2 style="color:blue">
<em>There is a big blackboard and a big eraser</em>
</h2>
```

New terms and **important words** are shown in bold. Words that you see on the screen, in menus or dialog boxes for example, appear in the text like this: "clicking on the **Next** button moves you to the next screen".

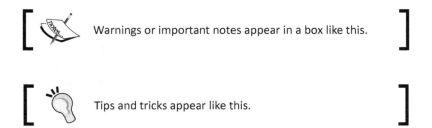

Warnings or important notes appear in a box like this.

Tips and tricks appear like this.

Reader feedback

Feedback from our readers is always welcome. Let us know what you think about this book—what you liked or may have disliked. Reader feedback is important for us to develop titles that you really get the most out of.

To send us general feedback, simply send an e-mail to feedback@packtpub.com, and mention the book title via the subject of your message.

If there is a book that you need and would like to see us publish, please send us a note in the **SUGGEST A TITLE** form on www.packtpub.com or e-mail suggest@packtpub.com.

If there is a topic that you have expertise in and you are interested in either writing or contributing to a book, see our author guide on www.packtpub.com/authors.

Customer support

Now that you are the proud owner of a Packt book, we have a number of things to help you to get the most from your purchase.

Downloading the example code for the book

You can download the example code files for all Packt books you have purchased from your account at http://www.PacktPub.com. If you purchased this book elsewhere, you can visit http://www.PacktPub.com/support and register to have the files e-mailed directly to you.

Errata

Although we have taken every care to ensure the accuracy of our content, mistakes do happen. If you find a mistake in one of our books—maybe a mistake in the text or the code—we would be grateful if you would report this to us. By doing so, you can save other readers from frustration and help us improve subsequent versions of this book. If you find any errata, please report them by visiting http://www.packtpub.com/support, selecting your book, clicking on the **let us know** link, and entering the details of your errata. Once your errata are verified, your submission will be accepted and the errata will be uploaded on our website, or added to any list of existing errata, under the Errata section of that title. Any existing errata can be viewed by selecting your title from http://www.packtpub.com/support.

Piracy

Piracy of copyright material on the Internet is an ongoing problem across all media. At Packt, we take the protection of our copyright and licenses very seriously. If you come across any illegal copies of our works, in any form, on the Internet, please provide us with the location address or website name immediately so that we can pursue a remedy.

Please contact us at copyright@packtpub.com with a link to the suspected pirated material.

We appreciate your help in protecting our authors, and our ability to bring you valuable content.

Questions

You can contact us at questions@packtpub.com if you are having a problem with any aspect of the book, and we will do our best to address it.

1
Matching Pictures

When we create exercises for e-Learning platforms, the main focus is to present well-organized information for the students. However, children with special education needs require unique activities. They like computers and they usually enjoy visually rich and interactive activities because they allow them to focus on solving simple or complex exercises. Graphics, videos, sounds and toy-like hardware are their best friends when they need to improve their skills. It is necessary to combine multimedia resources with funny environments to allow them to enjoy their homework. They don't need boring exercises. Luckily, Moodle is an open e-Learning platform that is indeed useful to support the implementation of the most exciting activities for children with special education needs.

We can combine Moodle, Web 2.0 tools, commercial and free software, and general purpose hardware devices to develop rich and interactive activities with pictures for children with **special education needs**.

In this chapter, Alice, a seven year old girl, goes to school. We will learn how to create activities related to her journey. By reading it and following the exercises we shall:

- ◆ Learn to create composite pictures
- ◆ Create activities to match composite pictures with sentences
- ◆ Search and organize 3D models to create a 3D scene
- ◆ Work with colors to define skill levels
- ◆ Create rich exercises to stimulate both the attention and the concentration
- ◆ Learn to take advantage of a gamepad and a digital pen to create funny exercises
- ◆ Add, run, and evaluate different kinds of rich and interactive activities

Matching composite pictures

It was a very nice day. The sun was shining in the sky and the birds flew happily.

The school playground was full of children ready to begin their first day in school. Alice was among them.

The bell rang. Everyone had to go to class. All the children sat down and opened their schoolbags. Alice saw a lot of interesting things in the classroom. Shall we help her sort them out?

Time for action – installing tools to manipulate 2D scalable clipart

We must first download and install some additional tools that will help us in searching, editing, combining, and converting 2D scalable clipart to the most appropriate file formats to use in Moodle and its related applications:

 The necessary tools will depend on the original 2D scalable clipart. However, we will be using some tools that will work fine with our examples.

1. Download the following files:

Application's name	Download link	File name	Description
Inkscape	`http://inkscape.org/download/?lang=en`	`Inkscape-0.47win32.exe`	This is a very complete free, open source, vector drawing program. This tool will enable us to import many vector assets in different popular file formats and export them to a format recognized by Moodle and Hot Potatoes.
Microsoft Office Home and Student 2007	`http://www.microsoft.com/office/trial/default.aspx`	`X12-30107.exe`	This is a commercial tool, but the trial offers a free fully functional version for 60 days. Microsoft Word 2007 will enable us to search vector assets in **Office Online Clip Art & Media**.

2. Run the installers and follow the steps to complete the installation wizards.

3. Once Inkscape's installation is completed, you will be able to load and edit many vector assets in different file formats, as shown in the following screenshot:

4. Once Office 2007 installation is completed, you will be able to use the powerful clipart search capabilities offered by Word 2007, as shown in the next screenshot:

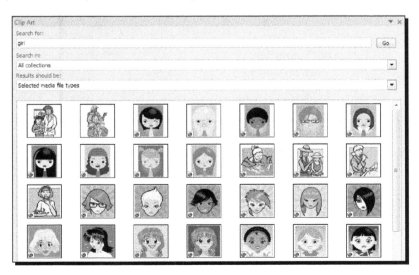

What just happened?

We installed Inkscape and Microsoft Office 2007. We now have the necessary tools to combine, edit, and convert scalable 2D clipart found in **Office Online Clip Art & Media** and export it to a format recognized by Moodle and Hot Potatoes.

Time for action – searching for 2D scalable clipart to combine inside a box

The creation of scalable vector graphics assets for a matching composite pictures exercise is very complex and involves professional skills. We are going to simplify this process by using existing clipart.

1. Create a new folder in Windows Explorer (`C:\School`).

2. Start Inkscape and minimize it. You will use it later.

3. Start Word 2007. You will be working in a new blank document.

4. Click on **Insert | Clip Art**. The **Clip Art** panel will appear on the right-hand side of the main window.

5. Click on the **Search in** combo box and activate the **Everywhere** checkbox. This way, Word will search for clipart in all the available collections, including the **Web Collections** as shown in the following screenshot:

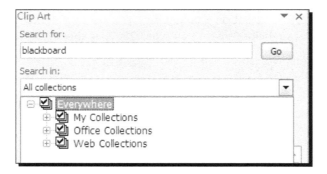

6. Click on the **Search for** text box and enter `blackboard`.

7. Click on the **Go** button. Word will begin downloading and displaying clipart related to the blackboard keyword, as shown in the next screenshot:

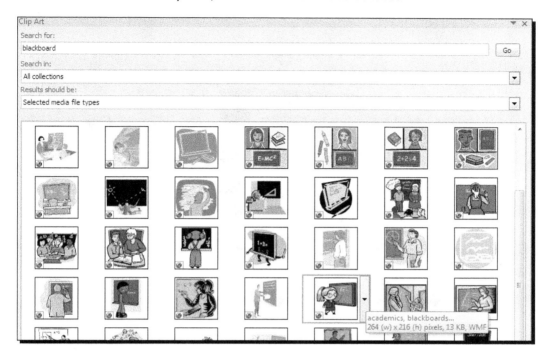

8. Position the mouse pointer over the desired clipart's thumbnail. Since you want to change the picture size without losing quality using Inkscape, make sure it is a **WMF (Windows Meta-File)** or an **EMF (Enhanced Meta-File)** file. Word displays the file format on the right-hand side of the tooltip that appears when you move the mouse pointer over each picture's thumbnail.

WMF is an old scalable vector format. Neither Moodle nor Hot Potatoes offer direct support to WMF graphics. However, using the next steps, we can also combine any vector formats supported by Inkscape, such as SVG (Scalable Vector Graphics), AI (Adobe Illustrator), PDF (Adobe PDF), and EMF (Enhanced Meta-File), among others.

9. Right-click on the desired clipart's thumbnail and select **Preview/Properties** in the context menu that appears. Word will display a new dialog box showing a larger preview of the scalable clipart and a temporary file name, as shown in the next screenshot:

10. Triple-click on the long path and file name shown after **File**. This way, you will be sure that the temporary file's full path is selected. Then, right-click on it and select **Copy** in the context menu that appears.

11. Next activate Inkscape—remember that it was running minimized. You can use *Alt + Tab* or *Windows + Tab*. Don't close the clipart's preview window.

12. Select **File | Import** from the main menu. Click on the **Type a file name button** (the pencil with a paper sheet icon) and paste the previously copied temporary file's full path in the **Location** text box. The path is going to be similar to `C:\Users\Username\AppData\Local\Microsoft\Windows\Temporary Internet Files\Content.IE5\171CJBOC\MCj03491330000[1].wmf`, as shown in the next screenshot:

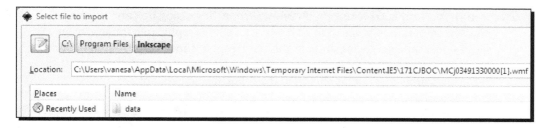

13. Click on the **Open** button. The previously previewed clipart will appear in Inkscape's drawing area, as shown in the following screenshot:

14. Return to Word 2007, close the **Preview/Properties** dialog box and repeat the aforementioned steps (6 to 13) for each vector graphic to combine inside a box—Inkscape's drawing area. In this case, repeat those steps searching for an `eraser`. Now, two scalable clipart items will appear with different sizes in Inkscape's drawing area, as shown in the following screenshot:

15. Select **File | Save** from Inkscape's main menu. Save the file as `image010101.svg` in the previously created folder, `C:\School`.

16. Now, repeat the aforementioned steps (6 to 14) to create a new drawing composed of two vector graphics, a `case` and `scissors`. Two new scalable clipart items will appear with different sizes in Inkscape's drawing area, as shown in the next screenshot:

17. Select **File | Save** from Inkscape's main menu. Save the file as `image010102.svg` in the previously created folder, `C:\School`.

What just happened?

We combined two pairs of 2D scalable clipart items in Inkscape's drawing areas. We searched for vector assets in **Office Online Clip Art & Media** and we imported the temporary files created by Word into Inkscape's drawing area.

We now have the following two boxes:

◆ `image010101.svg`: A blackboard and an eraser

◆ `image010102.svg`: A case and a pair of scissors

The exercise will look nice using these vector digital art assets.

> We used a naming convention for the pictures, as we want to keep everything well organized for our exercises. `image010101` means image for chapter 01; exercise 01; picture number 01.

Time for action – combining pictures with different sizes

We are now going to manipulate, resize, and save the new versions of the combined pictures for the exercise using Inkscape.

1. Open the vector graphic file in Inkscape (`C:\School\image010101.svg`).

2. Click on the blackboard picture to select it. Eight double-headed arrows will appear in a rectangle around the selection, as shown in the following image:

3. Drag-and-drop one of the diagonal double-headed arrows and scale the image both in the horizontal (X) and vertical (Y) directions. You can do it holding the *Ctrl* key down in order to maintain the original aspect ratio.

4. Next, click on the eraser picture to select it and enlarge it to match the blackboard's size.

5. Drag-and-drop the eraser to move it below the blackboard, as shown in the next screenshot:

6. Select **File | Save**, to save the changes made to the original Inkscape SVG file.

7. Select **File | Export Bitmap**. A dialog box showing many export options will appear. Enter 30 on the first dpi (Dots Per Inch) textbox.

8. Click on the **Drawing** button, and then on **Export**. Inkscape will export the drawing in **PNG** (Portable Network Graphics) format. The exported **bitmap graphics** with a big blackboard and a big eraser will be saved in C:\School\image010101.png.

9. Next, open the other vector graphic file in Inkscape (C:\School\image010102. svg).

10. Repeat the aforementioned steps (2 to 7) to export a new bitmap graphic with a big case and a pair of big scissors, as shown in the next screenshot. The exported bitmap graphic will be C:\School\image010102.png.

11. Click on the case picture to select it and shrink it.

12. Click on the scissors picture to select it and shrink it to match the new smaller case's size.

13. Drag-and-drop the scissors to move them below the case, as shown in the next screenshot:

14. Select **File | Save As**, to save the new manipulated vector graphic with a new name. Enter `image010103` as the new name and click on the **Save** button.

15. Select **File | Export Bitmap**. A dialog box showing many export options will appear. Click on the **Drawing** button, and then on **Export**. Inkscape will export the edited drawing in **PNG** format. The exported **bitmap graphics** file with a small case and a pair of small scissors will be `C:\School\image010103.png`.

16. Next open the previously manipulated vector graphic file in Inkscape (`C:\School\image010101.svg`).

17. Repeat the aforementioned steps (11 to 15) to edit the vector graphic and export a new bitmap with a small blackboard and a small eraser, as shown in the next image. Use `image010104` as the new Inkscape file. Thus, the new exported bitmap graphic will be `C:\School\image010104.png`.

What just happened?

We edited the two pairs of 2D scalable clipart pictures using Inkscape. As we had used vector graphics to create the drawings, we could change their size without losing quality and we exported the resulting images to the PNG format.

 PNG is an open, extensible image format with **lossless compression**. Both Moodle and Hot Potatoes work great with PNG images. We didn't use the **JPEG** (Joint Photographic Experts Group) format for these graphics, because it uses a **lossy compression** method, which removes some information from the image. As the exported images are small in size, we can use the PNG format.

We now have the following four bitmap graphics ready to be used in our matching composite pictures exercise:

- `image010101.png`: A big blackboard and a big eraser
- `image010102.png`: A big case and a pair of big scissors
- `image010103.png`: A small case and a pair of small scissors
- `image010104.png`: A small blackboard and a small eraser

Time for action – preparing texts using colors and fonts

First, we must download and install **Hot Potatoes** 6.3. Next, we will prepare the sentences for our matching composite pictures exercise.

1. If you do not have it yet, download and install Hot Potatoes 6.3 (`http://hotpot.uvic.ca/#downloads`).

2. Start Hot Potatoes and click on **JMatch**. A new window with the JMatch application will appear.

3. Enter `Matching composite pictures` in the **Title** textbox.

4. Click on the corresponding **Right (jumbled) items** textbox and enter the text shown in the next table for each row, as seen in the next screenshot:

Row number	Text to enter in the Right (jumbled) items textbox

1	`<h2 style="color:blue">`
	`<em>There is a big blackboard and a big eraser</em>`
	`</h2>`

2	`<h2 style="color:blue">`
	`<em>There is a big case and a pair of big scissors</em>`
	`</h2>`

3	`<h2 style="color:green">`
	`<em>There is a small case and a pair of small scissors</em>`
	`</h2>`

4	`<h2 style="color:green">`
	`<em>There is a small blackboard and a small eraser</em>`
	`</h2>`

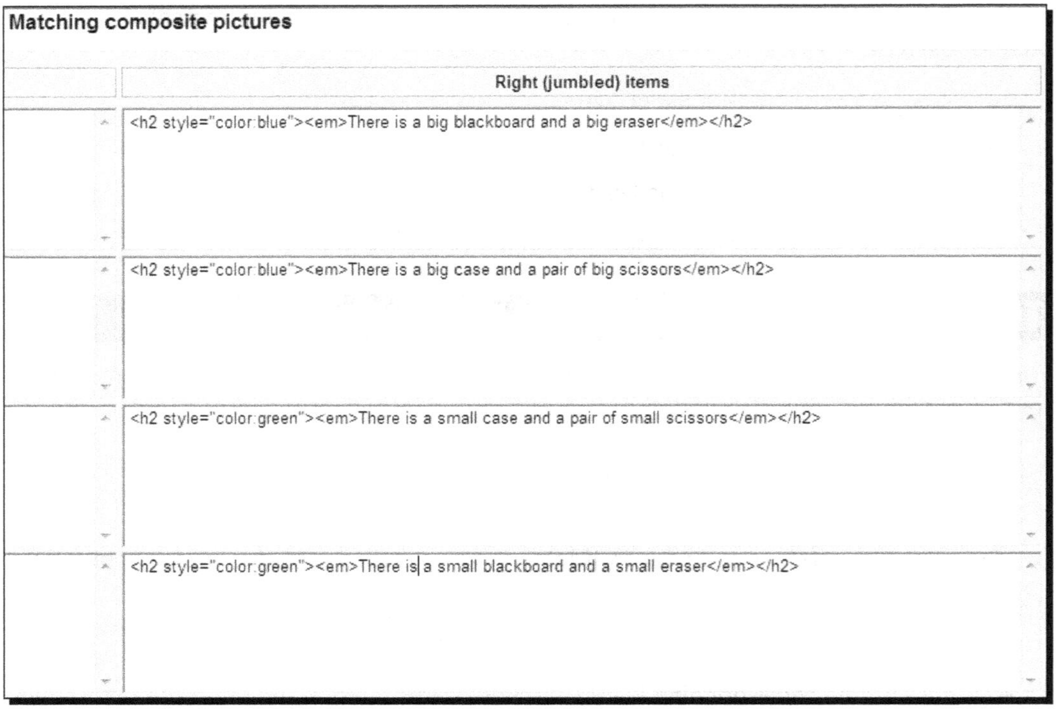

Matching composite pictures

	Right (jumbled) items
	`<h2 style="color:blue"><em>There is a big blackboard and a big eraser</em></h2>`
	`<h2 style="color:blue"><em>There is a big case and a pair of big scissors</em></h2>`
	`<h2 style="color:green"><em>There is a small case and a pair of small scissors</em></h2>`
	`<h2 style="color:green"><em>There is a small blackboard and a small eraser</em></h2>`

5. Select **File | Save** from JMatch's main menu. Save the file as `matching0101.jmt` in the previously created folder, `C:\School`.

6. Next select **File | Create Web Page | Drag/Drop Format**. JMatch will create a new web page. Save the new file as `matching0101.html` in the aforementioned folder.

7. A new dialog box will appear. Click on **View the exercise in my browser**. You want to preview the previously entered text with colors and fonts on the screen.

8. The default web browser will appear showing the matching exercise with a drag/drop format. You will be able to see the four sentences with a big font. Two of them are in blue (the ones talking about big things) and the other two are in green (the ones talking about small things), as shown in the next screenshot:

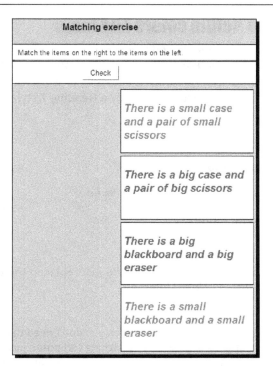

What just happened?

We installed Hot Potatoes 6 and we prepared the sentences for our matching composite pictures exercise, using a drag-and-drop format.

We used JMatch to edit and preview the following four sentences as items on the right-hand side:

- There is a big blackboard and a big eraser
- There is a big case and a pair of big scissors
- There is a small case and a pair of small scissors
- There is a small blackboard and a small eraser

Using HTML tags to define colors and fonts

We didn't want to use the default fonts and colors. We added **HTML code** to specify different colors for the aforementioned sentences. JMatch doesn't offer a simple way to select fonts and colors for the sentences. However, it allows us to work with standard HTML **tags**. Therefore, we used the following header to specify a Heading 2 style with a blue color and emphasized text:

```
<h2 style="color:blue"><em>
```

Next, we entered the plain text for the sentence:

```
There is a big blackboard and a big eraser
```

Finally, we used the following footers:

```
</em></h2>
```

We used the same tags for the other sentences. We just replaced the `color:blue` code by `color:green` in the sentences colored in green.

 HTML tags are a bit complex. However, you don't need to master the HTML standard in order to create a nice matching composite pictures exercise. You can replace the color name with other pure colors such as `red`, `black`, or `white`.

Working with red, green, and blue components to define customized colors

If we need other colors, we can use a dynamic HTML color-code chart or an HTML color picker, such as the ones offered by the **HTML Color Codes** website, `http://html-color-codes.info`.

We can click on one of the color boxes in the chart and the site will display the selected color code, as shown in the next screenshot:

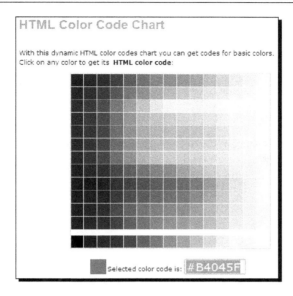

If we want to use a Heading 2 style with the previously selected color and emphasized text, we should use the following HTML tags as a header:

```
<h2 style="color:#B4045F"><em>
```

HTML codes define a color using a symbol (#) and a group of three two-digit hexadecimal numbers. Therefore, you will see the # followed by six letters (A-F) or numbers (0-9). The three two-digit hexadecimal numbers represent the intensity of the red, green, and blue colors. This way, combining the intensity of red, green and blue you can produce millions of different colors.

We can also move a vertical slider to choose the hue and then click into the color square in the HTML Color Picker and the site will display the selected color code, as shown in the following screenshot:

Time for action – organizing composite pictures and texts

We now have to add the composite pictures with different sizes to our exercise in JMatch:

1. Stay in the JMatch exercise, `matching0101`.

2. Click on the first **Left (ordered) items** textbox.

3. Select **Insert | Picture| Picture from local file** from JMatch's main menu. Choose the previously exported bitmap image `image010101.png` in `C:\School` and click on the **Open** button. A dialog box will appear displaying the image preview and some options, as shown in the next screenshot:

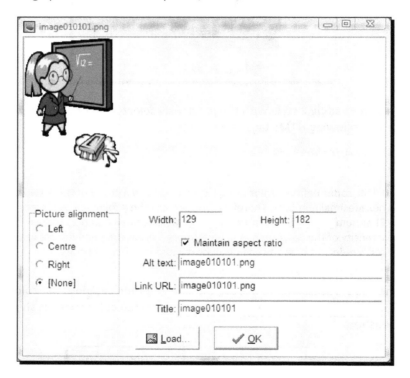

4. Click on **OK**. JMatch will show the following HTML code in the textbox:

    ```
    <img src="image010101.png" alt="image010101.png"
        title="image010101" width="129" height="182"></img>
    ```

5. Edit the HTML code in the textbox, adding the following header (prefix). We want to specify a background color for the picture.

    ```
    <h2 style="background:blue">
    ```

6. Add the following footer (suffix):

```
</h2>
```

7. The HTML code shown in the textbox should be as follows:

```
<h2 style="background:blue">
<img src="image010101.png" alt="image010101.png"
     title="image010101" width="129" height="182"></img></h2>
```

8. Click on the corresponding **Left (ordered) items** textbox and repeat the aforementioned steps (2 to 8) using the information shown in the next table. You have to replace the color name entered after the `background:` tag, with the color specified for each row.

Row number	Picture file name	Background color name
2	image010102.png	blue
3	image010103.png	green
4	image010104.png	green

9. The **Left (ordered) items** textboxes must show the HTML code for each picture as shown in the following screenshot:

	Left (ordered) items
1	`<h2 style="background:blue"><img src="image010101.png" alt="image010101.png" title="image010101" width="129" height="182"></img></h2>`
2	`<h2 style="background:blue"><img src="image010102.png" alt="image010102.png" title="image010102" width="127" height="139"></img></h2>`
3	`<h2 style="background:green"><img src="image010103.png" alt="image010103.png" title="image010103" width="76" height="72"></img></h2>`
4	`<h2 style="background:green"><img src="image010104.png" alt="image010104.png" title="image010104" width="57" height="71"></img></img></h2>`

10. Save the changes and select **File | Create Web Page | Drag/Drop Format**. Replace the existing web page and click on **View the exercise in my browser**.

11. The default web browser will appear showing the matching exercise with a drag/drop format. You will be able to see the four pictures and the jumbled sentences. Two of the pictures show a blue background (the pictures with big things) and the other two a green one (the pictures with small things), as shown in the next screenshot:

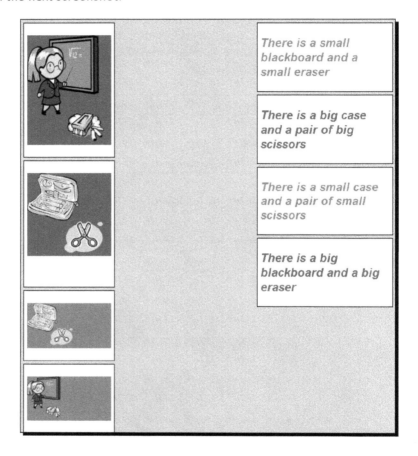

12. Perform the last two steps repeatedly. The jumbled sentences will change their order each time the matching exercise appears on the web browser.

What just happened?

We added the composite pictures with different sizes to our matching composite pictures exercise. We inserted the corresponding picture in the left-hand side for each sentence on the right-hand side.

When we run the exercise loading the web page created by JMatch, it jumbles the sentences on the right-hand side of the screen.

Using HTML tags to define background colors

We didn't want to use the default background colors for the pictures. We added **HTML code** to specify different background colors for the aforementioned composite pictures. As previously explained when defining colors for the text in the sentences, JMatch doesn't offer a simple way to select background colors for the pictures. Therefore, we had to use HTML tags again. We used the following header to specify a Heading 2 style with a blue background color:

```
<h2 style="background:blue">
```

We left the HTML code added by JMatch to insert the picture without changes and finally we used the following footer:

```
</h2>
```

We used the same tags for the other pictures. We just replaced the backgroundcolor:blue code with backgroundcolor:green in the pictures with a green background color.

 Everything we learned about defining customized color codes for the text foreground color (color property) also applies to the background color property.

Time for action – adding the activity to a Moodle course

We now have to add the matching composite pictures exercise to an existing Moodle course.

1. Log in to your Moodle server.

2. As we are going to add a Hot Potatoes exercise, you have to make sure that the **Hot Potatoes Quiz** activity module isn't hidden. Click on **Modules | Activities | Manage activities** in the **Site administration** panel. If the **Hot Potatoes Quiz** activity module appears in grey and displaying a closed eye icon in the **Hide/Show** column, you must click on this icon and it will change to an opened eye icon. This way, Moodle will enable this activity, as shown in the following screenshot:

Activity module	Activities	Version	Hide/Show	Delete	Settings
Assignment	0	2007101511	👁	Delete	Settings
Chat	0	2009031100	👁	Delete	Settings
Choice	0	2007101509	👁	Delete	
Database	0	2007101514	👁	Delete	Settings
Exercise	0	2007110500	👁	Delete	
Forum	3	2007101513			Settings
Glossary	0	2007101509	👁	Delete	Settings
Hot Potatoes Quiz	22	2007101513	👁	Delete	Settings

Site Administration [-]
- Notifications
- Users
- Courses
- Grades
- Location
- Language
- Modules
  - Activities
    - Manage activities
    - Assignment
    - Chat
    - Database
    - Forum
    - Glossary
    - Hot Potatoes Quiz
    - LAMS

Activities

3. Click on the desired course name (School). You can create a new course or use an existing one.

4. Click on **Turn editing on**. The web page will change to enable you to edit the **Weekly outline**.

5. Position the mouse pointer over the desired week under **Weekly outline** and click on the **Edit summary** icon (a small hand with a pencil).

6. Enter Exercise 1 in **Summary** and click on the **Save changes** button.

7. Next, click on the **Add an activity** combo box for the selected week and select **Hot Potatoes Quiz**, as shown in the next screenshot:

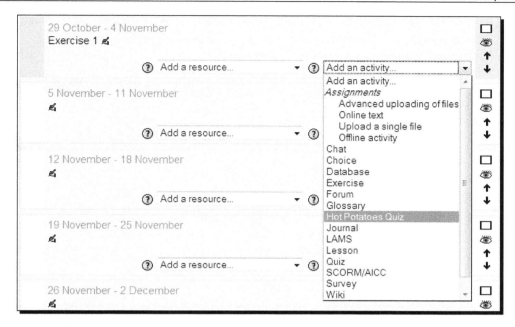

8. A new web page will appear displaying the title **Adding a new Hot Potatoes Quiz**. Click on the **Choose or upload a file** button and a pop-up window displaying information about files and folders will appear.

9. Click on the **Make a folder** button.

10. Enter chapter01 in the textbox and click on **Create**. Moodle will create a folder with this name and it will allow us to organize the necessary files for our exercise.

11. Click on **chapter01** (the recently created folder's hyperlink).

12. Click on the **Upload a file** button.

13. Click on the **Browse** button. Browse to the folder that holds the images and the files used in the exercise (C:\School) and select the file to upload, image010101.png. Then, click on **Open** and on the **Upload this file** button.

14. Repeat the aforementioned steps (12 to 13) for each of the files shown in the following list. You have to upload the following files in the chapter01 folder.

- image010102.png
- image010103.png
- image010104.png
- matching0101.html

15. Next, position the mouse pointer over the matching0101.html name and move it horizontally to the **Choose** action hyperlink in the same row. Then, click on **Choose**, as shown in the following screenshot:

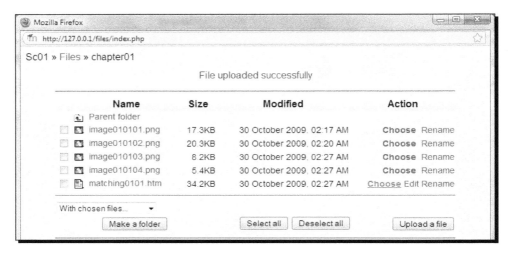

16. Moodle will display chapter01/matching0101.html in the **File name** textbox. This is the web page that will run the exercise previously created using JMatch.

17. Scroll down and click on the **Save and display** button, located at the bottom of the web page. The web browser will show the matching exercise with a drag/drop format, as shown in the next screenshot:

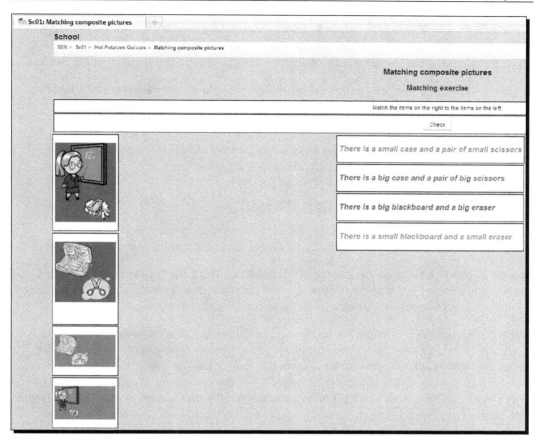

18. Click on the short course hyperlink on the top of the web page and the exercise will appear listed on the previously selected week, as shown in the following screenshot:

What just happened?

We added the matching composite pictures exercise to a Moodle course. Now, the students are going to be able to run the activity by clicking on its hyperlink on the corresponding week.

We created a new folder, chapter01. This folder will hold all the necessary files for the activities related to the school journey.

We then uploaded the four bitmap images and the HTML file created with JMatch (matching0101.html). This file has links to the bitmap images inserted with JMatch, therefore, it was very important to upload these image files.

Uploading multiple files in a ZIP folder

It is possible to upload all the necessary files for an exercise as a single ZIP file, also known as a ZIP folder. A ZIP file is a file with the .zip extension that contains many compressed files.

You can select **File | Create Zip Package | Create Drag/Drop Zip Package** from JMatch's main menu and enter the name for the new ZIP file. JMatch will create a ZIP file with all the necessary files to upload to Moodle in order to run the JMatch exercise.

You can then upload this single file to Moodle by following the previously explained steps. Once the file is uploaded, an **Unzip** command will appear at the right of the new ZIP file, under the **Action** column. You have to locate the mouse pointer over the ZIP file name and move it horizontally to the **Unzip** action hyperlink in the same row. Moodle will extract all the compressed files from this ZIP file and you will be able to choose the main HTML file, in this case, matching0101.html.

 You can also create a ZIP folder without using JMatch's function, include all the necessary files in it, and upload it to Moodle.

Time for action – running the matching composite pictures activity

It is time to run the activity as a student and to check the results as a teacher.

1. Click on the course name (School) and click on the **Switch role to** combo box (located on the left-hand side of the **Turn editing on** button) and select **Student**.

2. Click on the **Matching composite pictures** link on the corresponding week. The web browser will show the matching exercise with a drag/drop format.

3. Drag-and-drop each sentence to its corresponding image, as shown in the following screenshot:

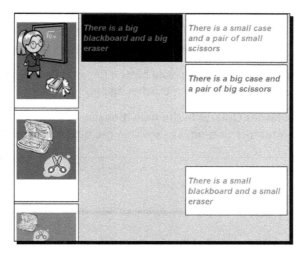

4. After repeating the aforementioned step for the four sentences, click on the **Check** button to test the results, as shown in the next screenshot:

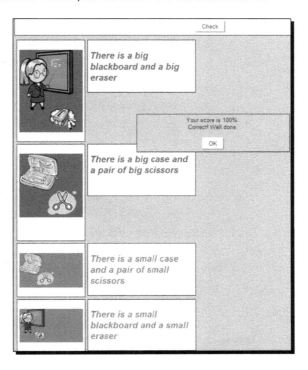

5. If the student's score is 100%, Moodle will save the results and will go back to the course web page.

6. Run the exercise with a different number of correct matches and click on the **Check** button each time. Moodle will remove the incorrect matches and will let you run the activity again. However, it will save the student's results for each attempt.

7. Click on the **Return to my normal role** button (located on the upper right-hand side corner of the web page). You are a teacher again.

8. Click on **Hot Potatoes Quizzes** in the **Activities** panel. The number of attempts will appear in the **Attempts** column, as shown in the next screenshot:

3 ☐	Update	Matching composite pictures	Never closed	100 / 100	View reports for 22 attempts (1 Users)	Regrade

9. Next, click on the **View reports** link for the row corresponding to the **Matching composite pictures** activity and Moodle will display details about all the attempts, grouped by user name, as shown in the next screenshot:

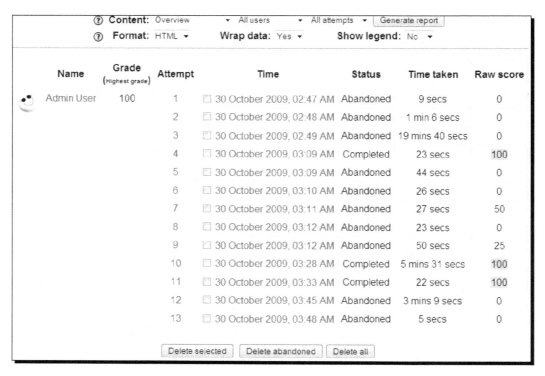

⑦ **Content:** Overview	▾	All users	▾	All attempts ▾	Generate report
⑦ **Format:** HTML ▾		**Wrap data:** Yes ▾		**Show legend:** No ▾	

Name	Grade (Highest grade)	Attempt	Time	Status	Time taken	Raw score
Admin User	100	1	☐ 30 October 2009, 02:47 AM	Abandoned	9 secs	0
		2	☐ 30 October 2009, 02:48 AM	Abandoned	1 min 6 secs	0
		3	☐ 30 October 2009, 02:49 AM	Abandoned	19 mins 40 secs	0
		4	☐ 30 October 2009, 03:09 AM	Completed	23 secs	100
		5	☐ 30 October 2009, 03:09 AM	Abandoned	44 secs	0
		6	☐ 30 October 2009, 03:10 AM	Abandoned	26 secs	0
		7	☐ 30 October 2009, 03:11 AM	Abandoned	27 secs	50
		8	☐ 30 October 2009, 03:12 AM	Abandoned	23 secs	0
		9	☐ 30 October 2009, 03:12 AM	Abandoned	50 secs	25
		10	☐ 30 October 2009, 03:28 AM	Completed	5 mins 31 secs	100
		11	☐ 30 October 2009, 03:33 AM	Completed	22 secs	100
		12	☐ 30 October 2009, 03:45 AM	Abandoned	3 mins 9 secs	0
		13	☐ 30 October 2009, 03:48 AM	Abandoned	5 secs	0

Delete selected	Delete abandoned	Delete all

What just happened?

In this activity, we worked with sentences and composite images. Our goal was that the child reads and understands the sentences alone, with the help of a therapist or a family member, so that he/she can run the exercise.

The activity consists of matching one sentence whose meaning belongs to a composite image. We applied the following concepts and resources:

◆ **Size notions**: For this reason, we have chosen school-related objects with different sizes.

◆ **Quantity notions**: We worked with composite images, showing more than one element per picture box.

◆ **Sensory perception resources**: We simplified the execution of the activity using colors. In this case, the sentences talking about big things use the background color found in the related composite pictures.

We can increase or decrease the complexity of this exercise using different combinations of colors. For example, if we want to create a simple activity, we can use the same foreground and background colors for each matching pair.

Discovering sentences related to 3D scenes

This morning, Alice gets up very happy. She opens her bedroom door and she sees Clifford, her puppy. He greets her wagging his tail and jumping.

Later, her mother calls her to have breakfast. After that, she prepares to go to school. Today, she has a problem; she doesn't know which school things fit in her bag. Can we help her?

Time for action – searching for 3D models to combine inside a 2D box

The creation and rendering of **3D models** for a discovering sentences exercise is very complex and involves professional skills. We are going to simplify this process by using existing free 3D models rendered in 2D bitmap images.

1. Start Inkscape and minimize it. You will use it later.

2. Open your default web browser and go to `http://sketchup.google.com/3dwarehouse`. This web page allows us to search for 3D models in Google 3D warehouse.

3. Enter `school bag` in the textbox, select **Models** in the combo box and click on the **Search** button. Many models matching the search criteria will appear as shown in the next screenshot:

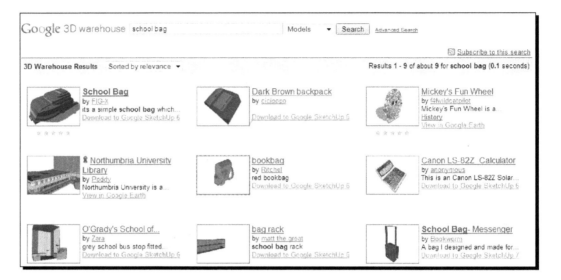

4. Click on the desired model's thumbnail. The default view for the rendered 3D model will appear.

5. Click on the **3D View** button located on the upper right-hand side corner of the 3D model.

6. Position the mouse pointer on the center of the 3D model. Press the mouse button and drag it horizontally to rotate the model until you get the desired view.

7. Position the mouse pointer on the center of the 3D model again. Right-click on it and select **Save picture as** in the context menu that appears, as shown in the next screenshot:

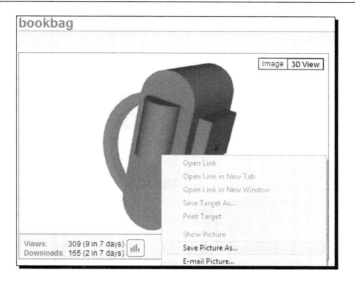

8. Since you want to change the picture size without losing quality using Inkscape, select **Bitmap (*.bmp)** in the **Save as type** combo box and save the file as `schoolbag.bmp` in the previously created folder, `C:\School`.

9. Now, activate Inkscape—remember that it was running minimized. You can use *Alt + Tab* or *Windows + Tab*.

10. Select **File | Import** from the main menu, select the previously saved file (`C:\School\schoolbag.bmp`), and click on the **Open** button. The rendered 3D model will appear in Inkscape's drawing area.

11. Now, go back to the web browser without closing Inkscape and repeat the aforementioned steps (2 to 10) for each 3D model to combine inside a box— Inkscape's drawing area. In this case, repeat those steps searching for the following things and saving the image files with the names shown in the following table:

Search for	Picture file name
book	book.bmp
calculator	calculator.bmp

12. The three rendered 3D models will now appear in Inkscape's drawing area, as shown in the next screenshot:

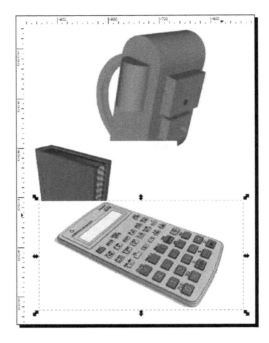

13. Select **File | Save** from Inkscape's main menu. Save the file as image010201.svg in the previously created folder, C:\School.

What just happened?

We combined three rendered 3D models in Inkscape's drawing areas. We searched for 3D models in **Google 3D warehouse** and we imported the bitmap files obtained from the desired views into Inkscape's drawing area.

We now have a picture with these three rendered 3D models, representing real-life shapes:

◆ A school bag

◆ A book

◆ A calculator

Time for action – organizing composite 3D models into a rendered 2D box

We are now going to move, resize, and save the new version of the combined rendered 3D models for the exercise using Inkscape.

1. Open the vector graphic file in Inkscape (C:\School\image010201.svg).

2. Resize and move each picture to create a drawing, as shown in the following screenshot:

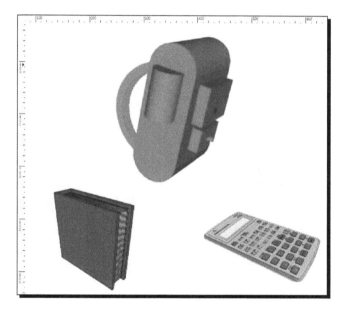

3. Select **File | Save**, to save the changes made to the original Inkscape SVG file.

4. Select **File | Export Bitmap**. A dialog box showing many export options will appear. Enter 90 on the first dpi (Dots Per Inch) textbox.

5. Click on the **Drawing** button, and then on **Export**. Inkscape will export the drawing in PNG format. The exported bitmap graphics with a school bag, a book, and a calculator will be C:\School\image010201.png.

What just happened?

We manipulated the bitmap images of the rendered 3D models using Inkscape. We could change their size and positions and we exported the resulting image to the PNG format.

The rendered 2D box is the exported bitmap graphic and represents a 3D scene.

Time for action – grouping text blocks and changing colors

It is time to create the text blocks with the possible answers for a pop quiz related to the 3D scene.

1. Start Hot Potatoes and click on **JQuiz**. A new window with the JQuiz application will appear.

2. Enter `Discovering sentences related to 3D scenes` in the **Title** textbox.

3. Select **Multiple-choice** in the combo box on the upper-right corner.

4. Click on the textbox below the title's textbox on the right-hand side of question number **1**.

5. Select **Insert | Picture| Picture from local file** from JQuiz's main menu. Select the previously exported bitmap image `image010201.png` in `C:\School` and click on the **Open** button. A dialog box will appear displaying the image preview and some options.

6. Click on **OK**. JQuiz will show the following HTML code in the textbox:
   ```
   <img src="image010201.png" alt="image010201.png"
         title="image010201" width="640" height="504"></img>
   ```

7. Click on the corresponding **Answers** textbox and enter the text shown in the next table for each row, as seen in the next screenshot:

Row label	Text to enter in the Right (jumbled) items textbox

A	`<h2 style="color:green">`
	
	`<em>There is a calculator and a book in the school bag.</em>`
	
	`</h2>`

B	`<h2 style="color:green ">`
	
	`<em>There is a calculator and a book under the school bag.</em>`
	
	`</h2>`

C	`<h2 style="color:green">`
	
	`<em>There is a calculator and four books next to the school bag.</em>`
	
	`</h2>`

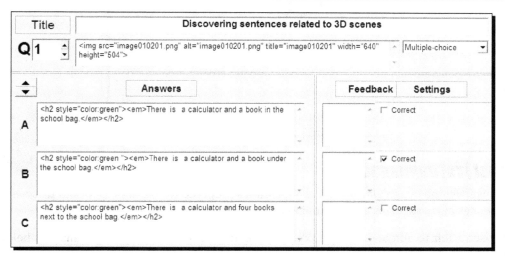

8. Activate the **Correct** checkbox corresponding to the row labeled with a **B**. This is the correct answer for the multiple-choice style quiz.

9. Select **File | Save** from JQuiz's main menu. Save the file as `quiz0102.jqz` in the previously created folder, `C:\School`.

10. Next, select **File | Create Web Page | Standard Format**. JQuiz will create a new web page. Save the new file as `quiz0102.html` in the aforementioned folder.

11. A new dialog box will appear. Click on **View the exercise in my browser**. You want to preview the exercise.

12. The default web browser will appear showing the image and the three possible answers. You will be able to see these three sentences with a big green font, as shown in the next screenshot:

What just happened?

We inserted the image with the 3D scene and we prepared the sentences for our discovering sentences exercise, using a multiple-choice format.

We used JQuiz to edit and preview the following three sentences as possible answers below the 3D scene:

- There is a calculator and a book in the school bag.
- There is a calculator and a book under the school bag.
- There is a calculator and four books next to the school bag.

We used our well-known HTML tags again to improve the fonts and color used for the sentences.

Time for action – adding the activity to a Moodle course

We now have to add the discovering sentences exercise to an existing Moodle course.

1. Log in to your Moodle server and make sure that the **Hot Potatoes Quiz** activity module isn't hidden.

2. Click on the desired course name (School) and then on **Turn editing on**.

3. Position the mouse pointer over the desired week under **Weekly outline** (a week later than the matching composite pictures exercise). Then, click on the **Edit summary** icon (a small hand with a pencil).

4. Enter Exercise 2 in **Summary** and click on the **Save changes** button.

5. Click on the **Add an activity** combo box for the selected week and choose **Hot Potatoes Quiz**.

6. A new web page will appear displaying the title **Adding a new Hot Potatoes Quiz**. Click on the **Choose or upload a file...** button and a pop-up window displaying information about files and folders will appear.

7. Click on **chapter01** (the folder created in our previous exercise).

8. Click on the **Upload a file** button and then on **Browse**. Browse to the folder that holds the images and the files used in the exercise (C:\School) and select the file to upload, image010201.png. Then, click on **Open** and on the **Upload this file** button.

9. Repeat the aforementioned step for the file generated by JQuiz, quiz0102.html.

10. Next, position the mouse pointer over the **quiz0102.htm** name and move it horizontally to the **Choose** action hyperlink in the same row. Then, click on **Choose**, as shown in the next screenshot:

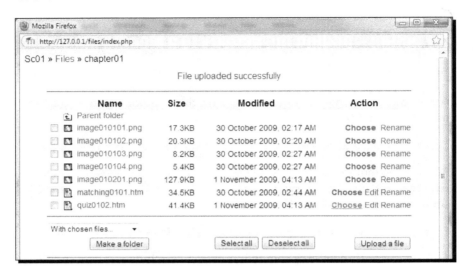

11. Moodle will display `chapter01/quiz0102.html` in the **File name** textbox. This is the web page that will run the exercise previously created using JQuiz.

12. Scroll down and click on the **Save and display** button, located at the bottom of the web page. The web browser will show the discovering exercise with a multiple-choice format, as shown in the next screenshot:

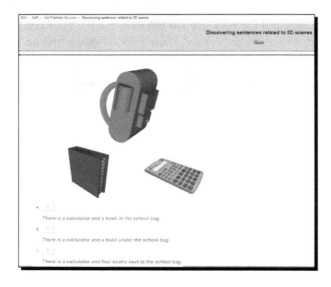

What just happened?

We added the discovering sentences related to 3D scenes exercise to a Moodle course. Now, the students are going to be able to run the activity by clicking on its hyperlink on the corresponding week.

We used the previously created folder, `chapter01`. We uploaded the bitmap image with the rendered 3D scene and the HTML file created with JQuiz (`quiz0102.html`).

Organizing the exercises' files using folders

We created a folder, `chapter01`, in which we uploaded all the files for both the matching composite pictures and the discovering sentences exercises. However, sometimes, we need to organize the exercises' files using additional folders.

For example, we can organize the files using the following structure:

- chapter01
  - exercise01
  - exercise02

We can create two sub-folders, `exercise01` and `exercise02`, in the `chapter01` folder. This way, all the files related to the second exercise would have to be uploaded in the `chapter01/exercise02` folder.

 The organization scheme chosen for the files will depend on the number of exercises and their relationship with your courses. However, in order to simplify your work, it is a good practice to keep all the files related to an exercise in a single folder. You can work with files in different folders; however, it will require you to work with complex paths in HTML code.

Time for action – running the discovering sentences activity

It is time to run the discovering sentences activity as a student.

1. Click on the course name (`School`) and switch your role to student.

2. Click on the **Discovering sentences related to 3D scenes** link on the corresponding week. The web browser will show the multiple-choice exercise.

3. Click on the button above the right-hand side sentence, as shown in the next screenshot. Moodle will save the results and go back to the course.

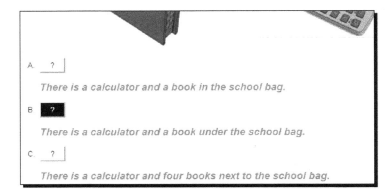

4. Repeat the aforementioned steps (1 to 3) and then click on the button above one of the wrong sentences. Moodle will display a message allowing you to try again and will show an X on the previously clicked wrong answer, as shown in the next screenshot. However, it will save your first wrong attempt in order to calculate a fair score.

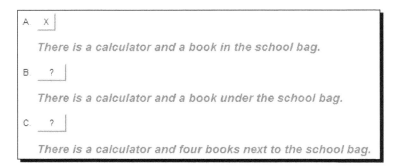

5. Now, click on the **View reports** link for the row corresponding to the **Discovering sentences related to 3D scenes** activity and Moodle will display details about all the attempts, grouped by user name, as shown in the next screenshot:

Grade (Highest grade)	Attempt	Time	Status	Time taken	Raw score
100	1	☐ 1 November 2009, 06:57 PM	Completed	5 secs	100
	2	☐ 1 November 2009, 06:57 PM	Completed	5 mins 1 sec	50

What just happened?

In this activity, we worked with sentences and a 3D scene. The objective was to select among several sentences the correct one describing the composite 3D image that was presented in the activity.

Why did we use 3D illustrations? We used them with the purpose of stimulating the motivation, because one of the features of these images is that they are realistic and children are attracted to them.

The activity consists of clicking on the sentence that explains the situation illustrated in the 3D scene. We applied the following concepts and resources in order to stimulate both the attention and the concentration:

- **Reading comprehension**: The child has to read and understand each of the sentences
- **Listening comprehension**: If the child can't read and understand the sentences alone, he/she can can run the exercise with the help of a therapist or a family member
- **Space notions**: The sentences describe the location of the elements within a specific space

We can also increase or decrease the complexity of this exercise using different combinations of colors. For example, if we want to create a simple activity, we can add a background color to the 3D scene and we can use this color as the foreground for the correct sentence.

Time for action – using a gamepad to solve the exercise

We can also use a **gamepad** instead of a mouse to solve the exercise. Its usage is easier and more attractive to those children who have **manual dyspraxia**.

We will use a USB gamepad, similar to the one used by the Sony Playstation 3 game console. We want to control the mouse pointer using the gamepad's right-hand side mini stick.

We have to configure the gamepad driver to map its left mini stick to the mouse pointer.

The student needs a USB gamepad with 4 axes and 2 mini sticks in order to complete the following exercise. This example is based on Windows operating systems.

1. Connect the USB gamepad to the computer and install its driver if you haven't already done so.

2. Go to **Control Panel | Game controllers**. Select the gamepad in the game controllers list and click on **Properties** (some drivers show the generic name **USB Network Joystick**). A dialog box will show the buttons for the gamepad, the mini sticks axes and the Point of View Hat (POV), as shown in the following picture:

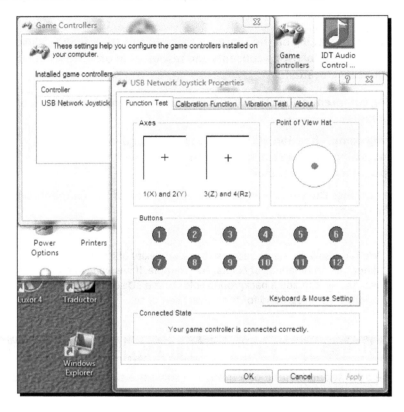

3. Disable the **analog mode** (the analog mode LED should be turned off). The gamepad must be in **digital mode** in order to allow us to map the right-hand side mini stick to the mouse's buttons.

4. You can test the relationship between the button numbers shown on the screen and the gamepad's pressed buttons using the aforementioned dialog box.

5. Click on the **Keyboard & Mouse Setting** button. A new dialog box will appear. It will allow you to change the gamepad mode and map its buttons to your mouse buttons.

6. Activate the checkboxes **Keyboard & Mouse mode** and **POV to arrow**.

7. Select **Left mouse button** in the **Key 1** combo box.

8. The values should be similar to the ones shown in the next screenshot:

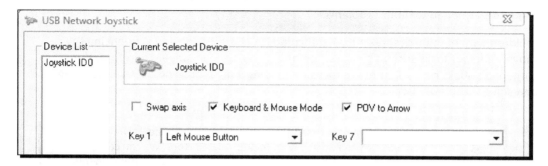

9. Click on **OK**.

10. Move the gamepad's left mini stick. The mouse pointer should change its position as the mini stick moves.

11. Control the gamepad's POV. The mouse pointer should change its position as it is pressed in different directions.

12. Press the gamepad's action button number 1 (on the upper right-hand side). It should work as the mouse's left button.

13. Run the discovering sentences activity as a student, following the previously explained steps. This time, use the gamepad instead of the mouse, as shown in the next image:

What just happened?

We configured the gamepad driver to map one of its mini sticks and one action button to the mouse pointer and the left mouse button. Therefore, you were able to execute the exercise using the gamepad without problems.

Children with manual dyspraxia have difficulties in coordinating and sequencing the movements for tasks such as gestures, pointing, and sign language. Therefore, the gamepad's sticks can help them to focus on moving a big mouse pointer on the screen and solve these exercises.

Sometimes, a gamepad isn't the most convenient device. However, it is cheap and easy to find in any computer-related store. We can configure gamepads as previously explained and we will be able to offer students different ways to move the mouse pointer. The same technique can be used for **joysticks** and **flightsticks**.

Understanding the gamepad as an input device

The gamepad is a complex input device. It usually offers many action buttons and two mini sticks, as shown in the following image (top view):

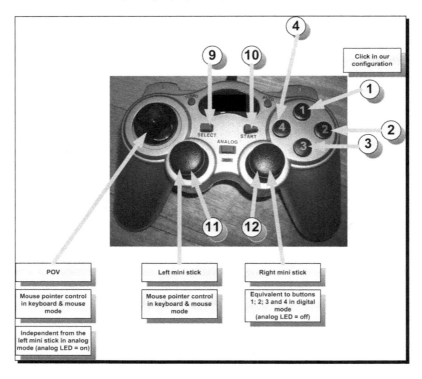

Each button number can be assigned to a different keyboard key or mouse button. Thus, we can take advantage of the 12 action buttons in this kind of gamepad.

 The action buttons 11 and 12 are triggered when the player pushes the mini stick (like clicking with a mouse button).

Depending on the manufacturer and the model, its four action buttons on the right-hand side can show different symbols or numbers, as shown in the following diagram:

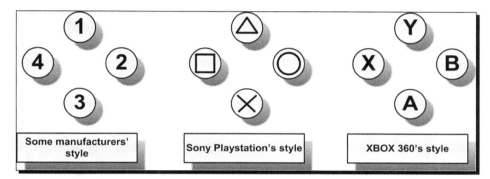

Have a go hero – dragging and dropping with a gamepad

You can also take advantage of the gamepad in the matching composite pictures exercise.

Configure the gamepad's mapping to simplify the drag-and-drop process used to solve the exercise.

Run the exercise as a student and create new versions of this exercise using different pictures, sentences, and color schemes.

Drawing an illustration according to speech bubbles

Alice is a very nice girl. She loves going to school, studying and doing her Math homework. She also is keen on playing every afternoon with her friends at break time. Her favorite weekday is Friday. The reason is that she has Art classes.

Every Friday Alice is very happy because together with her Art teacher they paint, model pictures, and draw. This class, her teacher suggested they do a very entertaining comic strip. They read it in the classroom and after that, the teacher asked them to draw the characters.

Can you draw with Alice?

Time for action – creating speech bubbles and filling them with text

The creation of a comic strip can be a very complex task. Luckily, there are many web pages that offer very simple interactive environments to create strips using speech bubbles and characters. Besides, we can export them to image formats compatible with Moodle and use them in exciting exercises.

1. Open your default web browser and go to `http:// stripgenerator.com`. This web page allows us to create simple comic strips.

2. Click on **Create New Strip!**. A new web page will appear displaying three boxes for a comic strip and many characters.

3. Click on the **Bubbles** button. A list of different bubbles will appear, as shown in the following screenshot:

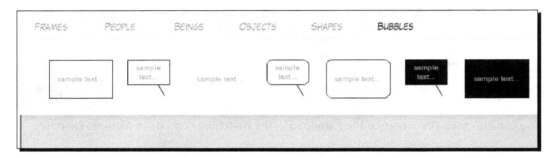

4. Position the mouse pointer over the desired bubble's thumbnail. Drag-and-drop it to the first box.

5. Double-click inside the new bubble in the box in order to select the original text. Enter `Today is Halloween`.

6. Change the bubble's size and direction by dragging and dropping the different rectangles that appear, as shown in the next screenshot:

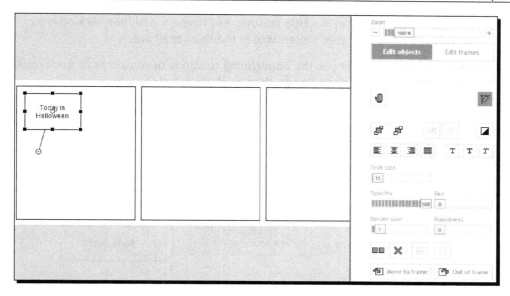

 You can also drag-and-drop the bubble to move it inside the box.

7. Repeat the aforementioned steps (4 to 6) to add speech bubbles and fill them with text using the following dialogues:

   ◆ Box number 1

   ❏ Today is Halloween

   ❏ What costume are you wearing?

   ◆ Box number 2

   ❏ I'm a princess

   ❏ I'm a butterfly! What about you, Alice?

   ◆ Box number 3

   ❏ Ohhhh....

   ❏ I'm a mummy

   ❏ How scary!!!!!

8. Click on the **Finish** button, located at the lower left-hand side corner.

9. Enter the desired title in the **Title** textbox, Halloween, and then click on **Next, last step**, because we aren't interested in the thumbnail preview.

10. The web page will offer you the opportunity to sign in or remain as an anonymous user. Click on **Remain anonymous**, then on **Publish** and the web page will create a bitmap image for the comic strip, as shown in the following image:

11. Position the mouse pointer on the center of the generated comic strip image. Right-click and select **Save picture as** in the context menu that appears.

12. Save the file as halloweenstrip01.png in the previously created folder, C:\School.

What just happened?

We created speech bubbles for a very simple comic strip with three boxes. We used the tools and the simple user interface provided by **stripgenerator.com**.

We could organize different kinds of speech bubbles, change their size, and enter the text to create a simple comic strip. Then, we exported the resulting image to the PNG format.

Time for action – adding the activity to a Moodle course

We now have to add the drawing and illustration according to speech bubbles to an existing Moodle course.

1. Log in to your Moodle server. Remember to click on the **Return to my normal role** button if necessary.

2. Click on the desired course name (School) and then on **Turn editing on**.

3. Edit the summary for a new week. Enter Exercise 3 in **Summary** and click on the **Save changes** button.

4. Click on the **Add an activity** combo box for the selected week and choose **Upload a single file**.

5. Enter Drawing with a digital pen in **Assignment name**.

6. Select Impact in font and 5 (18) in size—the first two combo boxes below **Description**.

7. Click on the **Font Color** button (a **T** with six color boxes) and select your desired color for the text.

8. Click on the big text box below **Description** and enter Draw an illustration of one of the characters according to the speech bubbles. This is the description of the student's goal for this exercise.

9. Press *Enter* and click on the **Insert Image** button (a mountain or a tree, according to the Moodle version). A new web page will appear displaying the title **Insert image**.

10. Click on **chapter01**.

11. Click on the **Browse** button. Browse to the folder that holds the comic strip image (C:\School) and select the file to upload, halloweenstrip01.png. Then, click on **Open** and on the **Upload** button. The label **File uploaded successfully** will appear inside the **File browser** box.

12. Next, click on the name of the recently uploaded file, `halloweenstrip01.png`. The image will appear in the **Preview** box, as shown in the next screenshot:

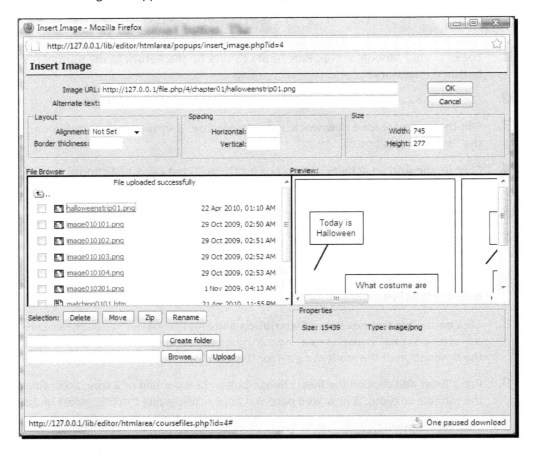

13. Enter `Halloween comic strip` in **Alternate text**. This text will appear if the web browser is not capable of downloading the image. It is a required field for this page.

14. Click on **OK**. The image will appear below the previously entered title. You can click on the **Enlarge editor** button (a diagonal arrow with two squares) and you will be able to view the title and the whole image, as shown in the next screenshot:

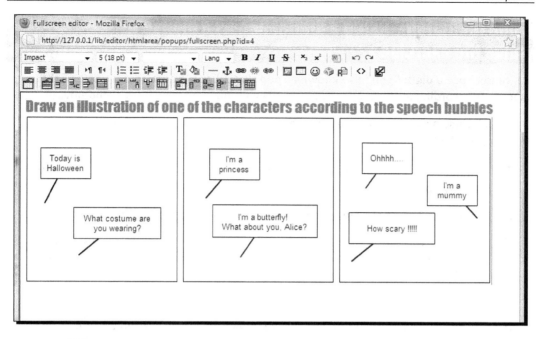

15. Close the enlarged editor's window.

16. Select 10MB in **Maximum size**. This is the maximum size for the file that each student is going to be able to upload as a result for this activity. However, it is very important to check the possibilities offered by your Moodle server with its Moodle administrator.

17. Scroll down and click on the **Save and display** button. The web browser will show the description and the previously uploaded image with the speech bubbles.

What just happened?

We added the drawing exercise to a Moodle course. The students are now going to be able to upload results for this activity after reading the goals and clicking on its hyperlink in the corresponding week.

We used the previously created folder, chapter01. We uploaded the bitmap image with the speech bubbles organized in a comic strip (halloweenstrip01.png). We added a title with a customized font and color using the description's editor.

The Upload a single file activity allowed us to describe the goals for the activity using a paragraph and an image.

Time for action – using a digital pen as a mouse to solve the exercise

It is time to use a **digital pen** (also known as **pen sketch**) as a mouse to draw one of the characters according to the speech bubbles. We will solve the activity as a student.

We can also use a classic mouse to solve the exercise. However, a digital pen is more appropriate.

1. Connect the USB digital pen to the computer and install its driver if you haven't already done so.

2. Click on the course name (School) and switch your role to student.

3. Click on the **Drawing with a digital pen** link on the corresponding week. The web browser will show the activity's description and the comic strip. Try to imagine one of the characters.

4. Start Inkscape.

5. Click on the **Draw calligraphic or brush strokes** button in the toolbar. This function will allow you to draw using a digital pen or a mouse, as shown in the next screenshot:

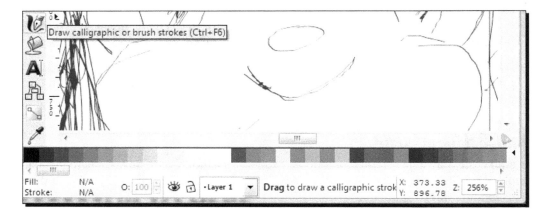

6. Now, imagine and draw the desired character on the tablet using the digital pen as a pencil, as shown in the next image:

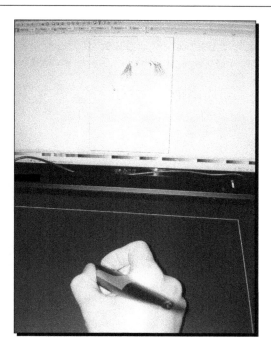

7. Select **File | Save** from Inkscape's main menu. Save the file as `mycharacter.svg` in your documents folder.

8. Select **File | Export Bitmap**. A dialog box showing many export options will appear. Enter `90` on the first dpi (Dots Per Inch) textbox.

9. Click on the **Drawing** button, and then on **Export**. Inkscape will export the drawing in PNG format. The exported drawing will be `mycharacter.png`.

10. Go back to your web browser and click on **Browse**. Browse to the folder where you saved the drawing, select it, and click on **Open**.

11. Next, click on **Upload this file** and the drawing in PNG format will be uploaded to the Moodle server. A **File uploaded successfully** message will appear if the file finished the upload process without problems. Click on **Continue**.

12. Now, the previously uploaded drawing in PNG format will appear below the instructions with the name **mycharacter.png**.

13. Finally, you will be able to download and open the uploaded drawing by clicking on the link that appears at the bottom of the page. The web browser is going to offer the default application to view this kind of file, as shown in the next screenshot.

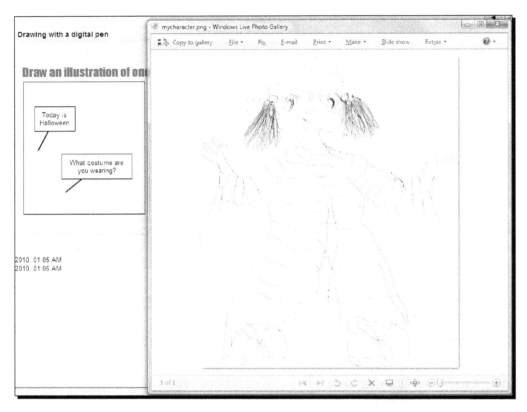

14. Don't forget to check the results for this exercise as previously learned.

What just happened?

In this activity, we created speech bubbles in a comic strip, using the online tools offered by `stripgenerator.com`. We asked the child to imagine and draw one of the characters of the comic strip using the digital pen.

This is an amusing and attractive activity for young children. They really enjoy working with a digital pen. We applied the following concepts and resources in order to stimulate both the attention and the concentration:

- ◆ **Reading comprehension**: The child has to read and understand the text found in the speech bubbles.

- ◆ **Listening comprehension**: If the child can't read and understand the comic strip alone, he/she can work with the help of a therapist or a family member, so that her/she can imagine the character.

- ◆ **Abstraction of situations**

- ◆ **Creativity**

Why did we use the digital pen? This device offers a great variety of resources to perform artistic activities. Furthermore, it is another resource for those children who have manual dyspraxia.

 The child usually has to work with the help of a therapist or a family member in order to solve this exercise using Inkscape, Moodle, and the digital pen. The child solves the exercise uploading his/her drawing to the upload a single file activity.

Tracing a drawing to solve the exercise

Children enjoy tracing drawings! Another alternative for solving this exercise is to trace an existing drawing using the digital pen.

You can do it by placing the model drawing on the tablet. You can then use the digital pen to draw over the existing lines, as shown in the next image:

You can add the model drawing as a bitmap image in the upload a single file activity. The student can print this image and trace the printed drawing using a digital pen. This way, you can begin measuring manual praxis.

Have a go hero – matching 3D scenes with 2D images

Your new activities are really engaging! You want to add a new matching pictures activity. However, you don't want to use text, just pictures on both sides.

Create a new matching composite pictures activity using JMatch. Add three 3D scenes on the left-hand side and three 2D pictures on the right-hand side. This way, the student will have to match the 3D scene with the corresponding equivalent 2D picture.

Use Inkscape to combine the 2D clipart and the 3D models for each picture. Create four pairs of images, combining the following elements:

- A pencil and a compass
- A piece of paper and an eraser
- A paint brush and colored pencils
- A pencil case and a school bag

Create a new Moodle exercise and run it as a student. Then, run the activity using a digital pen as a mouse to drag-and-drop the images to match each 2D picture with its corresponding 3D scene.

You can apply all the techniques learned in this chapter with many other Hot Potatoes exercises. We worked with JMatch and JQuiz to create visual exercises. However, this application offers many other interesting modules. The creation of other kinds of activities using Hot Potatoes is described in depth in *Moodle 1.9 for Teaching 7-14 Year Olds: Beginner's Guide* by Mary Cooch, Packt Publishing.

Pop quiz – creating attractive content for children

1. You can define a background color for a PNG image in a JMatch activity using:

    a. HTML tags

    b. A simple menu option

    c. A color context menu

2. You can define a font for a sentence in JMatch activity using:

   a. A simple combo box

   b. A font context menu

   c. HTML tags

3. JMatch allows you to insert pictures with the:

   a. SVG format

   b. PNG format

   c. TARGA format

4. In order to add a JMatch activity using many images to a Moodle course, you must:

   a. Upload the HTML file (`.html`) generated by JMatch and all the image files

   b. Upload only the HTML file (`.html`) generated by JMatch

   c. Upload only the JMT file (`.jmt`) saved by JMatch

5. In order to test an exercise as a student, you can:

   a. Click on the Student picture

   b. Restart the Moodle server

   c. Click on the **Switch role to** combo box and choose **Student**

6. You can find and rotate pictures of rendered 3D models in:

   a. Google 3D warehouse

   b. Microsoft Office Office Online Clip Art & Media

   c. Inkscape 3D warehouse

7. You can map a gamepad's mini stick to the:

   a. Mouse wheel

   b. Digital pen

   c. Mouse pointer

Summary

In this chapter, we have learned how to:

◆ Create rich activities using 2D and 3D clipart

◆ Use Inkscape to manipulate many different picture formats and export the results to the PNG format supported by both Moodle and Hot Potatoes

◆ Use JMatch and JQuiz to create visual exercises and then upload and run them on the Moodle server

◆ Take advantage of free 2D clipart, 3D models, and comic strip generation tools

◆ Work with general-purpose hardware in order to create activities that are even more engaging for children with special education needs

Now that we have learned how to create rich matching pictures activities, we're ready to prepare exercises to evaluate and work with abstraction and sequencing disabilities, which is the topic of the next chapter.

2

Working with Abstraction and Sequencing Disabilities

Abstraction is the ability to derive the correct general meaning from a particular word or symbol. It is a very basic intellectual task. However, instructions can combine words, symbols, and images. We can work a bit harder to create exercises that offer visually rich instructions to improve cognitive development in Moodle. This way, we can motivate children with minor abstraction and/or sequencing disabilities.

In this chapter, Alice goes to the zoo. We will learn how to create rich activities related to her journey. By following the exercises in this chapter we shall:

- ◆ Learn how to save portions of the screen as new pictures to use in new activities
- ◆ Make a gap fill activity changing pictures to words
- ◆ Prepare visually rich instructions
- ◆ Draw a scene that has to be painted using different colors
- ◆ Prepare instructions using visual patterns
- ◆ Create a visual yes/no multiple choice
- ◆ Use images and colors to evaluate sequencing and/or abstraction disabilities

Making a gap fill activity changing pictures to words

The big day finally arrived.

Alice and her friends went on excursion to the city zoo. Alice loves looking at animals; some of them such as the giraffe are very tall, others such as the rabbits are very small and soft, and some others roar like the lion.

Alice's favorite animals live in the aquarium of the zoo. Shall we go together and find out more about them?

Time for action – getting pictures of animals and nature

We are going to search for existing 2D clipart images of animals and nature. We will then convert them to 2D bitmap images using a simple tool to take snapshots of elements of the screen.

1. Create a new folder in Windows Explorer (C:\Zoo).

> The steps described are for the Windows operating system. However, you can also create this and the other exercises in all the other operating systems supported by Moodle, such as Linux and Mac OS X. You should use the default applications to work with the file systems and use different folder names.

2. Open your default web browser and go to http://office.microsoft.com/en-us/clipart/default.aspx. This web page allows us to search for free clipart in **Office Online Clip Art & Media**.

> You don't need Microsoft Office or Word installed in order to create this exercise because we aren't going to download the clipart.

3. Enter seal in the textbox and click on the **Search** button. The available clipart thumbnails related to the entered keyword will appear as shown in the next screenshot:

4. Click on the zoom icon located below the desired clipart thumbnail. A new window displaying a small preview of the clipart will appear.

5. Click on **Bigger preview** and this label will change to **Smaller preview**, as shown in the following screenshot. We want to use the big preview to take snapshots of the clipart using the same size.

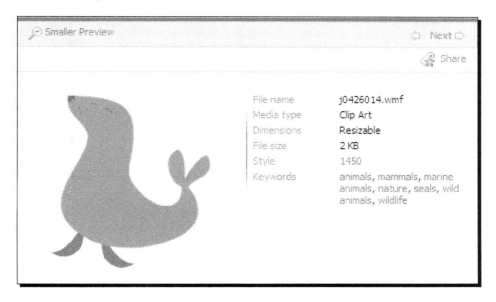

6. Start **Snipping Tool** (**Start Menu | All Programs | Accessories | Snipping Tool**) and a small window will appear. Click on the **Options** button, deactivate the **Show selection ink after snips are captured** checkbox, and click on **OK**.

 You can use the default screen capture keystrokes and applications provided by other operating systems and then edit the image file to achieve the same goal.

7. Click on the **New** button on the **Snipping Tool** toolbar. The screen's brightness will increase and the default mouse pointer will be replaced by a **precision select** cross.

8. Position the mouse pointer on the upper left-hand corner of the clipart preview and drag it to its lower right-hand corner. Whilst dragging the mouse, a rectangle will display the selected portion of the screen. Once you release the mouse's button, the **Snipping Tool** window will appear displaying the captured image, as shown in the next screenshot:

9. Select **File | Save as** from Snipping Tool's main menu. Select **Portable Network Graphic File (PNG) (*.PNG)** in the **Save as type** combo box and save the file as image020101.png in the previously created folder, C:\Zoo.

10. Next, go back to the web browser and repeat the aforementioned steps (3 to 9) to capture the bitmap image of another clipart picture. In this case, repeat those steps searching for `sea` and saving the captured image file as `image020102.png` in the same folder.

What just happened?

We searched for clipart previews in Office Online Clip Art & Media, through our web browser. Instead of working with Inkscape, this time we used the Snipping Tool application to capture the portion of the screen that showed the desired clipart's preview. This way, we could save the necessary images in the PNG format following just a few simple steps.

Snipping Tool is a very useful application to take screenshots of a rectangular area, a free-form area, specific windows, or the entire screen. Most modern Windows versions include this application: Windows 7, Windows Vista, and Windows XP Tablet PC Edition. You can use other applications to take screenshots instead of Snipping Tool in order to use the technique explained in this exercise.

We now have the following two bitmap graphics ready to be used in our completing dotted lines according to pictures exercise:

- ◆ `image020101.png`: A seal
- ◆ `image020102.png`: A photo of the sea

Time for action – preparing a cloze using images

It is time to prepare the sentence and the dotted lines and to organize the images for our cloze.

1. Start Hot Potatoes and click on **JCloze**. A new window with the JCloze application will appear.

2. Enter `Completing the dotted lines of the sentence according to the pictures` in the **Title** textbox.

3. Select **File | Save** from JCloze's main menu. Save the file as `cloze0201.jqz` in the previously created folder, `C:\Zoo`.

4. Click on the textbox below the title's textbox and enter `The seal lives in the sea.`

5. Position the cursor after the word `seal` and select **Insert | Picture| Picture from local file** from JCloze's main menu. Choose the previously saved bitmap image `image020101.png` in `C:\Zoo` and click on the **Open** button and then on **OK**. JCloze will use the default options to insert the image.

6. Now, position the cursor after the word `sea` and repeat the aforementioned step to insert the previously saved bitmap image `image020102.png` in `C:\Zoo`. JCloze will show the following HTML code in the textbox, as displayed in the next screenshot:

```
The seal
<img src="image020101.png" alt="image020101.png"
    title="image020101" width="216" height="232">
</img>
lives in the sea
<img src="image020102.PNG" alt="image020102.PNG"
    title="image020102" width="128" height="194">
</img>
```

Title	Completing the dotted lines of the sentence according to
The seal <img src="image020101.png" alt="image020101.png" title="image020101" width="216" height="232"></img> lives in the sea <img src="image020102.PNG" alt="image020102.PNG" title="image020102" width="128" height="194"></img>	

7. Select the word `seal` and click on the **Gap** button. The **Gapped word alternatives** dialog box will appear. Enter `It is an animal` in the **Clue** textbox and click on the **OK** button. The selected word will appear underlined and in red, as shown in the next screenshot:

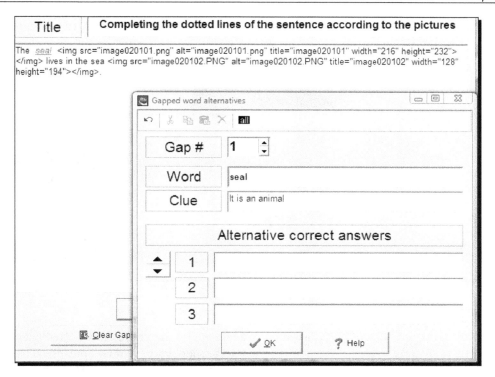

8. Next, select the word `sea` and click on the **Gap** button. The **Gapped word alternatives** dialog box will appear. This time, click on the **OK** button without entering information for a clue.

9. Select **File | Create Web Page | Standard Format**. JCloze will create a new web page. Save the new file as `cloze0201.htm` in the aforementioned folder. A new dialog box will appear. Click on **View the exercise in my browser**.

10. The default web browser will appear showing the cloze exercise with a standard format. You will be able to see a sentence with two textboxes, as shown in the next screenshot. You have to write the correct word according to each accompanying image. The **[?]** button allows you to get some help to discover the hidden word with a clue.

The _____ [?]   lives in the

What just happened?

We inserted the two images and prepared the sentence for our completing dotted lines according to pictures exercise. We defined the two gapped words and we specified a clue for one of them. Each gapped word is going to be represented by a textbox with an accompanying image.

We used JCloze to edit and preview the cloze exercise for the sentence The seal lives in the sea.

We inserted images of a seal and the sea in order to create a rich cloze exercise. This way, we offer additional stimulus and we present visual resources to simplify its resolution.

Time for action – adding the activity to a Moodle course

We now have to add the completing dotted lines according to pictures exercise to an existing Moodle course.

1. Log in to your Moodle server.

2. Click on the desired course name (Zoo). You can create a new course or use an existing one.

3. As we learned previously, follow the necessary steps to edit the summary for a desired week. Enter Exercise 1 in the **Summary** textbox and save the changes.

4. Click on the **Add an activity** combo box for the selected week and choose **Hot Potatoes Quiz**.

5. A new web page will appear displaying the title **Adding a new Hot Potatoes Quiz**. Click on the **Choose or upload a file** button and the already well-known pop-up window displaying information about files and folders will appear.

6. Follow the necessary steps to create a new folder, chapter02. It will allow us to organize the necessary files for our new exercise.

7. Click on **chapter02** (the recently created folder's hyperlink).

8. Click on the **Upload a file** button and then on the **Browse** button. Browse to the folder that holds the images and the files used in the exercise (C:\Zoo) and select the file to upload, image020101.png. Then, click on **Open** and on the **Upload this file** button.

9. Repeat the aforementioned step for each of the files shown in the following list. You have to upload all these files in the chapter02 folder.

   ❑ image020102.png

   ❑ cloze0201.htm

10. Next, position the mouse pointer over the **cloze0201.htm** name and move it horizontally to the **Choose** action hyperlink in the same row. Then, click on **Choose**, as shown in the next screenshot:

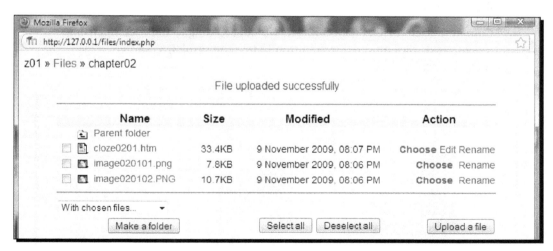

11. Moodle will display chapter02/cloze0201.htm in the **File name** textbox. This is the web page that will run the exercise previously created using JCloze.

12. Scroll down and click on the **Save and display** button, located at the bottom of the web page. The web browser will show the completing dotted lines according to pictures exercise with the two pictures.

What just happened?

We added the rich cloze exercise to a Moodle course. The students are now going to be able to run the activity by clicking on its hyperlink on the corresponding week.

We created a new folder, `chapter02`. This folder will hold all the necessary files for the activities related to the zoo journey.

Then, we uploaded the two images previously captured using Snipping Tool and the HTML file created with JCloze (`cloze0201.htm`). This HTML file has links to the two images inserted with JCloze.

Time for action – executing and completing the cloze with images

It is time to run the activity as a student and to check the results as a teacher.

1. Click on the course name (Zoo) and switch your role to student.

2. Click on the **Completing the dotted lines of the sentence according to the pictures** link on the corresponding week.

3. Complete each textbox with the right word, according to the accompanying image. Next, click on the **Check** button to test the results, as shown in the following screenshot:

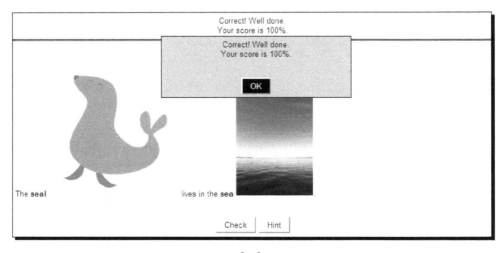

4. If the student's score is 100%, Moodle will save the results and will go back to the course web page.

5. Now, run the exercise with different numbers of correct words and click on the **Check** button each time. Moodle will tell you that some of your answers were incorrect and will let you run the activity again. However, the incorrect answers will appear in their original textboxes for you to change them. It will save the student's results for each attempt.

6. You can return to your normal role and check the number of attempts as done with the Hot Potatoes Quizzes activities.

[We ran a JCloze exercise. However, Moodle will show its statistics under Hot Potatoes Quizzes activities.]

What just happened?

In this activity, we worked with an incomplete sentence and two images. The objective was to complete the missing words according to the image located at the right-hand side of each textbox. The child can read, understand, and complete the missing words alone, with the help of a therapist or a family member, so that he/she can run the exercise.

The activity consists of writing the right word according to the related image. We applied the following concepts and resources in order to stimulate the attention, the concentration, and the abstraction capacity:

◆ **Reading comprehension**: The child has to read and understand the sentence with some missing words.

◆ **Listening comprehension**: If the child can't read and understand the sentence alone, he/she can work with the help of a therapist or a family member, so that he/she can run the exercise without needing to read or write.

◆ **Drawings and photographs**: They offer a visual mechanism to simplify the communication of different clues to guide the child to write the missing words. The child has to use his/her abstraction capabilities to solve the exercise.

◆ **Reading and writing**: The child has to write the missing words according to the accompanying images.

The zoo was our main stage for the exercise. It is usually considered a fun place for children. Besides, it offers a great number of resources and ideas to work with in fun exercises.

This exercise could be too difficult to solve for certain children, especially those with difficulties writing, or with reading comprehension problems. Besides, children who have manual dyspraxia could have great difficulties writing the words in the right place. In these cases, it is very important to work with the help of a therapist or a family member.

We can also increase or decrease the complexity of this exercise using additional clues, asking the student to complete words in many sentences, and adding more than one image per missing word. For example, if we want to create a simpler activity, we can write a short sentence with one missing word, three images related to that word, and a very descriptive clue.

Painting images according to the instructions

What a mess happened in the zoo! The monkey escaped and opened some of the other cages without being seen. All the animals were running and jumping. They were also being naughty around the zoo.

The zookeeper asked Alice and her friends for help. He wanted to find out where the animals were and especially the naughty monkey.

Luckily the lion did not escape!

Time for action – drawing the background using a digital pen

We are going to use a digital pen as a mouse to draw a picture. Later, the student will be able to paint the picture filling many closed areas.

We can also use a classic mouse to draw this picture. However, a digital pen is more appropriate to create realistic pictures with hand-drawing style.

1. Start **Paint (Start Menu | All Programs | Accessories | Paint)**.

You can use another bitmap or image editing application to run this exercise, such as GIMP. We will learn to work with GIMP in other exercises.

2. Position the mouse pointer on the lower right-hand corner of the white background (the drawing area) and drag it to fill the window. Once you release the mouse's button the white background will cover the bigger drawing area.

3. Click on the **Pencil** button in the toolbar. This function will allow you to draw using a digital pen or a mouse.

4. Next, click on the desired color for each element and draw a scene on the white background with the following elements using the digital pen as a pencil, as shown in the next screenshot:

- ❑ A monkey
- ❑ A toucan
- ❑ A pig
- ❑ Three clouds
- ❑ One tree

 Remember that you have to draw closed areas because the student will have to fill many of them according to the instructions provided in the exercise.

5. Select **File | Save as** from Paint's main menu. Select **PNG (*.PNG)** in the **Save as type** combo box and save the file as `image020201.png` in the previously created folder, `C:\Zoo`.

What just happened?

We used Paint to draw different shapes of animals in the zoo. We used closed areas to prepare them to be filled using the fill by color function. We used different brush colors because we will instruct the student to fill certain shapes with specific colors.

Paint is a simple yet useful application to create and edit bitmap images. All versions of Windows include this application. You can use other applications to create bitmap hand-drawn style drawing, such as Tux Paint. It is free computer art software for children. You can download it from `http://www.tuxpaint.org/`.

Time for action – preparing the instructions with images, colors, and fonts in Moodle

We are going to prepare the instructions for this activity using many portions of the previously created image.

1. Start **Paint** (**Start Menu | All Programs | Accessories | Paint**).

2. Open the bitmap image file in Paint (`C:\Zoo\image020201.png`).

3. Click on the **Select** button (a dotted rectangle) in the toolbar. This function will allow you to select rectangular areas of the drawing zone.

4. Position the mouse pointer on the upper left-hand corner of the desired area (the small clouds at the left of the Toucan) and drag it to the lower right-hand corner. Whilst dragging the mouse, a dotted rectangle will display the selected portion of the drawing area.

5. Select **Edit | Copy to** from Paint's main menu. Select **PNG (*.PNG)** in the **Save as type** combo box and save the file as `image020202.png` in the previously created folder, `C:\Zoo`. This way, you are saving just the selected area in a new bitmap image.

6. Repeat the aforementioned steps (3 to 5) for other areas and saving the image files with the names shown in the following table:

Area to select	Picture file name
The small clouds on the left-hand side of the toucan	image020202.png
The big cloud on the right-hand side of the toucan	image020203.png
The toucan above the tree	image020204.png
The grass below the tree	image020205.png

7. This way, you will have four images with four different parts of your original drawing. Now, return to your web browser.

8. Log in to your Moodle server.

9. Click on the desired course name (Zoo). As previously learned, follow the necessary steps to edit the summary for a desired week. Enter Exercise 2 in the **Summary** textbox and save the changes.

10. Click on the **Add an activity** combo box for the selected week and choose **Upload a single file**.

11. Enter Painting images according to the instructions in **Assignment name**.

12. Select Verdana in font and 5 (18) in size – the first two combo boxes below **Description**.

13. Select your desired color for the text.

14. Click on the big textbox below **Description** and enter Paint elements according to the instructions. This is the description of the student's goal for this exercise.

15. Press *Enter* and click on the **Insert Image** button (a mountain or a tree, according to the Moodle version). A new web page will appear displaying the title **Insert image**.

16. Follow the necessary steps to upload the file image020201.png in the previously created folder, chapter02. Remember to enter an alternate text and the image will appear below the previously entered title.

17. Follow the necessary steps to upload the four new images with the different areas of the original image in the same folder, chapter02.

18. Click on the **Insert Table** button (a grid). Enter 4 in **Rows** and 2 in **Cols**, to insert a new table with 4 rows and 2 columns, and then click on **OK**.

19. Next, enter the text with the instructions in the cells located on the left-hand side and the images at the right-hand side of each of the instructions, as explained in the following table. Remember to enter an alternate text for each image.

Text	Name of picture file to insert at the right of the text
Paint the small clouds at the left-hand side of the toucan blue	image020202.png
Paint the big cloud at the right-hand side of the toucan blue	image020203.png
Paint the toucan above the tree orange and black	image020204.png
Paint the grass below the tree green	image020205.png

20. Select each word that represents a color name and change its color to match it, as shown in the next screenshot. For example, blue in the sentence `Paint the small clouds at the left of the toucan blue`, should be in blue.

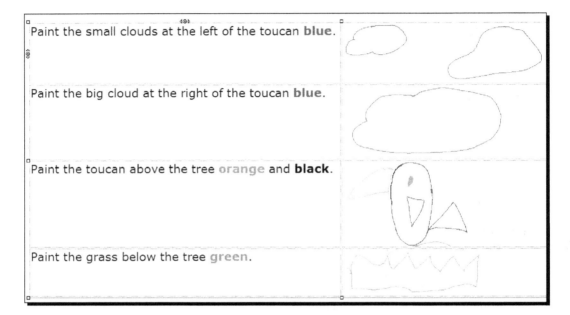

Paint the small clouds at the left of the toucan **blue**.

Paint the big cloud at the right of the toucan **blue**.

Paint the toucan above the tree orange and **black**.

Paint the grass below the tree green.

 Remember that you can click on the **Enlarge editor** button (a diagonal arrow with two squares) in order to edit the contents using a larger editing area.

21. Select 10MB in **Maximum size**. This is the maximum size for the file that each student is going to be able to upload for this activity. However, it is very important to check the possibilities offered by your Moodle server with its Moodle administrator.

22. Scroll down and click on the **Save and display** button. The web browser will show the main scene and the instructions with images and colors.

What just happened?

We added the painting exercise to a Moodle course. The students are now going to be able to upload the painted image with the results for this activity after reading the detailed goals by clicking on its hyperlink on the corresponding week.

We used the previously created folder, `chapter02`. We uploaded the main bitmap image with the closed areas to paint (`image020201.png`). We added a title with a customized font and color using the upload a single file editor and then we added sentences with instructions to paint the image using four images to show the area to be filled:

- `image020202.png`
- `image020203.png`
- `image020204.png`
- `image020205.png`

The description area of the upload a single file activity allowed us to explain the goals for the activity mixing several images with paragraphs and colors.

Time for action – executing the activity to paint images in Moodle

It is time to use a digital pen as a mouse to fill the closed areas according to the instructions. We will solve the activity as a student.

We can also use a classic mouse to solve the exercise. However, a digital pen makes it even more fun.

1. Connect the USB digital pen to the computer and install its driver if you haven't already done so.

2. Click on the course name (`Zoo`) and switch your role to student.

3. Click on the **Painting images according to the instructions** link on the corresponding week. The web browser will show the image with the scene and the four sentences with the instructions and the accompanying images.

4. Right-click on the image with the scene and select **Save picture as** in the context menu that appears. Save the file as `myzoo.png` in your documents folder. Your web browser will download the file to the selected folder.

In order to keep the instructions simple, we aren't including detailed step-by-step information about all the necessary steps that the students need in order to complete the exercise. However, most of the time, you should include the same steps that we are following to solve the exercise as instructions for the students. For example, you have to include the instructions to right-click and download the file for the children's parents.

5. Start **Paint** (**Start Menu | All Programs | Accessories | Paint**).

6. Open the recently saved bitmap image file in Paint, `myzoo.png`, located in your documents folder.

7. Click on the **Fill with color** button (a paint bucket) in the toolbar. This function will allow you to fill closed areas with the selected fill color.

8. Tap or click on the desired color in the color palette and then tap or click inside each closed area, according to the instructions. You'll be able to paint the original image as shown in the following screenshot:

9. Select **File | Save** from Paint's main menu.

10. Go back to your web browser and click on **Browse**. Browse to the folder that holds the exported drawing, select it, and click on **Open**.

11. Next, click on **Upload this file** and the exported drawing will be uploaded to the Moodle server. A **File uploaded successfully** message will appear if the file could finish the upload process without problems. Click on **Continue**.

12. The previously exported drawing in PNG format will now appear below the instructions with the name **myzoo.png**.

13. Don't forget to check the results for this exercise as previously learned.

What just happened?

In this activity, we created an image representing a scene of the zoo. We then used many portions of this scene to create visually rich instructions. We asked the child to fill certain elements of the image with the specified colors using the digital pen.

This is a fun activity for young children because they love painting pictures. We applied the following concepts and resources in order to stimulate both their attention and concentration:

◆ **Reading comprehension**

◆ **Pattern recognition**

◆ **Understanding simple tasks**: The child has to fill an exact element using the specified color

◆ **Understanding complex tasks**: The child has to fill the toucan using two colors

◆ **Executing simple and complex tasks**

◆ **Space notions**: The instructions describe the location of the elements to paint within a specific space

◆ **Sensory perception resources**: We simplified the execution of the activity using patterns, images, and colors. In this case, the color used to draw the line of each area is the same color that must be used to fill it

 As previously learned, we can also use a gamepad instead of a digital pen to solve the exercise. Sometimes, its usage is easier and more attractive to those children who have manual dyspraxia. It offers them more precision than the mouse pointer in many steps.

The child solves the exercise uploading his/her painted image to the upload a single file activity.

Have a go hero – painting silhouettes

The students enjoyed painting the scene related to the zoo. You want to add another painting exercise. However, you don't want to use another hand-drawn style picture. Instead, this time you will work with existing silhouette clipart.

Use Inkscape to combine silhouette clipart of many animals and nature elements, such as trees and clouds. Create a new scene using silhouettes and export the image to the PNG format.

Then, use Paint to copy many portions of this scene to new PNG images in order to create visually rich instructions mixing them with sentences.

Create a new Moodle exercise and run it as a student. Paint the silhouettes according to the instructions.

Remember that you have already learned how to combine existing clipart to create a bitmap image.

Have a go hero – using other tools to paint the image

Many students have played with their Start menu and now, they can't find the Paint application. However, all of them found a shortcut to Tux Paint.

Run the existing exercises as a student using Tux Paint instead of Paint in order to paint the elements with different colors.

Add the necessary instructions in the upload a single file activity to paint the elements using both Paint and Tux Paint. Use visually rich instructions explaining the necessary steps to the students.

Solving a yes/no multiple choice

Finally, Alice arrived home. Her mother was waiting for her anxiously to know how her first visit to the zoo was.

Alice told her mother that she played and had a lot of fun. She added that she met a lot of animals of different sizes, but she didn't remember the name of one animal.

Shall we help Alice to remember that animal's name?

Time for action – preparing several images and Boolean questions

We are first going to search for existing 2D clipart of two animals, a monkey and a cow. We will then convert them to 2D bitmap images using our well-known Snipping Tool.

Once we have the two images, we are going to prepare a sentence with a yes/no multiple choice format using Moodle's Quiz activity.

 A yes/no question is also known as a Boolean question. Boolean algebra is the algebra of two values, 0 and 1 or True and False.

1. Open your default web browser and go to `http://office.microsoft.com/en-us/clipart/default.aspx`. We are going to search for clipart in **Office Online Clip Art & Media**, again.

2. Following the same steps learned to find clipart for a seal and the sea in our first exercise, search for clipart for these animals. Save the snapshots taken by Snipping Tool with the names shown in the following table, in the previously created folder, C:\Zoo. The next picture displays sample images for these animals:

Animal	Picture file name
Monkey	image020301.png
Cow	image020302.png

image020301.png   image020302.png

3. Log in to your Moodle server and click on the desired course name (Zoo).

4. As we have learned previously, follow the necessary steps to edit the summary for a desired week. Enter Exercise 3 in the **Summary** textbox and save the changes.

5. Click on the **Add an activity** combo box for the selected week and select **Quiz**.

6. Enter `Boolean multiple choice` in **Quiz name**, then click on the **Save and display** button. Moodle will display the question bank for this quiz, as shown in the next screenshot:

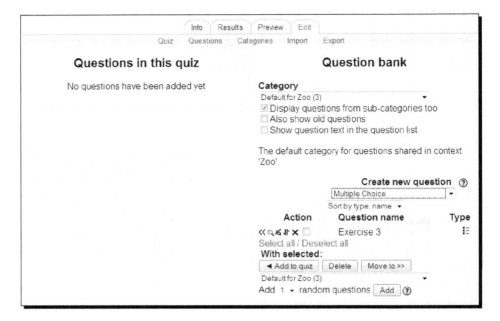

7. Click on the **Create new question** combo box and select **Multiple choice**. A new page asking for the necessary information to add a multiple choice question will appear.

8. Enter `Multiple choice` in **Question Name**.

9. Click on the big textbox below the **Question text** label. Use different fonts and colors to enter the sentences that define the goal and the question to answer using the multiple choice quiz, as shown in the next screenshot:

- ❑ Solving a Boolean multiple choice

- ❑ Which animal eats bananas, has a long tail, and climbs the tree?

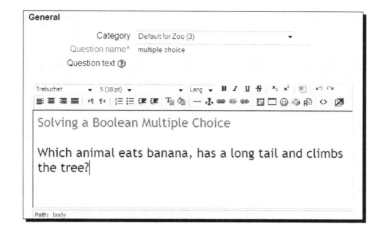

What just happened?

We searched for clipart previews in Office Online Clip Art & Media, through our web browser and we captured the desired portions using the Snipping Tool application. We now have the following two bitmap graphics ready to be used as visual answers in our Boolean multiple choice exercise:

- `image020301.png`: A monkey
- `image020302.png`: A cow

It is very important to avoid using descriptive names in the images because they could give the student undesired clues for the answer.

Next, we created a Quiz activity and we added a question for our Boolean multiple choice using the most appropriate question style.

Time for action – creating a YES button and a NO button with associated images

We now have to prepare the two possible answers using text and images.

1. Scroll down and go to the section named **Choice 1** (the first possible answer).

2. Enter A monkey in the **Answer** textbox inside the **Choice 1** section.

3. Click on the **Insert Image** button (a mountain) under the **Feedback** title inside the **Choice 1** section. A new web page will appear displaying the title **Insert image**.

4. Follow the necessary steps to upload the file `image020301.png` in the previously created folder, `chapter02`. Remember to enter an alternate text and the image will appear below the previously entered title.

> It is very important to avoid using descriptive names in the alternate text for these images because they could give the student undesired clues for the answer. In this case, we are inserting the image to be displayed as feedback. However, we are doing this in order to copy the complex HTML code generated to include this image accompanying the answer's text.

5. The monkey will appear in the Feedback's big textbox. Click on the **Toggle HTML Source** button (the one with the <> label) under the **Feedback** title inside the **Choice 1** section. The big textbox will display HTML code, a line similar to the following one:

```
<img hspace="0" height="216" border="0" width="211"
     vspace="0" title="image" alt="image"
src="http://127.0.0.1/file.php/5/image020301.png"/><br/>
```

6. Select all the text and press *Ctrl + C*. We want to copy the code to display the uploaded image.

7. Click on the **Answer** textbox inside the **Choice 1** section. Press *End* and then *Ctrl + V*. Now, the text in this textbox will be similar to the following:

```
A monkey
<img hspace="0" height="216" border="0" width="211"
vspace="0"
src="http://127.0.0.1/file.php/5/image020301.png"
alt="image" title="image"/><br/>
```

8. Select **100%** in the **Grade** combo box because this is the correct answer, as shown in the next screenshot:

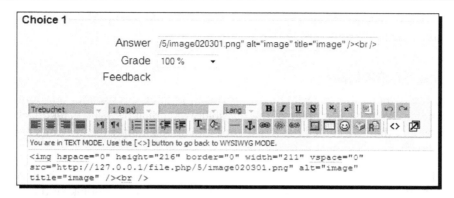

9. Scroll down and go to the section named **Choice 2** (the other possible answer).

10. Repeat the aforementioned steps (2 to 7) to define the second possible answer. In this case, repeat those steps under the section named **Choice 2**, enter A cow in the **Answer** textbox, and insert the image020302.png.

11. Select **None** in the **Grade** combo box under the section named **Choice 2** because this is the wrong answer.

12. Scroll down and click on the **Save changes** button, located at the bottom of the web page.

13. Moodle will display a question bank and the questions for the quiz. Now, activate the **Action** checkbox corresponding to the row labeled with the previously created question, **Multiple choice**. Then, click on the **Add to quiz** button. Moodle will add the question to our quiz, as shown in the following screenshot:

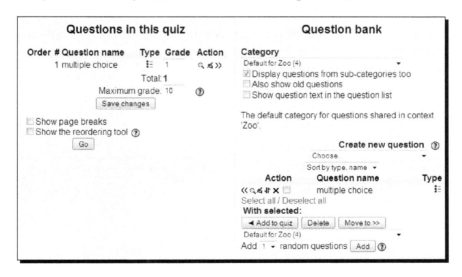

14. Click on the **Save changes** button. The Boolean multiple choice exercise with text and images in its possible answers is ready.

What just happened?

We added the two possible answers to our previously created question for our Boolean multiple choice. We took advantage of the possibility of adding pictures as feedback for each answer and then we copied the HTML code and added it after the answer's text. This way, the image will appear with the text.

Next, the students are going to be able to solve the multiple choice with two buttons with text and images after reading the question by clicking on its hyperlink on the corresponding week.

We used the previously created folder, chapter02. We uploaded the two bitmap images representing the possible answers to the question:

- image020301.png
- image020302.png

Inserting HTML code into the answer text allowed us to create a visually rich multiple choice.

Time for action – executing the activity

It is time to run the activity as a student and to check the results as a teacher.

1. Click on the course name (Zoo) and switch your role to student.

2. Click on the **Boolean multiple choice** link on the corresponding week.

3. Click on the **Attempt quiz now** button. The question and two radio buttons with text and images will appear, as shown in the next screenshot:

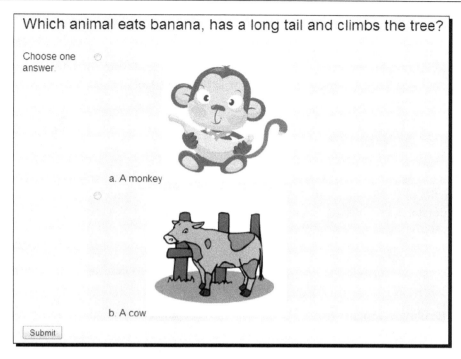

Which animal eats banana, has a long tail and climbs the tree?

Choose one
answer.

a. A monkey

b. A cow

Submit

4. Click on the corresponding radio button for the correct answer at the left-hand side of the image. Then, click on the **Submit** button, located on the lower left-hand corner.

5. Moodle will show the feedback, telling you whether the chosen answer was correct or not.

6. Next, click on the **Submit all and finish** button. Click on **OK** in the confirmation dialog box that appears and Moodle will display a review of the results for the activity:

   ❏ If the correct answer was chosen, it will appear with two images on a green background

   ❏ If the correct answer was not chosen, the correct one will appear with a single image on a green background

7. Click on the **Finish review** button, go back to the Moodle course, and return to your normal role.

8. Click on **Quizzes** in the **Activities** panel. The number of attempts will appear in the **Attempts** column.

9. Next, click on the **Attempts** link for the row corresponding to the **Boolean multiple choice** activity and Moodle will display details about all the attempts, grouped by user name.

What just happened?

In this activity, we worked with a question and two possible answers with radio buttons related to images of animals. The objective was to select the animal name according to the question and to the image located at the right-hand side of the radio button. The child can read, understand, and answer the question alone, with the help of a therapist or a family member, so that he/she can run the exercise.

The activity consists of clicking on the radio button for the correct animal according to the related image. We applied the following concepts and resources in order to stimulate the attention, the concentration, and the abstraction capacity:

*   **Reading comprehension**: The child has to read and understand the question and the animals' names.

*   **Associating concepts**: The child has to associate a question with the possible answers.

*   **Images**: They offer a visual mechanism to simplify the communication of different clues to guide the child to select the correct answer. The child has to use his/her abstraction and sequencing capabilities to answer the Boolean question.

*   **Long-term memory**: The child has to think which animal had the features explained in the question. He/She has to think about all the animals he knows and to associate the features with one of the possible answers displayed.

The zoo was our main stage for the exercise. It is usually considered a fun place for children. Besides, it offers a great number of resources and ideas to work with in fun exercises.

This exercise could be too difficult to solve for certain children, especially those with writing or reading comprehension problems. Besides, children who have manual dyspraxia could have great difficulties writing the words in the correct place. In these cases, it is very important to work with the help of a therapist or a family member.

 We can create Boolean multiple choices using the same pattern with different kinds of things. These kinds of visually rich activities are really engaging for children.

Have a go hero – preparing more Boolean questions

You already know how to create composite pictures with multiple elements. Create the following images with the help of existing clipart:

◆ A rabbit and a carrot

◆ A rabbit and a lemon

Next, create a Boolean multiple choice asking the student what the rabbit eats.

 Combining everything we learned in the previous chapter with the new activities developed during this one, you can create even more engaging and visually rich exercises for children with special education needs.

Pop quiz – discovering new tools and activities

1. You can use the Snipping Tool application to:
   a. Take screenshots of a rectangular area
   b. Increase an image's brightness value
   c. Create a Boolean multiple choice activity in an existing Moodle course

2. JMatch allows you to create a cloze exercise:
   a. Mixing just one picture and text
   b. Without pictures
   c. Mixing text and pictures

3. In order to define the gap word in a JCloze exercise, you must:
   a. Select the word in the sentence and click on the **Gap** button
   b. Triple-click on the word in the sentence
   c. Write the sentence without the gapped words and then enter them in the gapped words combo box

4. In order to check the number of attempts for a JCloze exercise added to a Moodle course, you must:
   a. Click on **Hot Potatoes Clozes** in the **Activities** panel
   b. Click on **JCloze Exercises** in the **Activities** panel
   c. Click on **Hot Potatoes Quizzes** in the **Activities** panel

5. In order to indicate the right answer for a Moodle's Boolean Quiz activity, you have to:

    a. Activate the **Right answer** checkbox

    b. Select 100% in the **Grade** combo box

    c. Select 0% in the **Grade** combo box

Summary

In this chapter, we have learned how to:

♦ Create many visually rich activities combining text and pictures

♦ Use Snipping Tool to capture different portions of the screen in order to export the results to the PNG format supported by both Moodle and Hot Potatoes

♦ Use JCloze, an upload a single file activity, and Moodle's Quiz to create visual exercises

♦ Take advantage of the HTML code generated by Moodle in order to add pictures to a question in a Moodle Quiz

♦ Work with Paint and a digital pen to create realistic activities that can provide further motivation for children with special education needs.

Now that we have learned how to create exercises to evaluate and work with abstraction and sequencing disabilities, we're ready to prepare exercises associating images and words, which is the topic of the next chapter.

3
Associating Images with Words

We can use images and pictures with many independent elements that are combined with words and sentences. It is possible to use many different applications in order to create exercises that challenge the student to associate images with words and sentences in a creative and visually rich Moodle experience. This way, we can train reading comprehension and the association of concepts in different scenarios.

In this chapter, Alice goes to the beach. We will learn how to create rich activities related to her journey. By reading this chapter and following the exercises we shall:

- ◆ Learn how to combine images with sounds to represent real-life situations
- ◆ Create activities to write sentences according to visual and sound resources
- ◆ Improve simple writing and composing skills
- ◆ Create a scene using many layers and different tools
- ◆ Create activities to drag-and-drop words inside a scene
- ◆ Use pictures, zones, elements, layers, words, and colors to evaluate the children's association capabilities and the reverse thinking process

Writing a sentence using two images

It was such a beautiful day on the beach. The sun was shining in the sky, the sand was clean and glittering, the sea was clear, blue, and full of waves to play with. A perfect day to go for a swim.

Alice and her little brother Kevin ran towards the sea together. They played, jumped, and slid with their body surfing boards and the waves. Suddenly, an animal appeared swimming between them. It was a dolphin. It jumped and threw water at them. Awesome! Alice was so happy because she had a new and very special friend on this vacation.

Time for action – looking for two images to generate the exercise

We are going to search for two royalty-free photos related to the beach in two specialized web pages. We are then going to use them to create a rich activity.

1. Create a new folder in Windows Explorer (C:\Beach).

2. Open your default web browser and go to http://animalphotos.info. This web page allows us to search for royalty-free animal photos.

3. Enter dolphin in the textbox and then click on the **Search** button. Browse through the results and select the desired photo of a single dolphin, as shown in the next image:

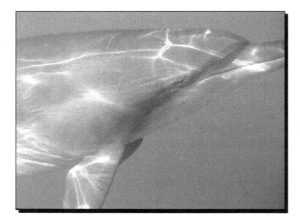

4. Right-click on the desired image with the dolphin and select **Save picture as** in the context menu that appears. Save the file as image030101.jpg in the previously created folder, C:\Beach.

5. Open your default web browser and go to `http://freedigitalphotos.net`. This web page allows us to search for, and download, royalty-free photos.

6. Enter `sea` in the textbox and then click on the **Go** button. The available photo thumbnails related to the entered keyword will appear. Browse through the results and select the desired photo of the sea, as shown in the next image:

7. Right-click on the desired image thumbnail with the sea and select **Save picture as** in the context menu that appears. Save the file as `image030102.jpg` in the previously created folder, `C:\Beach`.

What just happened?

We searched for two royalty-free photos related to the beach. In this case, we worked with two web pages, `http://animalphotos.info` and `http://freedigitalphotos.net`.

We now have the following two digital photos ready to be used in our writing sentences using two images exercise:

- `image030101.png`: A dolphin
- `image030102.png`: The sea and the shore

 It is very important to use photos in this exercise because the idea is to train the description of real-life scenarios.

Time for action – searching for related sounds

We have two digital photos and we want to add related sounds to them. We are going to search for MP3 files to use as sound effects for the scenes in **The Freesound Project** website (http://www.freesound.org/):

1. Open your default web browser and go to http://www.freesound.org. This web page allows us to search for, and download, sound files. It is necessary to register on this website in order to be able to download its files. The registration and access to its content are both free of cost.

 The Freesound Project website offers high-quality sounds with a Creative Commons License. The website offers thousands of samples. However, it does not offer songs.

2. Click on **Search** under **Search/Browse**.

3. Activate the **Filenames** checkbox. This way, the website will also search the file names of its sound files database.

4. Enter sea mp3 in the textbox and then click on the **Submit** button. The results with the details of many sound files will appear. You can click on the **Play** button on the left-hand side of each sound file's name and preview the recorded sound, as shown in the next screenshot:

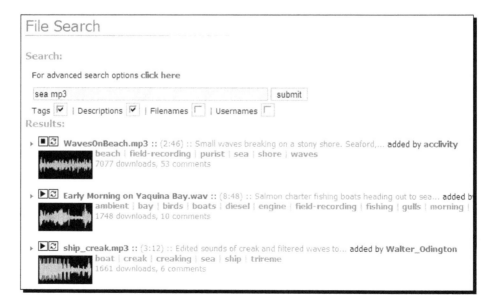

5. Click on the selected file name (`WavesOnBeach.mp3`) or on its waveform. A new page with more detailed information will appear (`http://www.freesound.org/samplesViewSingle.php?id=14777`), as shown in the next screenshot:

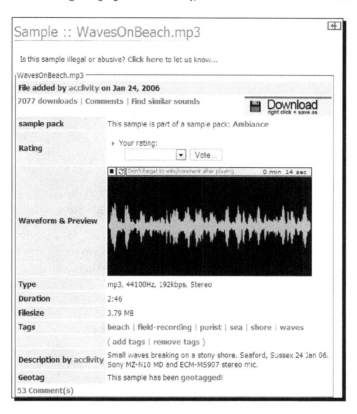

6. Check the license information about the chosen file.

7. Right-click on the **Download** label, located on the upper right-hand corner, and select **Save target as** in the context menu that appears. Save the file as `sound030102.mp3` in the previously created folder, `C:\Beach`. As this sound is related to the sea represented by the photo named `image030102.jpg`, we use the same name and another extension (`.mp3` instead of `.jpg`).

8. Next, go back to the web browser and repeat the aforementioned steps (2 to 7) to find and download sound related to a dolphin in MP3 format. In this case, repeat those steps searching for `dolphin mp3` and save the sound file as `sound030101.mp3` in the same folder. A nice recording of dolphins found on this website is `common_dolphins_isla_san_jose_16jan2002.mp3` (`http://www.freesound.org/samplesViewSingle.php?id=52099`).

What just happened?

We searched for two sound files in MP3 format because it is easy to integrate it into a Moodle exercise. We now have the following two digitalized sounds ready to be used in our writing sentences using two images and their related sounds exercise:

◆ `sound030101.mp3`: Dolphins on San Jose island

◆ `sound030102.mp3`: Waves on the beach

Time for action – activating the MP3 player in Moodle

As we are going to add the aforementioned sound files to our exercise in Moodle, we have to make sure that its multimedia plugins are enabled.

1. Log in to your Moodle server.

2. Click on **Modules | Filters | Manage filters** on the **Site Administration** panel.

3. If the **Multimedia Plugins** filter appears in grey and displays a closed eye icon in the **Disable/Enable** column, you must click on this icon to change it to an opened eye icon. This way, Moodle will enable the multimedia plugins, as shown in the next screenshot:

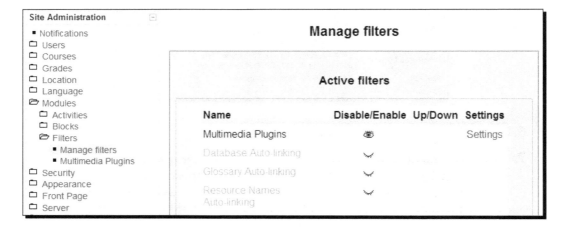

4. If you made changes, click on the **Save changes** button.

5. Next, click on **Modules | Filters | Multimedia Plugins** in the **Site Administration** panel.

6. Make sure that the **Enable .mp3 filter** checkbox is activated. If it is not, activate it and then click on the **Save changes** button.

What just happened?

We made the necessary changes in Moodle's configuration in order to make it possible to use its MP3 player. This way, we are going to be able to embed the sound files associated with the photographs, offering both visual and auditory perception resources in the exercise.

Time for action – integrating the visual and auditory resources in a Moodle exercise

We now have to upload the photos and their related sounds in order to add our exercise to an existing Moodle course.

1. Log in to your Moodle server.

2. Click on the desired course name (Beach). You can create a new course or use an existing one.

3. As previously learned, follow the necessary steps to edit the summary for a desired week. Enter Exercise 1 in the **Summary** textbox and save the changes.

4. Click on the **Add an activity** combo box for the selected week and select **Online text.**

5. Enter Writing a sentence in **Assignment name**.

6. Select Verdana in font and 5 (18) in size—the first two combo boxes below **Description**.

7. Select your desired color for the text.

8. Click on the big textbox below **Description** and enter Writing a sentence using two photos. This is the description of the student's goal for this exercise.

9. Press *Enter* and type Listen to its sound. Then, select this text and click on the **Insert Web Link** button (a chain). A new web page will appear displaying the title **Insert Link**.

10. Click on the **Browse** button and follow the necessary steps to create a new folder, chapter03. It will allow us to organize the necessary files for our new exercise.

11. Click on the **Browse** button. Browse to the folder that holds the sound files and the images used in the exercise (C:\Beach) and select the file to upload, sound030101.mp3. Next, click on **Open**, on **Upload** and on the file name link.

12. Moodle will display the URL for this sound file in the **URL** textbox. Enter Listen to its sound in the title textbox and click on **OK**.

13. Press *Enter* and click on the **Insert Image** button (a mountain or a tree according to the Moodle version). A new web page will appear displaying the title **Insert Image**.

14. Follow the necessary steps to upload the file image030101.png in the previously created folder, chapter03. Remember to enter an alternate text, and the image will appear below the previously entered title.

15. Remember that you can click on the **Enlarge editor** button in order to view all the instructions. Repeat the aforementioned steps (9 to 14) in order to add the second sound file, sound030102, and its related image, image030102.jpg. Take into account that it is not necessary to create the chapter03 folder again.

16. The online text assignment will display the title and the two **Listen to its sound** subtitles with their related photos, as shown in the next screenshot:

17. Finally, scroll down and select **Save and return to course**.

What just happened?

We added the writing sentences using two images and their related sounds exercise to a Moodle course. The students are now going to be able to write a sentence after watching the images and listening to their related sounds by clicking on its hyperlink in the corresponding week.

We used a new folder, `chapter03`. We uploaded the two MP3 sound files and their related images. We added a title and two hyperlinks to the MP3 sound files. As we had made sure that the multimedia plugins were enabled, Moodle is going to show a media player to allow the student to reproduce the MP3 sound file in their browsers.

The online text assignment allowed us to describe the goals for the activity mixing photos with their related sounds.

Time for action – writing the sentence

1. Click on the course name (`Beach`) and switch your role to student.

2. Click on the **Writing a sentence** link on the corresponding week. The web browser will show the two photos with a media player on top of each one. Click on the **Play** button on the right-hand side of the **Listen to its sound** label. You will be able to listen to the sound file associated with each image, as shown in the next screenshot:

 You can click on the **Play** button for both sounds. This way, you can listen to the waves on the beach and the sound made by dolphins at the same time.

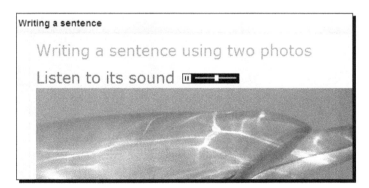

3. Click on the **Edit my submission** button. Moodle will display a big text area with an HTML editor.

4. Select `Verdana` in font and `5 (18)` in size.

5. Write a sentence, `The dolphin is swimming in the sea.` as shown in the next screenshot:

6. Click on the **Save changes** button. This way, Moodle will save the results for this exercise.

7. Don't forget to check the results for this exercise as previously learned.

What just happened?

In this activity, we worked with real-life images and sounds. Our goal in this exercise was that the child listen to the audio, watch the images, and then find their relationship. The child can work alone, or with the help of a therapist or a family member, so that he/she can understand and run the exercise.

The activity consists of writing a simple sentence considering the photos and their related sounds. We applied the following concepts and resources:

◆ **Visual and auditory perception resources**. We simplified the execution of the activity using sounds. The sound resources offer an additional source of information in order to simplify the identification of each element or scene.

◆ **Photographs**. They offer a perfect representation of a real-life scene. The child has to write a sentence about these photos.

◆ **Associating images**. The child has to associate two images in order to find a relationship between them and consider their related sounds. In this case, the sea is the animal's natural environment.

◆ **Simple writing and composing skills**. The child has to work with language structures, order, and coherence.

◆ **Motivation**. The real sound recordings and photographs usually increase the child's interest in this activity.

We can increase the complexity of this exercise using more images and just one sound. We can then also use complex photographs with many elements in different sizes. The main character in each picture can be the bigger one.

Putting words inside an image with structure

Great! Another vacation day!

Alice loved the beach. It was her favorite place to have fun, but she was scared of forgetting what she had learned in school after playing so much on the beach. Therefore, she had an idea. She asked her mother to help her write down everything that she found around her. She had so many things to write down, because the beach was full of people: some of them were sunbathing, others swimming in the sea; there were also children building sandcastles and others playing with balls.

Can we help her as well?

Time for action – creating a scene

We are going to create a scene using a background picture and then add other clipart inside it to represent each word.

1. Start Inkscape and minimize it. You will use it later.

2. Start Word 2007. You will be working in a new blank document.

In this case, we will use Word 2007 to search for clipart. However, you can also create a scene with other clipart libraries. We will also use other applications that provide high-quality clipart in other visually rich exercises.

3. Click on **Insert | Clip Art**. The **Clip Art** panel will appear on the right-hand side of the main window.

4. Click on the **Search in** combo box and activate the **Everywhere** checkbox. This way, Word will search for clipart in all the available collections, including the Web Collections.

5. Click on the **Search for** textbox and enter `Beach`.

6. Click on the **Go** button.

7. Position the mouse pointer over the desired clipart's thumbnail. Since you want to change the picture size without losing quality using Inkscape, remember to make sure that it is a **WMF** or an **EMF** file.

8. Right-click on the desired clipart's thumbnail and select **Preview/Properties** in the context menu that appears. Word will display a new dialog box showing a larger preview of the scalable clipart and a temporary file name.

9. Triple-click on the long path and file name shown after **File**. This way, you will be sure that the temporary file's full path is selected. Then, right-click on it and select **Copy** in the context menu that appears.

10. Now, activate Inkscape—remember it was running minimized. You can use *Alt* + *Tab* or *Windows* + *Tab*. Don't close the clipart's preview window.

11. Select **File | Import** from the main menu. Click on the **Type a file name button** (the pencil with a paper sheet icon) and paste the previously copied temporary file's full path in the **Location:** textbox. The path is going to be similar to `C:\Users\vanesa\AppData\Local\Microsoft\Windows\Temporary Internet Files\Content.IE5\WL240QUN\MCj04354940000[1].wmf`.

12. Click on the **Open** button. The previously previewed clipart, the background for our scene, will appear in Inkscape's drawing area, as shown in the next screenshot:

13. Return to Word 2007, and close the **Preview/Properties** dialog box.

14. Repeat the aforementioned steps (6 to 13) for each vector graphic to add to the previously shown background picture, the beach. The next image shows three possible pictures:

  ❑   A bucket and a shovel

  ❑   A beach ball

  ❑   A sandcastle

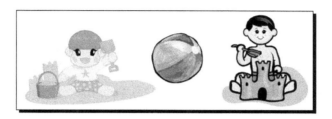

15. Click on one of the recently added pictures to select it. Eight double-headed arrows will appear in a rectangle around the selection. Drag-and-drop one of the diagonal double-headed arrows and scale the drawing both in the horizontal (X) and vertical (Y) directions. You can do it holding down the *Ctrl* key in order to maintain the original aspect ratio. Then, drag-and-drop the picture to the appropriate position inside the beach background.

16. Repeat the aforementioned step for the other two pictures to create a scene as shown in the next image:

17. Select **File | Save** from Inkscape's main menu. Save the file as image030201.svg in the previously created folder, C:\Beach.

What just happened?

We combined several scalable vector clipart images to create a representation of a scene on the beach. Inkscape allowed us to define a background and add different elements on top of it. Each element represents a different word.

Time for action – adding floating labels to the image

1. Click on the **Create and edit text objects** button (a big **A** with a cursor on the left-hand side) or press *F8*. This function allows you to add text with different fonts and colors in Inkscape's drawing area.

2. Select the desired font and size using the two combo boxes that appear on the upper left-hand corner of the window, below the main toolbar.

3. Repeat the aforementioned steps (1 to 2) to write the following words as labels, with a layout similar to the one shown in the next image:

    ❑ Sandcastle

    ❑ Umbrella

    ❑ Beach ball

    ❑ Sea

    ❑ Shovel

    ❑ Bucket

4. Once you enter each word, you can click on the desired color in the color palette. It is a good idea to use diverse colors to make it clear that they are different words.

5. Select **File | Save** from Inkscape's main menu in order to save the changes made to the original Inkscape SVG file.

6. Select **File | Export Bitmap**. A dialog box showing many export options will appear. Enter 72 on the first **dpi** (Dots Per Inch) textbox.

7. Click on the **Drawing** button, and then on **Export**. Inkscape will export the drawing in PNG format. The exported bitmap graphics with the beach scene and the words at the bottom will be saved at `C:\Beach\image030201.png`.

What just happened?

We created a representation of a scene on the beach using Inkscape and scalable vector clipart. We first added a background picture and then used vector graphics to add different elements related to specific words. We could change their size without losing quality and we could put them on top of the existing background.

We added text labels for each word that represents an element in the scene. Finally, we exported the resulting image to the PNG format.

Time for action – uploading the scene to Moodle

We now have to upload the original SVG file and its bitmap representation, in order to add our exercise to an existing Moodle course.

1. Log in to your Moodle server.

2. Click on the desired course name (`Beach`). You can create a new course or use an existing one.

3. As previously learned, follow the necessary steps to edit the summary for a desired week. Enter `Exercise 2` in the **Summary** textbox and save the changes.

4. Click on the **Add an activity** combo box for the selected week and select **Upload a single file**.

5. Enter `Dragging and dropping words` in **Assignment name**.

6. Select `Verdana` in font and `5 (18)` in size—the first two combo boxes below **Description**. Next, select your desired color for the text.

7. Click on the big textbox below **Description** and enter `Putting words inside an image with structure`. This is the description of the student's goal for this exercise.

8. Press *Enter* and click on the **Insert Image** button (a mountain or a tree, according to the Moodle version). A new web page will appear displaying the title **Insert image**.

9. Click on the `chapter03` folder link and then click on the **Browse** button. Browse to the folder that holds the exported drawing and select the file to upload, `image030201.png`. Then click on **Open** and on the **Upload** button. The label **File uploaded successfully** will appear inside the **File browser** box.

10. Next, click on the recently uploaded file name, `image030201.png`. The image will appear in the **Preview** box.

11. Enter `image` in **Alternate text** and click on **OK**. The image will appear below the previously entered title. Remember that you can click on the **Enlarge editor** button to view more information on the screen.

12. Press *Enter* and click on the **Ordered list** button (a list of 1, 2, and 3).

13. Write the detailed steps to complete the exercise.

- Open this picture using Inkscape
- Drag-and-drop each word to match the corresponding element in the picture
- Save and upload the new picture

14. Next, select the `picture` word written in the sentence that describes the first step.

15. Click on the **Insert Web Link** button (a chain). A new web page will appear displaying the title **Insert Link**.

16. Click on the **Browse** button and then on the `chapter03` folder link.

17. Click on the new **Browse** button that appears. Browse to the folder that holds the previously created Inkscape drawing with the scene (`C:\Beach`) and select the file to upload, `image030201.svg`. Next, click on **Open**, on **Upload**, and on the file name link, as shown in the next screenshot:

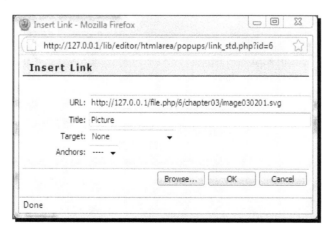

18. Moodle will display the URL for this Inkscape file in the **URL** textbox. Enter `picture` in the title textbox and click on **OK**. This way, the student is going to be able to download the Inkscape drawing by clicking on the word **picture** with a hyperlink, as shown in the next screenshot:

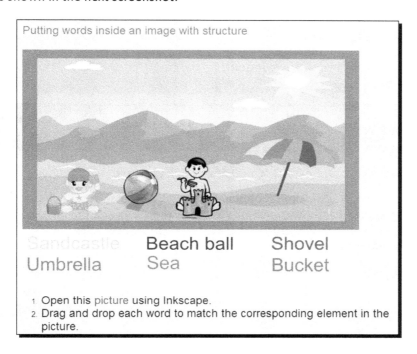

19. Select `100` in the **Grade** combo box.

20. Select `10MB` in **Maximum size**. This is the maximum size for the file that each student is going to be able to upload as a result for this activity. However, it is very important to check the possibilities offered by your Moodle server with its Moodle administrator.

21. Finally, scroll down and select **Save and return to course**.

What just happened?

We added the putting words inside an image with structure exercise to a Moodle course. The students are now going to be able to follow the instructions explained in the upload a single file assignment and download the Inkscape drawing to drag-and-drop words.

We defined a hyperlink to the Inkscape drawing because the students are going to use it to drag-and-drop each word to the corresponding zone of the scene.

The upload a single file assignment allowed us to describe the necessary steps to complete the activity, and it's also going to enable the students to upload their results as an Inkscape drawing.

 In this case, the necessary steps to complete the activity are just a few sentences in order to simplify the example. However, sometimes, it is necessary to write more instructions when you have to work with other applications such as Inkscape.

Time for action – running the exercise using a netbook's touchpad

1. Click on the course name (Beach) and switch your role to student.

2. Click on the **Dragging and dropping words** link on the corresponding week. The web browser will show the bitmap image of the scene and the instructions with the hyperlink to the Inkscape drawing. The picture word will appear in blue and underlined, indicating that it is a hyperlink.

3. Right-click on the **Picture** word with the hyperlink and select **Save Link As** in the context menu that appears. Save the file as mybeach.svg in your documents folder.

4. Click on the **Start or edit my journal entry** button. Moodle will display a big text area with an HTML editor.

5. Start **Inkscape** and open the previously saved file, mybeach.svg.

6. Drag each word below the image and drop it over the corresponding zone or element in the scene. You can use your finger to move the mouse pointer over the desired word, then press the left mouse pad button and drag the word with your finger without releasing the button. Once the word is over the desired zone or element in the scene, release the button. This way, you can play with your fingers whilst solving the exercise, as shown in the next image:

7. Once you have finished dragging and dropping each word, select **File | Export Bitmap**. A dialog box showing many export options will appear.

8. Click on the **Drawing** button and then on **Export**. Inkscape will export the drawing in PNG format. The exported drawing will be mybeach.png in your documents folder.

9. Go back to your web browser and click on **Browse**. Browse to the folder that holds the exported drawing and select the file to upload, mybeach.png. Then, click on **Open**.

10. The previously exported drawing in PNG format will now appear below the instructions with the name **mybeach.png**. You can click on the link and download this image with the words dropped over the corresponding elements in the scene. The next image shows an example of the solved exercise.

11. Don't forget to check the results for this exercise as previously learned.

What just happened?

In this activity, we created a drawing representing a scene on the beach. We asked the child to drag-and-drop each word below the scene to match the corresponding element or zone using a netbook and its touchpad.

The activity consists of watching the scene, reading the words, and understanding them and their relationship with elements in the scene. The child can then begin to drag-and-drop each word using any pointing device capable of dragging and dropping elements. We applied the following concepts and resources:

◆ **Associating images with words and reversibility**. The child has to associate an image with a word. This way, the exercise improves training in reverse thinking.

◆ **Reading comprehension**. The child has to read and understand simple words related to an existing scene.

◆ **Images composed of multiple layers**. There is a background scene, elements, and words that compose multiple layers for the complex scene. The child can identify himself/herself with the situation and develop his/her imagination while solving the exercise.

 We can increase the complexity of this exercise by adding more words and elements. This kind of visually rich activity is very useful to improve the child's vocabulary.

It is also possible to run this activity using a classic mouse, a gamepad's stick or a joystick. Working with different hardware devices can increase or reduce the complexity and help to work with diverse kinds of problems. The most appropriate hardware will depend on the child's disabilities.

New hardware such as a netbook and its touchpad usually offers additional motivation to the child.

Have a go hero – dragging and dropping pictures into the scene

You can increase the complexity of the previous activity in order to allow children to exercise pattern recognition and matching. Instead of working with words, add pictures similar to the elements found in the scene. However, the new pictures should be slightly different. For example, you can add an umbrella with different colors.

Add the new pictures organized at the bottom of the scene with the same layout previously explained for the words, in rows and columns.

The child can now recognize patterns, drag-and-drop each element over its similar element on the scene, and complete the new exercise.

 You can create different scenes with diverse skill levels and combine many activities using the tools that we have learned about so far.

Pop quiz – discovering new tools and activities

1. You can embed an MP3 sound file in Moodle by:
    a. Uploading it and inserting a web link to it
    b. Copying it to the sounds shared folder in the Moodle server
    c. Uploading it and clicking on the **Embed sound** button

2. In order to be able to reproduce an embedded MP3 file in Moodle:
    a. You have to install a multimedia plugin in the exercise
    b. You have to make sure that its multimedia plugins are enabled
    c. You have to make sure that the MP3 codec checkbox is activated in Moodle's multimedia control panel

3. An upload a single file assignment:
    a. Doesn't allow the student to upload files
    b. Allows the student to neither upload files nor write text
    c. Allows the student to upload files

4. A netbook's touchpad offers functions similar to:
   a. A keyboard
   b. A webcam
   c. A mouse

5. You can upload and add links to files in Moodle by:
   a. Selecting the text to hold the hyperlink and clicking on the **Insert Web Link** button (a chain)
   b. Clicking on the **Insert Web Link** button (a chain) without any selected text
   c. Clicking on the hyperlink manager in Moodle's Control Panel

Summary

In this chapter, we have learned how to:

◆ Create many visually rich activities combining images, sounds, scenes, layers, elements, words, and pictures

◆ Take advantage of Moodle's integrated multimedia plugins to add MP3 sound files related to images

◆ Work with many web pages that offer images and sounds, assignments, and Inkscape, in order to create attractive exercises in Moodle

◆ Use hyperlinks generated by Moodle in order to add sound and links to files that the student can download in order to solve the exercises

◆ Work with Inkscape and a netbook's touchpad to allow children with special education needs to use their fingers in order to drag-and-drop the words in the scene on a tiny screen

Now that we have learned to work with the association of images and words, we're ready to prepare exercises to develop sorting activities mixing words and pictures, which is the topic of the next chapter.

4
Developing Sorting Activities, Mixing Shapes and Pictures

We can use pictures representing situations, parts of sequences, and geometric shapes in order to develop sorting activities. It is possible to use many different applications to create exercises that challenge the student to order certain elements in many creative visually rich experiences in Moodle. This way, we can train time management capabilities, visual perception, and size and space notions in different scenarios.

In this chapter, Alice goes to the supermarket. We will learn how to create rich activities related to her shopping experience. By reading this chapter and following the exercises we shall:

- ◆ Create activities to sort jumbled pictures
- ◆ Learn to represent a real-life temporal sequence with pictures
- ◆ Improve pattern recognition skills
- ◆ Combine geometric shapes with pictures and text to evaluate children's pattern recognition capabilities
- ◆ Prepare an activity to work with a multi-touch screen in order to help children drag-and-drop elements with their fingers

Ordering the temporal sequence

Alice loves going to the supermarket with her mother because she usually buys her a few gifts—cookies, candies, among others. This time, she had to draw a few pictures about her activities during the weekend as homework for the school. The new visit to the supermarket was a great opportunity to watch many situations and get some good ideas for her drawings.

Time for action – getting three pictures to represent a temporal sequence

We are going to search for existing 2D clipart related to different situations whilst shopping in a supermarket. We are then going to convert them to 2D bitmap images using the Snipping Tool application to take snapshots of elements of the screen.

1. Create a new folder in Windows Explorer (`C:\Supermarket`).

2. Open your default web browser and go to `http://office.microsoft.com/en-us/clipart/default.aspx`. This web page allows us to search for free clipart in **Office Online Clip Art & Media**.

3. Enter **grocery stores** in the textbox and click on the **Search** button. The available clipart thumbnails related to the entered keywords will appear.

4. Select **Clip art** in **Filter by type**. This way, the search results will be filtered to display only vector graphics.

5. Click on the zoom icon located below the desired clipart thumbnail. A new window displaying a small preview of the clipart will appear.

6. Click on **Bigger preview** and this label will change to **Smaller preview**. We want to use the big preview to take snapshots of the clipart using the same size.

7. Start **Snipping Tool (Start Menu | All Programs | Accessories | Snipping Tool)** and capture the clipart preview as previously learned. Save the file in the Portable Network Graphic File (PNG) format as `image040101.png` in the previously created folder, `C:\Supermarket`. This way, we have the first image of the sequence, a woman selecting items in the grocery store, as shown in the next image:

8. Return to the web browser and repeat the aforementioned steps (3 to 7) to capture the bitmap image of another clipart image. In this case, repeat those steps searching for `cashier` and saving the captured image file as `image040102.png` in the same folder. This way, we have the second image of the sequence, a cashier checking-out the items, as shown in the next image:

9. Return to the web browser and repeat the aforementioned steps (3 to 7) to capture the bitmap image of the third clipart image. In this case, repeat those steps searching for `grocery shopping` and saving the captured image file as `image040103.png` in the same folder. This way, we have the third image of the sequence, the items in the car's trunk, as shown in the next image:

What just happened?

We searched for clipart previews in Office Online Clip Art & Media, through our web browser. We then used our well-known Snipping Tool application to capture the portion of the screen that showed the preview of the desired clipart. This way, we could save three images in the PNG format by following just a few simple steps.

We now have the following three bitmap graphics, representing three different situations whilst shopping in a supermarket, ready to be used in our ordering the temporal sequence exercise:

- `image040101`: A woman choosing items in a grocery store
- `image040102`: A cashier checking-out the items
- `image040103`: A shopping cart and the items in the car's trunk

Time for action – creating the mixed temporal sequence using images

1. It is time to organize the images for our mixed temporary sequence.

2. Start Hot Potatoes and click on **JMix**. A new window with the JMix application will appear.

3. Enter `Ordering the temporal sequence` in the **Title** textbox.

4. Select **File | Save** from JMix's main menu. Save the file as `jmix0401.jmx` in the previously created folder, `C:\Supermarket`.

5. Click on the big textbox below **Main sentence**.

6. Select **Insert | Picture | Picture from local file** from JMix's main menu. Select the previously saved bitmap image `image040101.png` in `C:\Supermarket` and click on the **Open** button and then on **OK**. JMix will use the default options to insert the image.

7. Press *Enter* and repeat the aforementioned step to insert the previously saved bitmap image `image040102.png` in `C:\Supermarket`.

8. Press *Enter* again and repeat the aforementioned step to insert the previously saved bitmap image `image040103.png` in `C:\Supermarket`. JMix will show the following HTML code in the textbox, as displayed in the next screenshot:

```
<img src="image040101.PNG" alt="image040101.PNG"
        title="image040101" width="300" height="232"></img>
<img src="image040102.PNG" alt="image040102.PNG"
```

```
                    title="image040102" width="215" height="235"></img>
    <img src="image040103.PNG" alt="image040103.PNG"
                    title="image040103" width="350" height="234"></img>
```

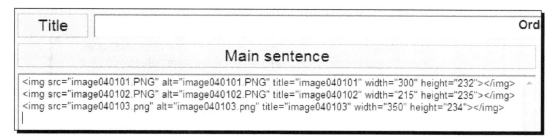

9. Select **File | Create Web Page | Drag/drop Format**. JMix will create a new web page. Save the new file as `jmix0401.htm` in the aforementioned folder. A new dialog box will appear. Click on **View the exercise in my browser**.

10. The default web browser will appear showing the three images that compose the sequence. They will appear jumbled, with a random order, as shown in the next screenshot:

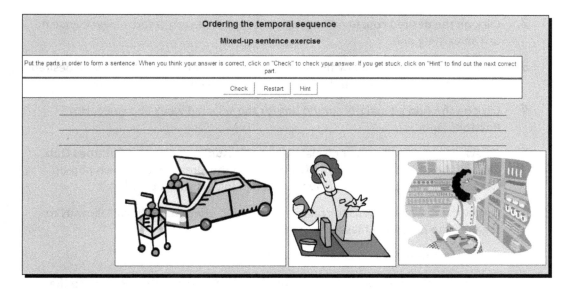

11. Go back to JMix. Select **File | Create Zip Package | Create Drag/Drop Zip Package** from the main menu and enter the name for the new ZIP file, `jmix0401.zip`. JMix will create a ZIP file with all the necessary files to upload to Moodle in order to run the JMix exercise.

What just happened?

We inserted the three images to prepare an ordered sequence for our exercise. Instead of putting the parts in order to form a sentence, we used the capabilities offered by JMix to create a visually rich mixed-up sequence exercise.

 JMix is designed to work with words as parts of a sentence. However, as the images are expressed as HTML code, we were able to add each picture as a word of a visual sentence.

We added each picture following the order for the sequence. When we run the exercise loading the web page created by JMix, it jumbles the pictures on the bottom of the screen. Therefore, we don't have to worry about jumbling them.

Time for action – adding the activity to a Moodle course

We now have to add the ordering a temporal sequence exercise to an existing Moodle course.

1. Log in to your Moodle server.

2. Click on the desired course name (Supermarket). You can create a new course or use an existing one.

3. As previously learned, follow the necessary steps to edit the summary for a desired week. Enter Exercise 1 in the **Summary** textbox and save the changes.

4. Click on the **Add an activity** combo box for the selected week and select **Hot Potatoes Quiz**.

5. A new web page will appear displaying the title **Adding a new Hot Potatoes Quiz**. Click on the **Choose or upload a file** button and the already well-known pop-up window displaying information about files and folders will appear.

6. Follow the necessary steps to create a new folder, chapter04. It will allow us to organize the necessary files for our new exercise.

7. Click on **chapter04** (the recently created folder's hyperlink).

8. Click on the **Upload a file** button and then on the **Browse** button. Browse to the folder that holds the images and the files used in the exercise (C:\Supermarket) and select the ZIP file to upload, jmix0401.zip. Next, click on **Open** and on the **Upload this file** button.

9. Position the mouse pointer over the **jmix0401.zip** name and move it horizontally to the **Unzip** action hyperlink in the same row. Next, click on **Unzip | OK**, and Moodle will extract all the compressed files from this ZIP file.

10. Next, position the mouse pointer over the **Jmix0401.htm** name and move it horizontally to the **Choose** action hyperlink in the same row. Then click on **Choose**, as shown in the next screenshot:

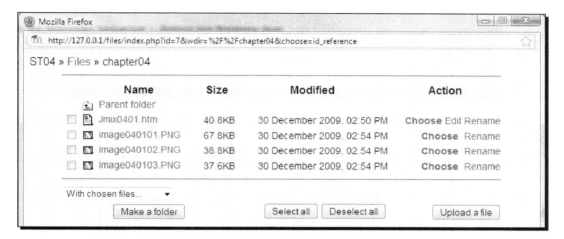

11. Moodle will display `chapter04/jmix0401.htm` in the **File name** textbox. This is the web page that will run the exercise created previously using JMix.

12. Scroll down and click on the **Save and display** button, located at the bottom of the web page. The web browser will show the exercise with the three jumbled pictures that must be dragged and dropped to prepare the ordered sequence.

What just happened?

We added the rich ordering a temporal sequence exercise to a Moodle course. Now, the students are going to be able to run the activity by clicking on its hyperlink in the corresponding week.

We created a new folder, `chapter04`. This folder will hold all the necessary files for the activities related to the visit to the supermarket.

We then uploaded and decompressed a ZIP file that contained the three images previously captured using Snipping Tool and the HTML file created with JMix (`jmix0401.htm`). This HTML file has links to the three images inserted with JMix.

Time for action – ordering the sequence by dragging and dropping images

It is time to run the activity as a student and to check the results as a teacher.

1. Click on the course name (Supermarket) and switch your role to student.

2. Click on the **Ordering the temporal sequence** link on the corresponding week. The web browser will show the exercise with a drag/drop format.

3. Drag-and-drop each image to its corresponding place to compose the ordered sequence of events that usually happens when visiting a supermarket. You have to drop each image over the first line, creating the ordered sequence from left to right, as shown in the next screenshot:

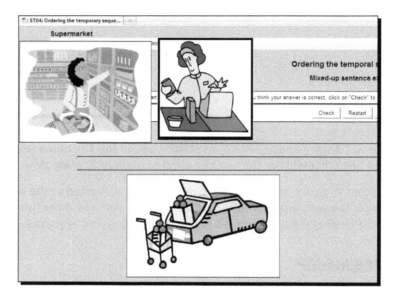

4. After dropping all the images to their corresponding positions in order to compose the visual sequence, click on the **Check** button to test the results.

5. If the student's score is 100%, Moodle will save the results and will go back to the course web page.

6. Run the exercise with different wrong sequences and click on the **Check** button each time. Moodle will display the resulting sequence ordered by the student and the part of the answer that is in its right place, as shown in the next screenshot. Besides, it will let you run the activity again. However, it will save the student's results for each attempt.

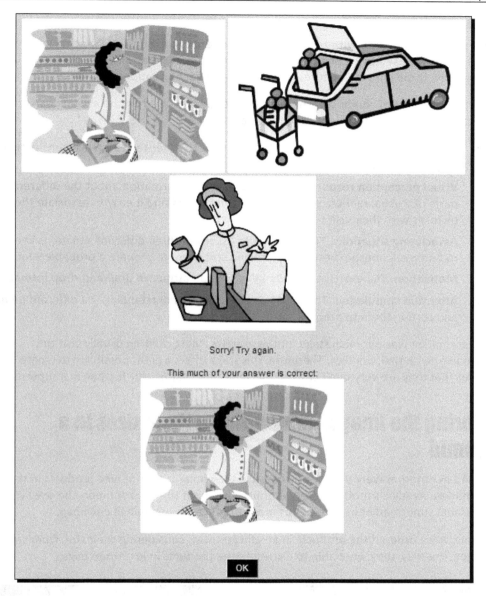

Sorry! Try again.

This much of your answer is correct:

OK

7. You can return to your normal role and check the number of attempts as done with the Hot Potatoes Quizzes activities.

We ran a JMix exercise. However, Moodle will show its statistics under Hot Potatoes Quizzes activities.

What just happened?

In this activity, we worked with a usual real-life sequence consisting of shopping in a supermarket. We used three pictures to represent different situations. The child has to look at the three jumbled pictures and understand each situation.

The activity consists of composing the temporal sequence based on the existing parts. We applied the following concepts and resources:

- ◆ **Time management capabilities**. The child has to order the sequence considering the time at which a situation happens.
- ◆ **Visual perception resources**. The pictures offer information about the different parts of a usual real-life sequence. The child would find it easy to associate the pictures with their visit to the supermarket.
- ◆ **Associating situations**. The child has to associate three different situations in order to find a relationship between them and sort them to prepare a probable sequence.
- ◆ **Motivation**. The exercise is challenging with an attractive drag-and-drop format.
- ◆ **Attention stimulation**. The child has to focus on understanding the different pictures and sorting them to prepare a probable sequence.

The supermarket was our main stage for the exercise. Most children usually visit the supermarket with their families. Therefore, this stage offers a great possibility to create activities that they are very familiar with, the situations that usually happen in a supermarket.

Ordering the images according to their sizes in a pyramid

Alice and her mother were very happy because they bought a lot of nice products in the supermarket. As Alice's mother is very enthusiastic about the environment, she uses very big reusable supermarket bags to put as many products as possible in each bag.

This time, Alice ordered the products in an efficient way, considering their size, from smaller to bigger. This way, they were able to distribute the products in just three bags.

Time for action – building the pyramid

We are first going to download and install Edraw Max 5.1. We will then prepare a diagram of a pyramid with three parts for our ordering the images according to their sizes exercise.

1. Start Word 2007 and minimize it. You will use it later.

2. If you do not have it yet, download and install the free trial version of Edraw Max 5.1 (`http://www.edrawsoft.com/download.php`).

3. Start Edraw Max 5.1. A new window with the graphics software will appear, displaying the start page.

4. Click on **Basic diagram** under **Template categories** and then double-click on **Blank drawing** under **Templates**. A new drawing area will appear.

5. Click on the textbox below **Libraries**. Enter `pyramid` and click on the arrow button (**Start search**). Edraw will display all the predefined shapes in its installed templates that comply with the word entered in the search criteria, as shown in the next screenshot:

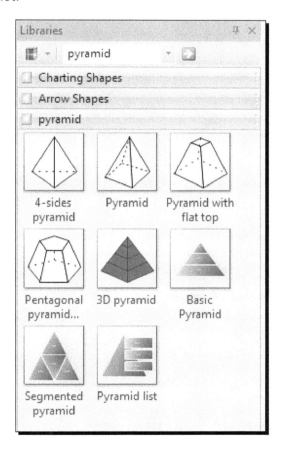

6. Click on the **Basic Pyramid** icon on the previously shown search results.

7. Drag-and-drop the **Basic Pyramid** icon into the drawing area. The shape of a pyramid composed of three parts will appear in the drawing area, as shown in the next screenshot:

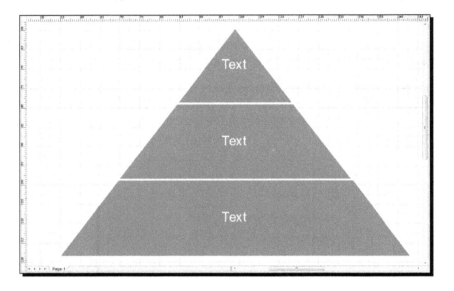

8. Double-click on each part of the pyramid and erase its default text.

9. Select the pyramid. Click on **Shape format | Rotate & Flip | -90** on the ribbon. The pyramid will now appear drawn from left to right.

10. Press *F3* and the **Shape format** dialog box will appear. Click on **Fill | Gradient fill** and select the desired colors to fill each part with a linear gradient. You can also add other effects to each part of the pyramid.

11. Click on **Shape format | Grouping | Ungroup** on the ribbon. Each part of the pyramid will now be an independent shape. Therefore, you can move each part as desired to separate them as needed.

12. Next, activate Word 2007—remember it was running minimized.

13. Search for a `milk bottle` scalable vector clipart image, as explained in previous exercises.

14. Right-click on the desired clipart's thumbnail and select **Preview/Properties** in the context menu that appears. Word will display a new dialog box showing a larger preview of the scalable clipart and a temporary file name.

15. Triple-click on the long path and file name shown after **File**. This way, you will be sure that the temporary file's full path is selected. Then right-click on it and select **Copy** in the context menu that appears.

16. Next, activate Edraw. You can use *Alt + Tab* or *Windows + Tab*. Don't close the clipart's preview window.

17. Click on **Insert | Picture** on the ribbon. Paste the previously copied temporary file's full path in the **File name** text box and click on the **Open** button. The previously previewed clipart will appear in Edraw's drawing area.

18. Resize this graphic to make it fit into the first part of the pyramid, the triangle on the left-hand side.

 The necessary steps to move and resize the inserted picture are the same as the ones previously learned to move and resize a graphic in Inkscape's drawing area.

19. Duplicate this graphic by copying and pasting it. Move the copy inside the next part of the pyramid, the trapezoid in the middle. Resize this copy to make it bigger than the first copy.

20. Duplicate this new graphic by copying and pasting it. Move the copy inside the next part of the pyramid, the last trapezoid on the right-hand side. Resize this copy to make it the biggest one, as shown in the next screenshot:

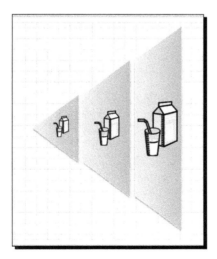

21. Click on **View | Gridlines** on the ribbon. This way, the **Gridlines** checkbox will be deactivated and the background gray dotted lines will disappear from Edraw's drawing area. You will thus be able to take snapshots of the three different parts of the pyramid with a white background and without the gridlines.

22. Following the same steps learned in previous exercises, take snapshots of the different parts of the pyramid using Snipping Tool and save the resulting image files with the names shown in the following table, in the previously created folder, `C:\Supermarket`. The next screenshot displays sample images for the snapshots using Paint to view them:

Part of the pyramid	Picture file name
Left (triangle)	image040201.png
Middle (trapezoid)	image040202.png
Right (trapezoid)	image040203.png

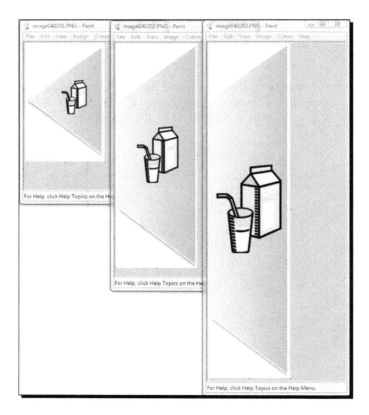

What just happened?

We installed the free trial version of Edraw Max 5.1. This versatile graphics software allows us to create and edit professional-looking flowcharts and charts using its extensive predefined symbols and templates. The free trial version has some limitations when exporting the graphics to other formats. However, it is very useful to create our pyramid. If you like the trial version, you can buy the full version.

We combined the pyramid shape found in Edraw's templates with a scalable clipart image. We searched for a vector asset in **Office Online Clip Art & Media** and we imported the temporary files created by Word into Edraw's drawing area.

You can also build a pyramid like the one used in this exercise using Inkscape or any other vector drawing software. The key advantage of using Edraw was the possibility to drag-and-drop an existing definition of a pyramid's shape. Nonetheless, it isn't difficult to draw a pyramid by drawing a few lines to create each part.

We then copied and pasted the clipart in the different parts of the pyramid with different sizes. Finally, we used our well-known Snipping Tool application to capture three portions of the screen that showed each part of the pyramid. This way, we could save three images in the PNG format following just a few simple steps.

We now have the following three bitmap graphics, representing three parts of a pyramid, from left to right, ready to be used in our ordering the images according to their sizes in a pyramid:

- ◆ image040201: The first part of the pyramid, with the smallest picture
- ◆ image040202: The second part of the pyramid, with a big picture
- ◆ image040203: The third part of the pyramid, with the biggest picture

Time for action – creating the mixed parts of the pyramid using images

It is time to organize the images for our exercise.

1. Start Hot Potatoes and click on **JMix**. A new window with the JMix application will appear.

2. Enter Ordering the images according to their sizes in the pyramid in the **Title** textbox.

3. Select **File | Save** from JMix's main menu. Save the file as `jmix0402.jmx` in the previously created folder, `C:\Supermarket`.

4. Click on the big textbox below **Main sentence**.

5. Select **Insert | Picture| Picture from local file** from JMix's main menu. Choose the previously saved bitmap image `image040201.png` in `C:\Supermarket` and click on the **Open** button. Enter `97` in the **Width** textbox and then click on **OK**. JMix will resize the height to maintain the image's aspect ratio according to the new width and will insert the image using the new size.

6. Press *Enter* and repeat the aforementioned step to resize and insert the previously saved bitmap image `image040202.png` in `C:\Supermarket`.

7. Press *Enter* again and repeat the aforementioned step to resize and insert the previously saved bitmap image `image040203.png` in `C:\Supermarket`. JMix will show the following HTML code in the textbox, as displayed in the next screenshot:

```
<img src="image040201.PNG" alt="image040201.PNG"
     title="image040201" width="97" height="150"></img>
<img src="image040202.PNG" alt="image040202.PNG"
     title="image040202" width="97" height="275"></img>
<img src="image040203.PNG" alt="image040203.PNG"
     title="image040203" width="97" height="407"></img>
```

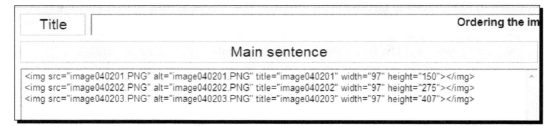

8. Select **File | Create Web Page | Drag/Drop Format**. JMix will create a new web page. Save the new file as `jmix0402.htm` in the aforementioned folder. A new dialog box will appear. Click on **View the exercise in my browser**.

9. The default web browser will appear showing the three images that compose the pyramid. The same picture with different sizes will appear inside each of the pyramid's parts. They will appear jumbled, with a random position, as shown in the next screenshot:

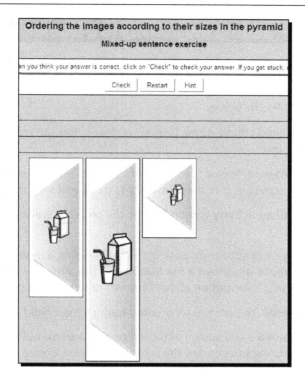

10. Go back to JMix. Select **File | Create Zip Package | Create Drag/Drop Zip Package** from the main menu and enter the name for the new ZIP file, `jmix0402.zip`. JMix will create a ZIP file with all the necessary files to upload to Moodle in order to run the JMix exercise.

What just happened?

We inserted the three images to build a pyramid for our exercise, considering both the pyramid's shape and the sizes of the pictures that appear inside each of the pyramid's parts. We used the capabilities offered by JMix, as done in our previous exercise, to create a visually rich mixed-up figures exercise.

We added each image that represents a specific part of the pyramid following the order for building a pyramid from left to right (bottom-to-top). As previously explained, JMix is going to jumble the pictures each time the students run the exercise using a randomly generated order.

Time for action – adding the activity to a Moodle course

We now have to add the ordering the images according to their sizes in a pyramid exercise to an existing Moodle course.

1. Log in to your Moodle server.

2. Click on the desired course name (Supermarket). You can create a new course or use an existing one.

3. As previously learned, follow the necessary steps to edit the summary for a desired week. Enter Exercise 2 in the **Summary** textbox and save the changes.

4. Click on the **Add an activity** combo box for the selected week and select **Hot Potatoes Quiz**.

5. A new web page will appear displaying the title **Adding a new Hot Potatoes Quiz**. Click on the **Choose or upload a file** button and the already well-known pop-up window displaying information about files and folders will appear.

6. Click on **chapter04** (the previously created folder's hyperlink).

7. Click on the **Upload a file** button and then on the **Browse** button. Browse to the folder that holds the images and the files used in the exercise (C:\Supermarket) and select the ZIP file to upload, jmix0402.zip. Then click on **Open** and on the **Upload this file** button.

8. Position the mouse pointer over the **jmix0402.zip** name and move it horizontally to the **Unzip** action hyperlink in the same row. Then click on **Unzip**, click on **OK** and Moodle will extract all the compressed files from this ZIP file.

9. Next, position the mouse pointer over the **jmix0402.htm** name and move it horizontally to the **Choose** action hyperlink in the same row. Then click on **Choose**, as shown in the following screenshot:

10. Moodle will display `chapter04/jmix0402.htm` in the **File name** textbox. This is the web page that will run the exercise previously created using JMix.

11. Scroll down and click on the **Save and display** button, located at the bottom of the web page. The web browser will show the exercise with the three jumbled parts of a pyramid that must be dragged and dropped to build the pyramid from left to right.

What just happened?

We added the rich building a pyramid exercise to a Moodle course. Now, the students are going to be able to run the activity by clicking on its hyperlink on the corresponding week.

We used the previously created folder, `chapter04`. We uploaded and decompressed a ZIP file that contained the three images previously captured using Snipping Tool to represent each part of the pyramid and the HTML file created with JMix (`jmix0402.htm`) to create the drag-and-drop activity. This HTML file has links to the three images inserted with JMix as HTML code to define each element that Moodle will jumble and the student will have to order.

Time for action – ordering the sequence by dragging and dropping images with the mouse

It is time to run the activity as a student and to check the results as a teacher.

1. Click on the course name (`Supermarket`) and switch your role to student.

2. Click on the **Ordering the images according to their sizes in the pyramid** link on the corresponding week. The web browser will show the three parts of the pyramid and will let the student solve the exercise with a drag/drop format.

3. Drag-and-drop each part of the pyramid to its corresponding place to compose a pyramid from left to right, considering both the shape of a pyramid and the sizes of the pictures found inside each part, as shown in the next screenshot:

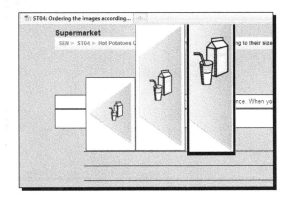

4. After dropping all the parts of the pyramid in their corresponding position to compose the pyramid, click on the **Check** button to test the results.

5. If the student's score is 100%, Moodle will save the results and will go back to the course web page.

6. Run the exercise with different incorrect solutions and click on the **Check** button each time. Moodle will display the resulting wrong pyramid shape ordered by the student and the part of the answer that is in its right place, as shown in the next screenshot. Besides that, it will let you run the activity again. However, it will save the student's results for each attempt.

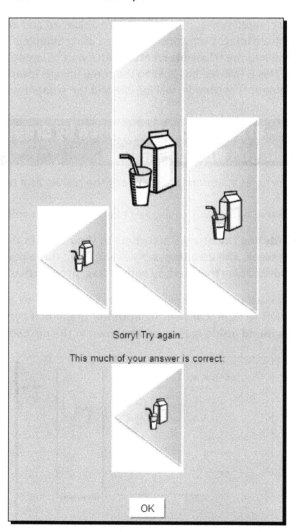

7. You can return to your normal role and check the number of attempts as done with the Hot Potatoes Quizzes activities.

What just happened?

In this activity, we worked with geometric shapes with different sizes. We used three pictures to represent three parts of a pyramid, drawn from left to right. Besides, we added a picture inside each part of the pyramid to provide the child with the same picture in different sizes, to use as an additional reference. The child has to look at the three jumbled pictures and understand the sorting activity.

The activity consists of composing the pyramid from left to right based on the existing parts as well as considering the size of the pictures inside each part, from smaller to bigger. We applied the following concepts and resources:

- **Size notions**. For this reason, we have chosen the shape of a pyramid and a carton of milk with different sizes.
- **Pattern recognition**. The child has to recognize the shape of a pyramid and its rotation.
- **Space notions**. The child has to locate the different parts of a rotated pyramid within a specific space.
- **Motivation**. The exercise is challenging with an attractive drag-and-drop format.
- **Attention stimulation**. The child has to focus on detecting the differences in the sizes and the different parts of a pyramid in order to sort them.

 As previously learned, we can also use a gamepad or a digital pen to solve the exercise. Sometimes, its usage is easier and more attractive to those children who have manual dyspraxia. It offers them more precision to drag-and-drop each part.

Time for action – executing the exercise using a multi–touch screen

It is also possible to make this exercise more attractive by executing it in a multi-touch screen.

> You need a multi-touch screen device compatible with Moodle web browsers' requirements in order to complete this activity.

1. Click on the course name (Supermarket) and switch your role to student.

2. Click on the **Ordering the images according to their sizes in the pyramid** link on the corresponding week. The web browser will show the three parts of the pyramid and will let the student solve the exercise with a drag/drop format.

3. Point one finger to each part of the pyramid and drag it to its corresponding place to compose a pyramid from left to right, as shown in the next image:

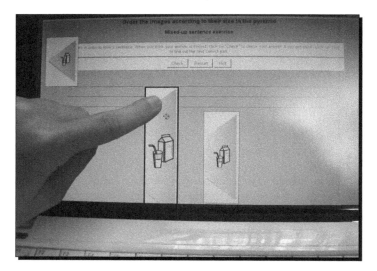

4. Once you finish dragging each part, you can drop it by separating the finger from the screen.

5. After dragging and dropping all the parts of the pyramid to their corresponding position, using your fingers to compose the pyramid, tap on the **Check** button to test the results.

To tap is the gesture equivalent to a click with the mouse. In order to tap, you have to position your finger on the desired element, push the screen and then separate your finger from the screen.

What just happened?

We took advantage of the popular multi-touch screen to use a finger as a mouse pointer. Therefore, you were able to execute the exercise using your fingers without problems.

Children with manual dyspraxia have difficulties in coordinating and sequencing the movements for tasks such as gestures, pointing, and sign language. Therefore, working with a multi-touch screen can help them to coordinate these complex movements in many steps. They can try many times to point one finger to a big picture and drop it. As the exercise uses big pictures, it is easier to improve the gestures working with these kinds of activities and a multi-touch screen.

 Nowadays, multi-touch screens are more popular than they were a few years ago. Therefore, they are not so expensive and they are easy to find. They are very useful to help children with difficulties when working with a classic mouse. However, the exercises must be solved with patience.

Have a go hero – increasing the skill level by creating a more complex pyramid

You can increase the complexity of the last exercise in order to allow children to exercise pattern recognitions and size notions.

Create a new pyramid with five parts. Use big numbers inside each part of the pyramid. This way, the child can sort the pyramid with the help of numbers.

Create a new pyramid with seven parts. Use different pictures with diverse sizes inside each part of the pyramid. This way, the child can sort the pyramid with the help of the different size of each picture. However, in this case, it is a more complex exercise because all the pictures are different, so the child has to pay more attention to recognize the differences in their size.

Combine a sequence inside four parts of a pyramid. This way, the child will work with all the resources explained for both exercises.

Pop quiz – developing visually rich sorting activities

1. JMix allows you to:

    a. Draw pictures to create visually rich mixed-up exercises.

    b. Use Visual Basic code to define each word of a sentence. Therefore, you can create visually rich mixed-up exercises.

    c. Use HTML code to define each word of a sentence. Therefore, you can create visually rich mixed-up exercises.

2. If the student runs a JMix exercise with a wrong solution in Moodle and clicks on the **Check** button, Moodle will:

    a. Display the resulting wrong sequence ordered by the student and the part of the answer that is in its right place.

    b. Display the complete correct sequence.

    c. Display the exercise another time without offering any additional clue.

3. In order to solve a JMix drag-and-drop exercise with jumbled images:

    a. The student must click on each image and Moodle places it on its corresponding place over the first line, creating the ordered sequence from left to right.

    b. The student must press the number accompanying each image. This way, Moodle places it on its corresponding place over the first line, creating the ordered sequence from left to right.

    c. The student must drag-and-drop each image to its corresponding place over the first line, creating the ordered sequence from left to right.

4.. A multi-touch screen allows you to drag-and-drop elements using:

    a. A keyboard.

    b. Your fingers.

    c. A mouse.

5. Using HTML code, you can:

    a. Only define each word of a JMix sentence as plain text.

    b. Define each word of a JMix sentence as a picture.

    c. Only define each word of a JMix sentence as a picture.

6. To tap is:

   a. The gesture equivalent to a double-click with the mouse.

   b. The gesture equivalent to a click with the mouse.

   c. The gesture equivalent to dropping an element with the mouse.

Summary

In this chapter, we have learned how to:

◆ Develop many visually rich sorting activities combining geometric shapes with pictures and text

◆ Take advantage of JMix's capabilities to work with HTML code in order to add pictures that can be dragged and dropped by the student

◆ Work with several applications to create pictures that represent a jumbled temporal sequence

◆ Use Edraw to create a pyramid combined with clipart and to split it in many different pictures

◆ Take advantage of a multi-touch screen in order to allow the children to drag-and-drop elements with their fingers

Now that we have learned to work with sorting activities, we're ready to create exercises for short-term and long-term memory improvement, which is the topic of the next chapter.

5
Creating Exercises to Improve Short-term Memory

We can organize the information in many creative ways combined with the addition of animations and nice effects. It is possible to use several different applications to create exercises that challenge the student to memorize different kind of visual elements for a short period of time. This way, we can help them to improve their short-term memory in different scenarios.

In this chapter, Alice has many birthday parties. We will learn how to to create rich activities related to her parties. By reading this chapter and following the exercises we shall:

◆ Learn how to create animated virtual cards

◆ Create visual activities to find matching pairs

◆ Improve short-term memory management

◆ Exercise audio pattern recognition and matching

◆ Create slide shows with animations and convert them into videos

◆ Create activities to memorize words, pictures, or sounds

Finding pairs of matching animations

The big day finally arrived. Today is Alice's birthday!

Her mother is extremely busy organizing her party.

Everything must be ready before the children arrive, her mother thought. Alice and her friends arrived after school so as to celebrate together, as well as have fun, eat sweets, and blow out the candles. They were enjoying themselves a lot that day, until the sky grew dark and it started to rain. How sad! They couldn't play in the garden; therefore, Alice had an idea—why not play a finding the matching pairs game until it stops raining? What fun!

Time for action – generating the animated virtual cards

We are first going to download and install JClic Author 0.2.0.5. We will then search for animated graphics in order to create virtual cards for our find the matching pairs exercise.

1. Create a new folder in Windows Explorer (C:\Birthday party).

2. Start Word 2007 and minimize it. You will use it later.

3. Run JClic Author 0.2.0.5 from its web page (http://clic.xtec.cat/en/jclic/download.htm) by clicking on the JClic author hyperlink. You can also download and install it instead of running it from its web page by clicking on one of the **Installers** hyperlinks.

 JClic requires the free Java Runtime Environment (also known as JRE) for both the teacher and the students' computers. You can download and install its latest version from http://java.sun.com.

4. If you decided to download and run the standalone installer, you will have to start JClic Author by clicking on its icon.

5. The first time you run this application, it will ask you for the name of a folder in which to store the data files and program settings. The default folder is C:\Program files\JClic. Click on **OK** or specify a different folder.

6. Select **File | New Project** from JClic's main menu. A new dialog box will appear. Enter the following values for each textbox, as shown in the next screenshot, and then click on **OK**:

    □   jclic0501 in **Project name**.

    □   jclic0501 in **File name**. JClic will save the complete project in a compressed file, jclic0501.jclic.zip.

    □   A new jclic0501 sub-folder in the previously created folder, C:\Birthday party, in **Folder**, C:\Birthday party\jclic0501.

7. Click on the **Project** tab. Enter `Finding the matching pairs` in the **Title** textbox.

8. Activate the **Event sounds** checkbox under **User interface**. By default, this option will play sounds associated with many events during the activity.

9. Next, start Word 2007. You will be working in a new blank document.

10. Click on **Insert | Clip Art**. The **Clip Art** panel will appear on the right-hand side of the main window.

11. Click on the **Search in** combo box and activate the **Everywhere** checkbox. Click on the **Results should be** combo box and deactivate all the options. Next, activate the **Animated GIF (*.gif)** checkbox in **All media types | Movies**, as shown in the next screenshot. This way, Word will search for animated bitmap files in all the available collections, including the Web Collections.

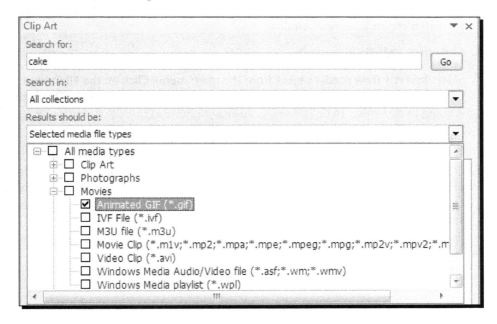

12. Click on the **Search for** textbox and enter `Birthday cake`, then click on **Go**.

13. Position the mouse pointer over the desired animated clipart's thumbnail. As you want to use bitmaps with animation effects, remember to make sure it displays many frames in the preview. Right-click on it and select **Preview/Properties** in the context menu that appears. Word will display a new dialog box showing a larger preview of the animated clipart, playing the short animation, and a temporary file name. For example, the next image shows the ten frames that compose the animation for a birthday cake:

14. Triple-click on the long path and file name shown after **File**. This way, you will be sure that the temporary file's full path is selected. Then right-click on it and select **Copy** in the context menu that appears.

15. Next, activate JClic Author. You can use *Alt + Tab* or *Windows + Tab*. Don't close the animated clipart's preview window.

16. Click on the **Media library** tab.

17. Select **Insert | New media object** from the main menu. Click on the **File name** textbox and paste the previously copied temporary file's full path in it. The path is going to be similar to `C:\Users\vanesa\AppData\Local\Microsoft\Windows\Temporary Internet Files\Content.IE5\PD1W3KEI\MMj03365690000[1].gif`.

18. Click on the **Open** button. JClic will ask your confirmation to copy the file to the project's folder; click **Yes**. The previously previewed animated clipart, the first virtual card for our find the matching pairs game, will appear in JClic's media library, as shown in the next screenshot:

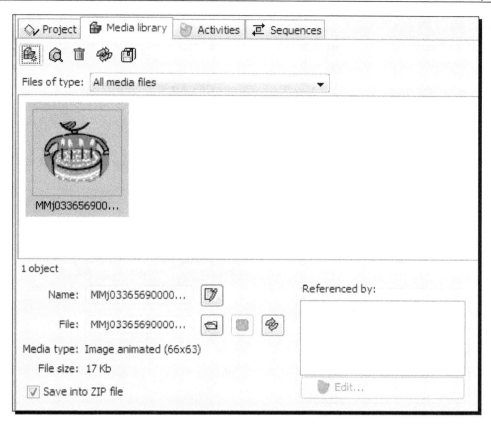

19. Return to Word 2007, and close the **Preview/Properties** dialog box.

20. Repeat the aforementioned steps (9 to 19) for each animated bitmap to add as a virtual card for the game. The next image shows the first frame of two possible animations, as a result of searching for the following keywords:

- ❑ Balloons
- ❑ Gift

What just happened?

We ran JClic Author 0.2.0.5. This software allows us to create diverse rich multimedia education activities.

We searched for animated graphics in **Office Online Clip Art & Media** and we imported the temporary files created by Word into JClic's media library.

We now have the following three animated graphics available in the media library to be used as virtual cards for our game:

◆ A birthday cake

◆ Balloons

◆ A gift

The graphics are animated **Graphics Interchange Format (GIF)** files. This bitmap image format with **lossless compression** supports animations by defining many frames in a single file. As JClic also supports animated GIF files as multimedia resources, we can use these files to reproduce simple animations in each virtual card for the find the matching pairs exercise.

The exercise will look nice using these animated graphics and it will be more attractive than virtual cards displaying static images.

In this case, we didn't use a naming convention for the pictures because they are part of JClic's media library for this project and they are saved in the same ZIP file. Therefore, it won't be necessary to upload many different files to Moodle. However, if you develop many activities in the same project, you would instead rename the multimedia resources using a naming convention.

Time for action – organizing the virtual cards

We are now going to associate the previously added multimedia resources to a new finding pairs activity.

1. Stay in JClic Author.

2. Click on the **Activities** tab and select **Insert | New activity** from the main menu. Select **Finding pairs** in the list shown in the **New activity** dialog box. Enter `Finding pairs of matching animations` in the **Name of the activity** textbox and click on **OK**. JClic will add the new activity to the project and will display new tabs with dozens of options for it, as shown in the next screenshot:

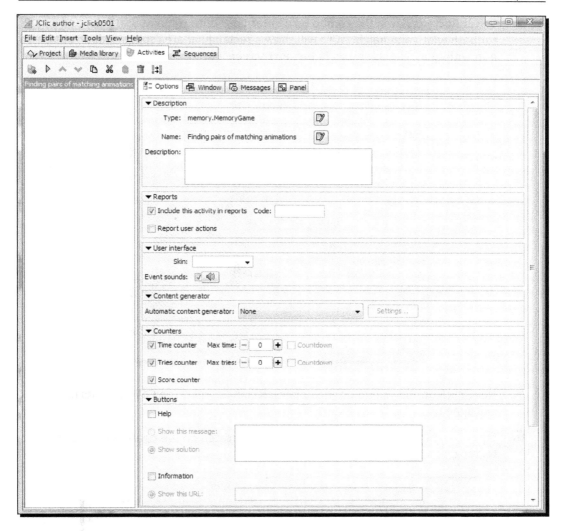

3. Click on the **Panel** tab related to the new activity and then on the **Grid** tab.

4. Select **Rectangular** in the combo box; enter 2 for both columns and rows and 140 for both width and height. JClic will show a rectangular area split into four squares, a grid with four cells, as shown in the next screenshot:

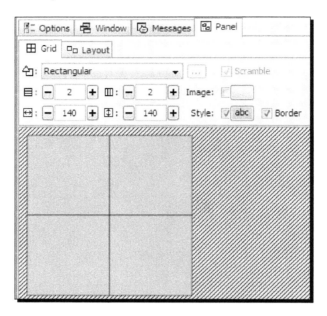

5. Next, click on the square on the upper left-hand corner. The **Cell contents** dialog box will appear.

6. Enter Cake in **Text** and click on the up arrow located on the right-hand side of this textbox, as shown in the next screenshot:

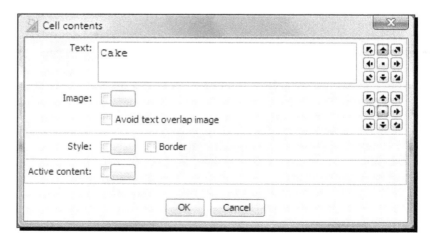

7. Click on the button located on the right-hand side of the **Image** label. The **Multimedia object selection** dialog box will appear. Click on the different animated graphics shown in the list and select the one that displays the preview of the animation of the birthday cake, as shown in the next screenshot:

8. Click on **OK** and then **OK** on the **Cell contents** dialog box. The upper left-hand cell will display the **Cake** text at the top and the selected animated bitmap at the center.

9. Next, repeat the aforementioned steps (5 to 8) for the other two animated bitmaps to display them in different cells with their corresponding text. The next screenshot shows three cells with text and animated bitmaps and one empty cell:

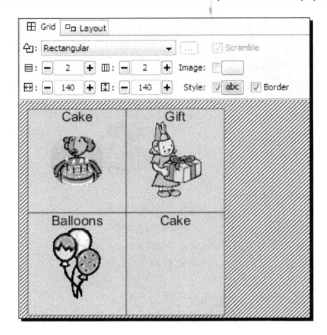

10. Select **File | Save** from JClic's main menu. A dialog box will ask you whether to add the activity to a sequence. Click on **Yes** and JClic will create a new sequence with the activity included in it.

11. Click on the **Sequences** tab. Select **Exit JClic** in the **Action** combo box under **Forward arrow** and activate the **Move on automatically** checkbox. This way, JClic will end once the activity is finished. Deactivate the **Show button** checkbox under **Back arrow**.

12. Select **File | Save** from JClic's main menu to save the changes made to the project.

13. Next, select **View | Preview Activity**. JClic will show a new window with eight grey cells. They represent eight flipped virtual cards. The number of cells is double the four cells created previously because you have to match pairs (4 x 2 = 8). Each time you preview the activity, JClic will scramble the virtual cards and present them in a random order.

14. Click on one of the grey cells. The card will flip and a hidden animated bitmap will appear with its corresponding text. Remember that there are going to be two empty cells.

15. You now have to click on one of the other grey cells to flip the virtual card and find the matching pair. The new card will flip. If it is the pair of the previously flipped card, they will remain flipped and you can go on with the other cells. If it isn't the pair, the previously flipped card will flip again and you will have to try to find the pair for this new card. The next screenshot shows the completed activity with all the pairs discovered:

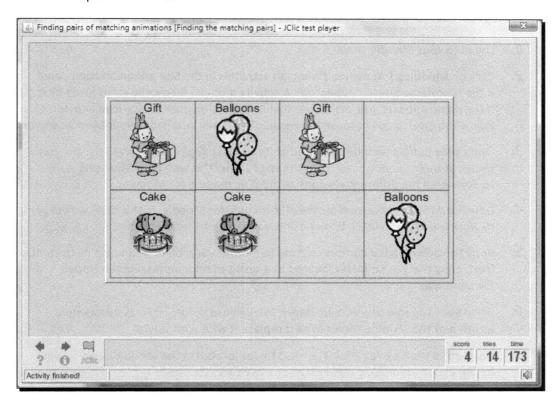

What just happened?

We created a finding pairs activity using JClic and the previously added animated bitmaps. We used the capabilities offered by JClic to create visually rich virtual cards for our exercise, mixing text and animated graphics. As the virtual cards are animated, the exercise is more complex to solve than using static pictures.

We added text and linked each animated bitmap to each cell. JClic displayed the changes made in each virtual card in a preview panel. As previously explained, JClic is going to jumble the virtual cards each time the students run the exercise using a randomly generated order.

Time for action – installing a module to integrate JClic and Moodle

We now have to add the find the matching pairs exercise to an existing Moodle course. Firstly, it is necessary to install a JClic module that allows us to add JClic projects and activities to Moodle and to analyze the results of their execution. You have to follow these steps in order to install JClic activities with access to your Moodle server.

1. Log in to your Moodle server.

2. Click on **Modules | Activities | Manage activities** in the **Site administration** panel. If the **JClic** name doesn't appear as an activity module, follow the steps given next. If the name appears, just make sure that it displays an opened eye icon and don't follow the given steps because the module is already installed in your Moodle server.

3. Open your default web browser and go to `https://projectes.lafarga.cat/projects/jclicmoodle/downloads/files`. This web page allows us to download the different versions of the JClic module for Moodle.

4. Download the latest version for the JClic module for Moodle. In this case, we are going to work with version 0.1.0.10 and its file name is `jclicmoodle-0.1.0.10.zip`.

5. Copy the downloaded compressed file to a temporary folder and unzip its contents. Next, copy the `jclic` folder created as a result of uncompressing the zipped file contents.

6. Go to your Moodle server main folder. We will use `C:\Moodle` as an example location of the Moodle server folder; replace it with your folder.

7. Next, go to the `server\moodle\mod` folder located in the Moodle server main folder, in our example, `C:\Moodle\server\moodle\mod`.

8. Paste the previously copied `jclic` folder. As a result, you will see a new `jclic` folder in the `mod` sub-folder, in our example, `C:\Moodle\server\moodle\mod`.

9. Log in to your Moodle server as the administrator, `Admin` user.

10. Click on **Notifications** under **Site Administration**.

11. Moodle will create all the necessary new tables in the underlying database to support the requirements of the new module. Once it finishes, it will display a message, as shown in the next screenshot. Click on **Continue**.

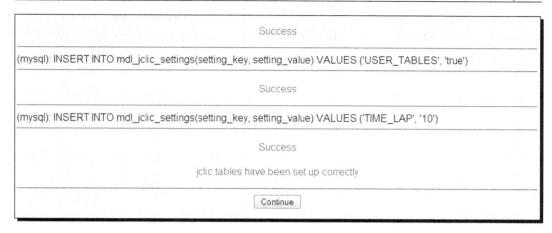

12. Click on **Modules | Activities | Manage activities** in the **Site administration** panel. You should see **JClic** listed as one of the activity modules, as shown in the next screenshot:

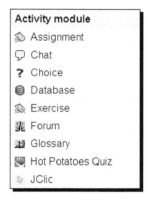

What just happened?

We installed a module to allow Moodle to add JClic activities and to check the results of these exercises. We are now going to be able to add the previously created find the matching pairs exercise and many other new activities created with JClic.

 The previously explained steps require some knowledge on Moodle administration procedures. The configuration and customization of Moodle is described in depth in *Moodle Administration* by *Alex Büchner*, Packt Publishing.

Time for action – adding the activity to a Moodle course

Now that we are sure that the JClic module is installed, we can add the previously created activity to an existing Moodle course.

1. Log in to your Moodle server.

2. Click on the desired course name (Birthday party). You can create a new course or use an existing one.

3. As previously learned, follow the necessary steps to edit the summary for a desired week. Enter Exercise 1 in the **Summary** textbox and save the changes.

4. Click on the **Add an activity** combo box for the selected week and choose **JClic**.

5. A new web page will appear displaying the title **Adding a new JClic to week**.

6. Enter Finding the matching pairs in the **Name** textbox.

7. Enter Click on each card and find its matching pair in the **Description** textbox. Select the desired font and color for this text.

8. Click on the **Choose or upload a file** button; the already well-known pop up window displaying information about files and folders will appear.

9. Follow the necessary steps to create a new folder, chapter05, and then click on its hyperlink.

10. Click on the **Upload a file** button and then on **Browse**. Browse to the folder that holds the JClic project (C:\Birthday party\jclick0501) and select the file to upload, jclick0501.jclic.zip. Then click on **Open** and on the **Upload this file** button.

11. Next, position the mouse pointer over the **jclick0501.jclic.zip** name and move it horizontally to the **Choose** action hyperlink in the same row. Then click on **Choose**, as shown in the next screenshot:

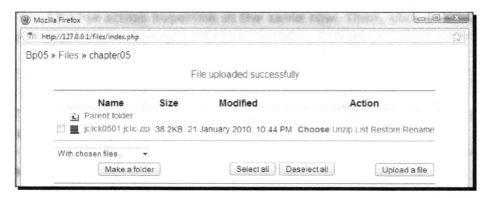

12. Moodle will display `chapter05/jclick0501.jclic.zip` in the **File name** textbox. This is the ZIP file that contains all the files with the JClic project and its activity.

13. Select `1` in **Maximum number of trials**.

14. Scroll down and click on the **Save and return to course** button, located at the bottom of the web page.

What just happened?

We added the animated finding the matching pairs exercise to a Moodle course. The students are now going to be able to run the activity by clicking on its hyperlink in the corresponding week.

We created a new folder, `chapter05`. This folder will hold all the necessary files for the activities related to the visit to the birthday party.

We then uploaded just one ZIP file that contains many compressed files with the multimedia resources and the definitions for the JClic project and single activity. This file contains the three animated bitmap graphics; therefore, it wasn't necessary to upload these files separately.

Time for action – finding the matching pairs by flipping virtual cards

It is time to run the activity as a student and to check the results as a teacher.

1. Click on the course name (`Birthday party`) and switch your role to student.

2. Click on the **Finding the matching pairs** link on the corresponding week. The web browser will show the exercise. The JClic panel that displays the activity can take some time to load.

3. Click on one of the grey cells and try to find its pair, as shown in the next screenshot:

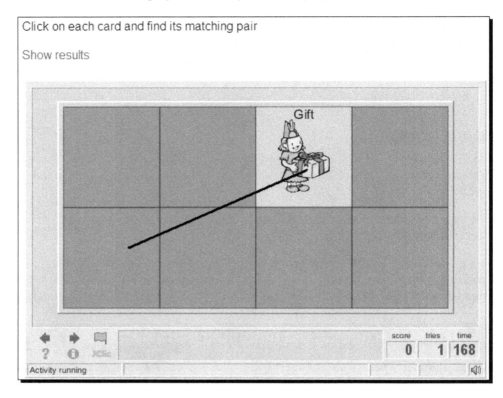

4. Each time you miss a pair, the JClic application will play a sound indicating a mistake. Each time you match a pair, it will play a sound indicating a successful operation.

5. After matching all the pairs, the activity will finish and you will be able to check your results by clicking on **Show results**.

6. You can return to your normal role and check the number of attempts as done with the previous activities. Remember that they are going to appear grouped in JClic activities.

What just happened?

In this activity, we created the virtual cards using animated graphics of typical situations related to a birthday party. The child has to discover the animation and the text hidden in each virtual card and find its matching pair.

The activity consists of clicking on each virtual card to flip it and to solve the exercise as soon as possible. We applied the following concepts and resources in order to help to improve short-term memory:

◆ **Linking patterns**. The child has to match pairs of animated graphics and pairs of words.

◆ **Motivation**. The exercise is challenging with attractive animations and sounds. The sounds are predefined in JClic for this kind of activity.

◆ **Short-term memory**. The child has to remember the location of each animated graphic and/or its text. Thus, the child works hard with his/her short-term memory.

◆ **Attention stimulation**. The child has to focus on memorizing the location of the different animated graphics to find the matching pair as soon as possible. As the exercise uses animated graphics instead of static pictures, they have to pay more attention and the exercise is more funny.

 As previously learned, we can also use a gamepad or a multi-touch screen instead of the mouse to solve the exercise. In this case, their usage would simplify the execution of the activity by those children who have manual dyspraxia.

We can increase the complexity of these kinds of exercises using text without the animated graphics. However, the exercise could be a bit boring.

Have a go hero – adding sounds to a finding the matching pairs activity

JClic Author offers the possibility to customize the sound related to each event in an activity. You can do it by clicking on the **Options** tab and then on the **Event sounds** button under **User Interface**. The **Edit event sounds** dialog box will allow you to select a sound for the following events of a finding pairs activity:

◆ Start of activity

◆ Click on object

◆ Correct action

◆ Incorrect action

◆ Activity finished OK

◆ Activity finished with errors

You can click on the button for each of the aforementioned events and use an audio file previously added to JClic's media library.

Additionally, you can associate a sound to each virtual card by clicking on the **Active content** button in the **Cell contents** dialog box, and then clicking on **Play sound** and selecting an audio file previously added to JClic's media library.

Create a different version of the last exercise in order to allow children to exercise audio pattern recognition and matching. Instead of adding text in each virtual card, associate a sound to be played when the virtual card is flipped. This way, children can memorize both the image and the associated sound related to each card.

Working with a list of words organized in rows

Alice and her little brother Kevin wanted to prepare a surprise party for her mother's birthday.

They worked together all afternoon cooking and decorating the birthday cake. Some more things were needed if they wanted it to be a fantastic party. So Alice decided to prepare a list of things to buy, things that were missing. It is going to be both a great surprise for their mother and an unforgettable party.

Time for action – creating an animation with a list of words

We are first going to create an animated slide with many words organized in different rows.

1. Start PowerPoint 2007. You will be working in a new blank presentation.

 Microsoft PowerPoint 2007 is a commercial product and it is part of Microsoft Office 2007 in its different versions, including Home and Student. However, as previously explained, the trial offers a free fully functional version for 60 days. You can use other tools like OpenOffice Impress to create the presentation.

2. Click on **Home | Layout | Blank** on the ribbon. This way, the text blocks will disappear from the slide and you will be able to work with a blank one.

3. Click on **Insert | WordArt** on the ribbon. A drop-down list containing many fonts with nice effects will appear. Select the desired effect and color by clicking on the corresponding decorated letter A. A new **WordArt** text block will appear on the slide displaying **Your Text Here**.

4. Select the aforementioned text in the block and enter the following words, pressing *Enter* in order to create a new line for each of them:

   ❑ Hat

   ❑ Gift

- ❏ Balloon
- ❏ Confetti
- ❏ Mask

5. Drag-and-drop the text block to the center of the slide, as shown in the next screenshot. You can also achieve this goal by clicking on **Format | Align | Align Center** and then on **Format | Align | Align Middle**, on the ribbon.

6. Keep the text block selected and click on **Animations** on the ribbon. Then select **By 1st Level Paragraphs** under **Fade** in the **Animate** drop-down list. Click on the **Preview button** and you will see a preview of the animation effect. Each word will appear one after the other with a fade effect. Once the animation finishes, all the words will be visible in the slide.

7. Next, click on **Animations | Custom Animation** on the ribbon. A new panel will appear.

8. Click on the expand button after **Hat** on the **Custom Animation** panel. The panel will now display the five words, as shown in the next screenshot:

9. Next, select the five words shown in the list in the **Custom Animation** panel. Then select **After Previous** in **Start** and **Slow** in **Speed**. This way, the words will fade in slowly one after the other.

10. Click inside the selected text block on the slide.

11. Click on the **Add Effect | Exit | Blinds**. The **Add Effect** button is located on the upper left-hand corner of the **Custom Animation** panel.

12. A new animation will be listed after **Mask**. Click on the expand button located at the bottom of the list on the **Custom Animation** panel. The panel will now display the five words for the exit animation effect, as shown in the next screenshot:

13. Next, select the five words shown in the list for the exit animation effect in the **Custom Animation** panel. Then, select **After Previous** in **Start**, **Horizontal** in **Direction** and **Slow** in **Speed**. This way, the words will be blinded slowly one after the other.

14. Click on the **Preview button** and you will see a preview of both the entry and exit animation effects. Each word will appear one after the other with a fade effect.

15. Once the animation finishes, all the words will be visible in the slide and then they will start to disappear one after the other with a blind effect, as shown in the next sequence:

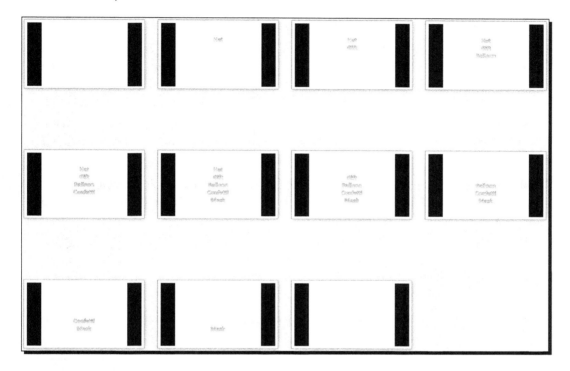

16. Click on the office button, located on the upper left-hand corner of the window and select **Save**. Save the file as `powerpoint0502.pptx` in the previously created folder, `C:\Birthday party`.

What just happened?

We used PowerPoint to create and preview a slide show that displays a list of five words organized in rows. The slide show uses a fade effect to animate the exhibition of each word. This way, the student will be able to read the five words as they appear and then, the slide show applies a blind effect to animate the disappearance of each word.

Time for action – exporting a video with animated words

It is very difficult to display a slide show with animations created in PowerPoint in a web browser. Therefore, it is convenient to convert the PowerPoint slide show to a video file compatible with the multimedia plugins available in a Moodle default installation.

We are first going to download and install Wondershare PPT to Video 6 (6.0.3.11). We will then load the previously created PowerPoint 2007 file to this software and we will export a video in the **Flash Video (FLV)** format.

1. Close PowerPoint 2007. It is necessary to close it before running the conversion process.

2. If you do not have it yet, download and install the free trial version of Wondershare PPT to Video 6 (`http://www.ppt-to-dvd.com/ppt-to-video-overview.html`).

3. Start Wondershare PPT to Video 6. A new dialog box will display the days remaining for the trial version's expiration. Click on **Evaluate** if you are using the trial version and a new window will appear with two big buttons.

4. Click on **Convert to Video Files From PowerPoint**. A new conversion wizard will appear displaying the three steps to convert an existing PowerPoint slide show to a video file: **Import**, **Settings**, and **Export**.

5. Click on the **+ Add** button. Select the previously created PowerPoint slide show `powerpoint0502.pptx` in `C:\Birthday Party` and click on the **Open** button. A thumbnail representation of the slide show will be added to the list of files to import. Click on **Next**.

6. Select **PowerPoint to FLV** in **Format** and **640 x 480** in **Resolution**, as shown in the next screenshot. Then click on **Next**.

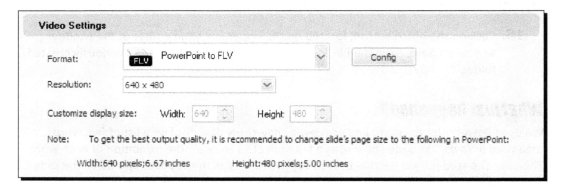

7. Select `C:\Birthday Party` as the **Output folder** for the exported video. Then, click on **Start**. Wondershare PPT to Video will perform the conversion process and will create a sub-folder with the date and the time of the conversion in the previously specified folder to save the new video file. For example, if the conversion finishes on January 24, 6:57 p.m., the new file will be `C:\Birthday Party\01-24 18 57\powerpoint0502.FLV`, as shown in the next screenshot.

8. Finally, click on **Close**.

What just happened?

We installed the free trial version of Wondershare PPT to Video 6. This software allows us to convert PowerPoint slideshows to many video formats. The free trial version includes a watermark in the exported video and is limited to 30 days. However, it is very useful to create our video for our exercise. If you like the trial version, you can buy the full version.

We converted the previously created PowerPoint slide show, including all its animations and effects, to a Flash Video (FLV) format. We selected this format because it is easy to integrate it in a Moodle exercise.

Time for action – adding the activity to a Moodle course

As we are going to add the aforementioned video file to our exercise in Moodle, we have to make sure that its multimedia plugin is enabled. We already learned how to do it for MP3 audio files in previous chapters. We then have to upload the video file in order to add our exercise to an existing Moodle course.

1. Log in to your Moodle server.

2. Follow the previously learned steps to make sure that the multimedia plugins are enabled.

3. Next, click on **Modules | Filters | Multimedia Plugins** in the **Site administration** panel.

4. Make sure that the **Enable .flv filter** checkbox is activated. If it is not, activate it and click on the **Save changes** button.

5. Click on the desired course name (Birthday party). You can create a new course or use an existing one.

6. As previously learned, follow the necessary steps to edit the summary for a desired week. Enter `Exercise 2` in the **Summary** textbox and save the changes.

7. Click on the **Add an activity** combo box for the selected week and select **Online text**.

8. Enter `Working with a list of words organized in rows` in **Assignment name**.

9. Select `Verdana` in font and `5 (18)` in size—the first two combo boxes below **Description**.

10. Select your desired color for the text.

11. Click on the big textbox below **Description** and enter `Writing the words you see in the video`. This is the description of the student's goal for this exercise.

12. Press *Enter* and type `Watch the video`. Then select this text and click on the **Insert Web Link** button (a chain). A new web page will appear displaying the title **Insert Link**.

13. Click on the **Browse** button and navigate to the previously created folder, `chapter05`.

14. Click on the **Browse** button. Browse to the folder that holds the previously exported video file (`C:\Birthday Party\01-24 18 57`) and select the file to upload, `powerpoint0502.flv`. Then click on **Open**, on **Upload**, and then on the file name link.

15. Moodle will display the URL for this audio file in the **URL** textbox. Enter `Watch the video` in the title textbox and click on **OK**.

16. The online text assignment will display the title and subtitle with the hyperlink, as shown in the next screenshot:

17. Finally, scroll down and select **Save and return to course**.

What just happened?

We added the working with a list of words organized in rows exercise to a Moodle course. The students are now going to be able to write the words they memorize after watching the video by clicking on its hyperlink on the corresponding week.

We uploaded the Flash Video (FLV) file, then we added a title and an hyperlink to this file. As we had made sure that the necessary multimedia plugin was enabled, Moodle is going to show a media player to allow the student to view the video file in their browsers.

The online text assignment allowed us to describe the goals for the activity originally created with a PowerPoint slide show.

Time for action – writing the memorized words

It is time to run the activity as a student and to check the results as a teacher.

1. Click on the course name (Birthday party) and switch your role to student.

2. Click on the **Working with a list of words organized in rows** link on the corresponding week. The web browser will show the video with a media player at the right-hand side of the subtitle. Click on the **Play** button located on the lower left-hand corner of the video panel. You will be able to view the video file with the animated words, as shown in the next screenshot:

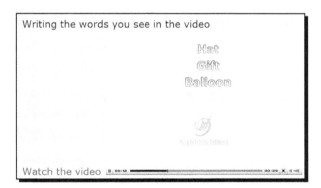

 As we used the trial version of Wondershare PPT to Video 6, it added a watermark with the software manufacturer's name in the video.

3. Watch the video and try to memorize the five words. You can also watch the video in full screen mode by clicking on the button located at the left-hand side of the volume control.

4. Click on the **Edit my submission** button. Moodle will display a big text area with an HTML editor.

5. Select Verdana in font and 5 (18) in size.

6. Write the words that you remember, as shown in the next screenshot:

7. Click on the **Save changes** button. This way, Moodle will save the results for this exercise.

8. Don't forget to check the results for this exercise as previously learned.

What just happened?

In this activity, we worked with a video displaying a list of words, organized in rows, appearing and disappearing. The objective was to make the child memorize the words shown and let him/her write the words that he/she remembers. The child can watch the video, read, and memorize the words as they appear and then write the remembered ones, with the help of a therapist or a family member, so that he/she can run the exercise.

The activity consists of reading and writing words. We applied the following concepts and resources:

◆ **Short-term memory**. The child has to memorize the words as they appear in the video. Then, he/she has to write the remembered ones without a time-limit. Thus, the child works hard with his/her short-term memory.

◆ **Reading comprehension**. The child has to read, understand, and remember each of the words in a short period of time.

◆ **Motivation**. The exercise is challenging with attractive animations and effects. As the exercise uses words related to a birthday party, they are usually attractive to children.

◆ **Attention stimulation**. The child has to focus on memorizing each word as soon as possible. As the exercise uses animations instead of static words, they have to pay more attention and the exercise is more fun.

This exercise could be too difficult to solve for certain children, especially those who have difficulty writing or have reading comprehension problems. In these cases, it is very important to work with the help of a therapist or a family member.

Have a go hero – adding pictures and using a webcam to record the results

Create a different version of the last exercise as an upload a single file assignment in order to allow children to record the results using a webcam and its incorporated microphone. This way, instead of writing the words by editing the submission for the online text assignment, they can record and upload their voice with their memorized words in the upload a single file assignment.

The child can record his/her voice using Windows Sound Recorder (**Start | All Programs | Accessories | Sound Recorder**), as shown in the next screenshot:

You can also use Audacity, free software that allows you to record and encode sounds. We will learn to use this software in *Chapter 9, Writing Guided Sentences and Paragraphs*.

Create another version using pictures instead of words. You can apply the same animation effects to pictures included in a PowerPoint slide shown, as previously learned with text blocks.

Pop quiz – discovering new tools and activities

1. An animated GIF file:
    a. Supports animations by defining just two frames in a single file.
    b. Supports animations by defining many frames in many files.
    c. Supports animations by defining many frames in a single file.

2. JMatch allows you to add multimedia files to the activities through its:
    a. Media library.
    b. Clipart gallery.
    c. Multimedia resource manager.

3. JClic Author:

    a. Allows you to customize the sound related to each event in an activity.

    b. Offers default sounds related to each event in an activity and you cannot change them.

    c. Allows you to customize the sound related to the activity finished with errors. You cannot customize the sound associated to the other events.

4. A JClic project file can contain:

    a. Just one activity.

    b. Many compressed activities and their related multimedia resources.

    c. Just the multimedia resources of an activity. The activities are saved in different files identified with the `.act` extension.

5. JClic requires:

    a. The free Java Runtime Environment (also known as JRE) for both the teacher and the students' computers.

    b. The free Java Runtime Environment (also known as JRE) for the teacher's computer. The student's computer doesn't need the JRE installed.

    c. The Special HTML Interpreter (also known as SHI) for both the teacher and the students' computers.

Summary

In this chapter, we have learned how to:

- ◆ Create many visually rich activities combining animations, effects, text, pictures, and sounds.

- ◆ Work with several tools to create realistic activities that can improve the student's short-term memory management

- ◆ Use JClic Author to create a finding pairs of matching animations exercise

- ◆ Use animated GIF graphics to represent each virtual card

- ◆ Install a module to integrate the new JClic activity in Moodle

- ◆ Create a slide-show with PowerPoint and use Wondershare PPT to Video 6 in order to export a video in the Flash Video (FLV) format, compatible with Moodle

- ◆ Use an online text assignment to create a visual exercise that enables the student to view the slide show and to memorize the list of words organized in rows, shown with nice animations and effects

Now that we have learned how to create exercises for short-term memory improvement, we're ready to prepare exercises to reduce attention deficit disorder, which is the topic of the next chapter.

6
Reducing Attention Deficit Disorder Using Great Concentration Exercises

We can reduce Attention Deficit Disorder working with different kinds of visually rich puzzles. It is possible to use many different applications to create exercises that help the student to improve their focus on achieving certain goals in a short period of time. This way, we can help them to reduce their Attention Deficit Disorder in different scenarios.

In this chapter, Alice visits the Aquarium. We will learn how to create visually rich puzzles related to her journey. By reading this chapter and following the exercises we shall:

- ◆ Learn how to create virtual pieces of a puzzle based on a photo
- ◆ Create an exchange puzzle
- ◆ Work with multi-touch devices to solve a puzzle and improve the student's interest in executing exercises
- ◆ Create visual and interactive activities to find words in a grid with letters
- ◆ Combine videos, sounds, photos, letters, and words to improve long-term memory management

Solving a puzzle

Alice and her little brother Kevin went to the Aquarium. They saw exciting fishes everywhere. Additionally, they enjoyed watching ducks with dazzling colors in an artificial lake.

One of the things Alice liked most about the visit was the plumage of one of the ducks, so she took a nice picture of the duck. Would you like to solve a puzzle using this picture?

Time for action – choosing a high definition picture adequate for a puzzle

We are going to search for royalty-free high definition photos related to the aquarium in a specialized web page. We are then going to use one to create a puzzle.

1. Create a new folder in Windows Explorer (`C:\Aquarium`).

2. Open your default web browser and go to `http://animalphotos.info`. This web page allows us to search royalty-free and high resolution animal photos. We need animals that we can find in an aquarium.

3. Enter `duck` in the textbox and then click on the **Search** button. The available photos' thumbnails related to the entered keyword will appear. Scroll down and up and click on the desired photo of a single duck. A new web page will appear, displaying the higher resolution version of the selected image, as shown in the next image:

The original URL for this image with a Creative Commons License is:
`http://farm3.static.flickr.com/2320/2312123237_d6464e7874.jpg`.

4. Right-click on the photo and select **Properties** in the context menu that appears. A new dialog box will appear displaying the properties for the image. Check its dimensions or resolution. It should be higher than **600 x 400** pixels, as shown in the next screenshot:

5. If the resolution for the chosen picture is lower than **600 x 400** pixels, you should select another picture with a higher resolution. If the resolution is higher than **900 x 700** pixels, you can reduce the size of your web browser's window and check the properties again until the dimensions shown are lower than this value and at least **600 x 400** pixels.

Most modern web browsers reduce the size of the picture shown in this page according to the window size when the image is larger than the window. Thus, you can take advantage of this feature when you have an image with a resolution higher than the one needed for the puzzle.

6. Start **Snipping Tool (Start Menu | All Programs | Accessories | Snipping Tool)** and capture the image as previously learned. Save the file in the **Portable Network Graphic File (PNG)** format as `image060101.png` in the previously created folder, `C:\Aquarium`. This way, we have the image of a nice duck with the desired resolution to create a puzzle.

What just happened?

We searched for a royalty-free photo related to the aquarium. In this case, we worked with our well-know web page, `http://animalphotos.info`.

We made sure that the image has the appropriate resolution to create a puzzle. We now have the digital photo of a duck ready to be used in our puzzle.

[It is very important to use photos with the specified resolution for this exercise because we want to create a big puzzle with a specific number of pieces.]

Time for action – generating an exchange puzzle

We are now going to generate an exchange puzzle with the photo of the duck and our well-known JClic Author.

1. Run JClic Author 0.2.0.5 from its web page or by clicking on its icon.

2. Select **File | New Project** from JClic's main menu. A new dialog box will appear. Enter the following values for each textbox and then click on **OK**:

   - ❑ `puzzle0601` in **Project name**.
   - ❑ `puzzle0601` in **File name**. JClic will save the complete project in a compressed file, `puzzle0601.jclic.zip`.
   - ❑ A new `puzzle0601` sub-folder in the previously created folder, `C:\Aquarium`, in **Folder**, `C:\Aquarium\puzzle0601`.

3. Click on the **Project** tab. Enter `Solving the puzzle` in the **Title** textbox.

4. Click on the **Media library** tab.

5. Select **Insert | New media object** from the main menu. Select the previously saved image `image060101.png` in `C:\Aquarium` and click on the **Open** button. JClic will ask your confirmation to copy the file to the project's folder; click on **Yes**. The photo of the duck that will be converted to a puzzle will appear in JClic's media library.

6. Click on the **Activities** tab and select **Insert | New activity** from the main menu. Select **Exchange puzzle** in the list shown in the **New activity** dialog box. Enter `Puzzle` in the **Name of the activity** textbox and click on **OK**. JClic will add the new activity to the project and will display new tabs with dozens of options for it, as shown in the next screenshot:

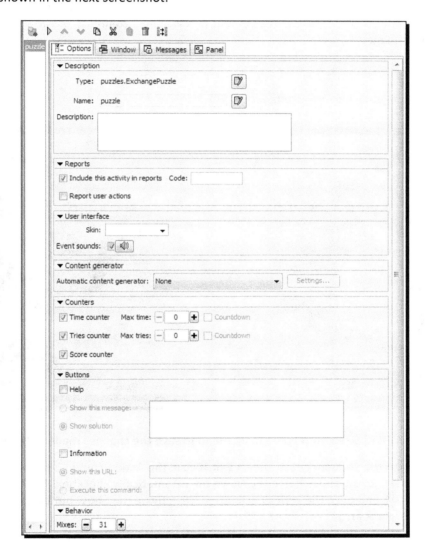

7. Click on the **Panel** tab related to the new activity.

8. Click on the button located on the right-hand side of the **Image** label. The **Multimedia object selection** dialog box will appear. Select the photo of the duck (image060101.png) and click on **OK**.

9. Select **Jigsaw with curved unions** (or curved edges) in the combo box, enter 2 for rows, 3 for columns, 247 for width, and 245 for height. JClic will show the duck split into six pieces with curved unions (2 rows and 3 columns), as shown in the next image:

10. Select **File | Save** from JClic's main menu to save the changes made to the project.

11. Click on the **Sequences** tab. Select **Exit JClic** in the **Action** combo box under **Forward arrow** and activate the **Move on automatically** checkbox. This way, JClic will end once the activity is finished. Deactivate the **Show button** checkbox under **Back arrow**.

12. Select **File | Save** from JClic's main menu again.

13. Next, select **View | Preview Activity**. JClic will show a new window with six scrambled pieces of the photo of the duck. They represent six pieces of a puzzle. Each time you preview the activity; JClic will scramble the virtual pieces and present them in a random order, as shown in the next image:

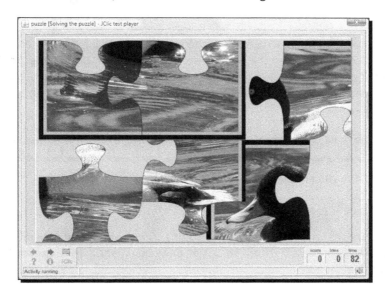

14. Drag-and-drop each piece to its corresponding position in order to solve the puzzle. When a piece is dropped in its right place, if there is another piece in this position, JClic will move it to another place to avoid an unordered piece to be hidden, as shown in the next image:

What just happened?

We created an exchange puzzle activity using JClic and the previously selected photo of the duck. We used the capabilities offered by JClic to create visually rich virtual pieces with teeth for our puzzle. As the photo of the duck has a thick black border, it can be used as a guideline to find the right place for each piece.

We linked the photo of the duck with the exchange puzzle activity, configured the desired shape and number of pieces and the puzzle's size on the screen. JClic displayed the changes made in each parameter in a preview panel. As previously explained, JClic is going to scramble the virtual pieces each time the students run the exercise using a randomly generated order.

Time for action – adding the activity to a Moodle course

We now have to add the exchange puzzle to an existing Moodle course.

1. Log in to your Moodle server.

2. Make sure that the module to allow adding JClic projects and activities to Moodle is installed. The necessary steps to perform the installation were explained in *Chapter 5, Creating Exercises to Improve Short-term Memory*.

3. Click on the desired course name (Aquarium). You can create a new course or use an existing one.

4. As previously learned, follow the necessary steps to edit the summary for a desired week. Enter Exercise 1 in the **Summary** textbox and save the changes.

5. Click on the **Add an activity** combo box for the selected week and choose **JClic**. A new web page will appear displaying the title **Adding a new JClic to week**.

6. Enter Solving the puzzle in the **Name** textbox.

7. Enter Drag and drop each part to its right place to solve the puzzle in the **Description** textbox. Select the desired font and color for this text.

8. Click on the **Choose or upload a file** button and the already well-known pop-up window displaying information about files and folders will appear.

9. Click on the **Upload a file** button and then on **Browse**. Browse to the folder that holds the JClic project (C:\Aquarium\puzzle0601) and select the file to upload, puzzle0601.jclic.zip. Then click on **Open** and on the **Upload this file** button.

10. Next, position the mouse pointer over the **puzzle0601.jclic.zip** name and move it horizontally to the **Choose** action hyperlink in the same row. Then, click on **Choose**, as shown in the next screenshot:

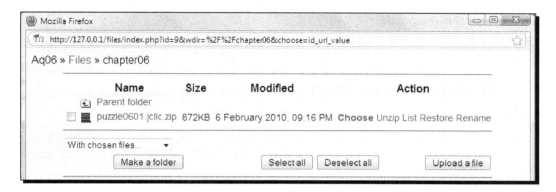

11. Moodle will display `chapter06/puzzle0601.jclic.zip` in the **File name** textbox. This is the ZIP file that contains all the files with the JClic project and its activity, the puzzle.

12. Enter `750` in **Width** and `550` in **Height**.

13. Select `1` in **Maximum number of trials**.

14. Scroll down and click on the **Save and return to course** button, located at the bottom of the web page.

What just happened?

We added the exchange puzzle exercise to a Moodle course. The students are now going to be able to run the activity by clicking on its hyperlink in the corresponding week.

We created a new folder, `chapter06`. This folder will hold all the necessary files for the activities related to the visit to the aquarium.

Then, we just uploaded one ZIP file that contains many compressed files with the photo of the duck and the definitions for the JClic project and single activity.

Time for action – solving the puzzle using a gamepad

It is time to run the activity as a student and to check the results as a teacher. It is possible to run the activity using a mouse; however, this time, we are going to take advantage of a gamepad to solve the puzzle.

1. Configure the gamepad's mapping to simplify the drag-and-drop process used to solve the exercise. The necessary steps to perform this configuration were explained in *Chapter 1, Matching Pictures*.

2. Click on the course name (Aquarium) and switch your role to student.

3. Click on the **Solving the puzzle** link on the corresponding week. The web browser will show the exercise. The JClic panel that displays the activity can take some time to load.

4. Move the gamepad's left mini stick to position the mouse pointer over the desired virtual piece.

5. Press the gamepad's action button number 1 (on the upper right-hand side).

6. Move the gamepad's left mini stick and the virtual piece will change its position according to the mini stick movement. Use the mini stick to position the virtual piece in its correct place, as shown in the next image:

7. Press the gamepad's action button number 1 (on the top right-hand side) to leave the virtual piece in the selected position. Each time you drop a virtual piece in its correct place, the JClic application will play a sound indicating a successful operation. Each time you drop a virtual piece on a wrong place, the JClic application will play a sound indicating a mistake.

8. After solving the puzzle, the activity will finish and you will be able to check your results by clicking on **Show results**.

9. You can return to your normal role and check the number of attempts as done with the previous activities. Remember that they are going to appear grouped in JClic activities.

What just happened?

In this activity, we created the virtual pieces of a puzzle using an image related to an aquarium. The child has to drag-and-drop the virtual pieces to solve the puzzle and discover the complete image.

We applied the following concepts and resources in order to help to reduce attention deficit disorder:

◆ **Attention stimulation**. The child has to focus on finding the right place for each virtual piece. The gamepad requires the child to work with both the stick and the button. This way, the child usually finds the activity fun.

◆ **Motivation**. The exercise is a challenging traditional game, a jigsaw puzzle game.

◆ **Photograph**. It offers a perfect representation of a real-life scene, in this case, a duck in an artificial lake in an aquarium. The child has to solve the puzzle to discover the duck.

◆ **Pattern recognition**. The child has to join different virtual pieces to build a complete image.

 As previously explained, we can also use the mouse or a multi-touch screen instead of the gamepad to solve the exercise. In this case, the gamepad's use makes the activity more attractive and requires more attention to solve it.

Time for action – solving the puzzle using a multi-touch device

It is also possible to make this exercise more attractive executing it with a multi-touch device working as a multi-touch mouse. We must first download and install **Logitech Touch Mouse Server**. We will then solve the puzzle using the multi-touch device.

> You need an iPhone, iPod Touch, or an iPad connected to your computer through a Wi-Fi or any other kind of compatible network in order to complete this activity. The following instructions explain the necessary steps to run this software on Windows. However, you can also run it on Mac OS X.

1. Go to **Control Panel | System** and a new window displaying the basic information about your computer will appear. Check the value shown for **System type**. The possible values are **32-bit Operating System** or **64-bit Operating System**, as shown in the next screenshot:

System	
Manufacturer:	Dell
Model:	Studio 1555
Rating:	**5.0** Windows Experience Index
Processor:	Intel(R) Core(TM)2 Duo CPU P8600 @ 2.40GHz 2.40 GHz
Memory (RAM):	4.00 GB
System type:	32-bit Operating System

2. Open your default web browser and go to `http://www.logitech.com/touchmouse`. This web page allows us to download the different versions of the Logitech Touch Mouse Server. This software allows you to use an iPhone, iPod Touch, or an iPad to control the mouse of your computer.

3. Click on **Downloads** and then on **Choose OS** and select your Windows version. Then, click on **Select File** and choose the file according to your operating system, 32-bit or 64-bit, considering the results of the previosuly explained step 1. For example, for Windows 7, 32-bit, you must select **touchmouse1.0.exe (32-bit)**, as shown in the next screenshot:

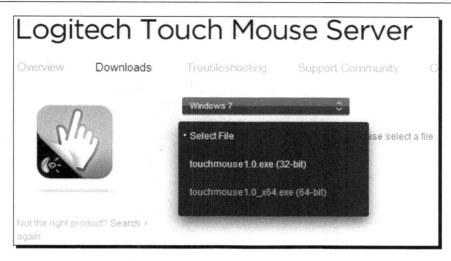

4. Scroll down and click on the **Download software** button. Start the downloaded installer and follow the steps to finish the installation process. By default, the Logitech Touch Mouse Server application will start automatically when the operating system starts. You can change this configuration by double-clicking on its tray icon and deactivating the option **Start this application automatically when Windows starts**.

5. Next, install **Logitech Touch Mouse** application on an iPhone, iPod Touch, or on an iPad. Then start this application on the device.

6. Select the desired server, in this case, the name of the PC that is running the previously explained server software, as shown in the next image:

7. Once the server is connected, a panel will appear in the device that will allow you to control the mouse pointer of your computer with your fingers, as shown in the next image:

8. Follow the steps explained in the previous section to start the exchange puzzle activity as a student. Once the puzzle is displayed, take the multi-touch device and control the mouse pointer by dragging your fingers on the previously shown dark panel.

9. Use your finger to position the mouse pointer over the desired virtual piece, as shown in the next image:

10. Tap the **Left** button that appears on the device's upper left-hand side corner.

11. Drag your finger over the dark panel and the virtual piece will change its position according to your finger's movement. Use your finger to position the virtual piece in its correct place.

12. Tap the **Left** button again to leave the virtual piece in the desired location.

13. After solving the puzzle, the activity will finish and you will be able to check your results by tapping or clicking on **Show results**.

What just happened?

We took advantage of the popular multi-touch screen offered by the iPhone, iPod Touch, and iPad to use the fingers as a remote mouse. Therefore, you were able to solve the puzzle using your fingers.

These devices are very popular. With the help of the free software created by Logitech, you can take advantage of this device to offer another creative and attractive way of solving an exchange puzzle.

Have a go hero – creating a puzzle based on a vector graphic

JClic Author offers the possibility to customize the shape of the virtual pieces for the exchange puzzle. You can do it by clicking on the ... button located at the right-hand side of the shape type selection combo box.

The **Shaper properties** dialog box will allow you to specify the tooth height and width. Besides, you can also activate the **Random distribution** checkbox to create shapes with random tooth distributions.

You can also change the shape of the virtual pieces by choosing one of the following options in the shape type selection combo box:

- Cuts
- Jigsaw with curved unions
- Jigsaw with rectangular unions
- Jigsaw with triangular unions
- Rectangular

 The software calls the edges for the pieces unions.

Use a scalable vector graphic and export it to a bitmap image as learned in Chapter 1, *Matching Pictures*, in the Matching composite pictures section. Use this image to create a new exchange puzzle with eight virtual pieces and choose one of the aforementioned shape types.

Once you have created the exchange puzzle with JClic Author, click on each virtual piece (cell) and add a number as the text associated to it. Numbers can help the student to solve the puzzle. For example, if the puzzle has two rows and four columns, the numbers shown in each piece with its corresponding part of the image would be as shown in the following table:

1	2	3	4
5	6	7	8

Looking for words in a word search puzzle

It was a sunny day at the Aquarium.

Alice and Kevin had a lot of fun. They fed the dolphins, played basketball with the seals, and watched the whales moving their tails.

She didn't want to forget the animals that they had seen in the Aquarium. Thus, she created a word search puzzle using the names of many animals. Do you want to play?

Time for action – creating a background picture by combining two images

We are first going to combine two images to create a background picture for our word search puzzle.

1. Open your default web browser and go to `http://animalphotos.info`. In this case, search for photos of the following animals in an aquarium, capture and save the image files with the names shown in the following table, in the previously created folder, `C:\Aquarium`. The next screenshot shows an example of two images:

Search for	Picture file name
dolphin	image060201.png
whale	image060202.png

image060201.PNG   image060202.PNG

2. Start **Paint** (**Start Menu | All Programs | Accessories | Paint**).

3. Open the first image file in Paint, C:\Aquarium\image060201.png.

4. Select **Edit | Paste from** and select the second image, C:\Aquarium\
image060201.png. This image will appear with a dotted border.

5. Next, drag the second image to a position such that both the dolphin and the whale
are visible in a merged picture, as shown in the next image:

6. Select **File | Save as** from Paint's main menu. Select **PNG (*.PNG)** in the **Save as
type** combo box and save the file as image060203.png in the previously created
folder, C:\Aquarium.

What just happened?

We searched for two royalty-free photos related to the aquarium and we merged them in a single image by using Paint. We now have a digital photo with both a dolphin and a whale to use as a background in our word search puzzle. The child will have to find the words related to the background picture.

Time for action – generating a word search puzzle with letters and pictures

We are now going to generate a word search puzzle with a photo of a dolphin and a whale, and our well-known JClic Author.

1. Run JClic Author 0.2.0.5 from its web page or by clicking on its icon.

2. Select **File | New Project** from JClic's main menu. A new dialog box will appear. Enter the following values for each textbox and then click on **OK**:

    ❑ word0602 in **Project name**.

    ❑ word0602 in **File name**. JClic will save the complete project in a compressed file, word0602.jclic.zip.

    ❑ A new word0602 sub-folder in the previously created folder, C:\Aquarium, in **Folder**, C:\Aquarium\word0602.

3. Click on the **Project** tab. Enter Finding the words related to the background picture in the **Title** textbox.

4. Click on the **Media library** tab.

5. Select **Insert | New media object** from the main menu. Choose the previously saved image image060203.png in C:\Aquarium and click on the **Open** button. JClic will ask your confirmation to copy the file to the project's folder; click **Yes**. The photo with a dolphin and a whale that will be used as a background will appear in JClic's media library.

6. Click on the **Activities** tab and select **Insert | New activity** from the main menu. Select **Word search** in the list shown in the **New activity** dialog box. Enter Word in the **Name of the activity** textbox and click on **OK**. JClic will add the new activity to the project and will display new tabs with dozens of options for it.

7. Click on the **Window** tab related to the new activity.

8. Click on the button located on the right-hand side of the **Image** label. The **Multimedia object selection** dialog box will appear. Select the previously added photo, image060203.png, and click **OK**. Activate the **Tiled** checkbox and select **Absolute position** under **Game window**. A preview for the window will appear with the whale and the dolphin as a background, as shown in the next screenshot:

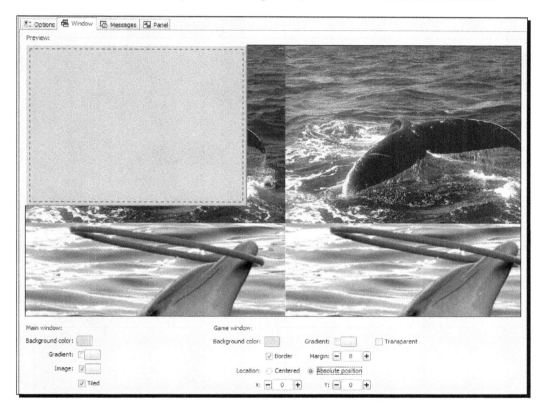

9. Next, click on the **Panel** tab related to the new activity and then on the **Grid A** panel inside it.

10. Enter 8 for both rows and columns, 45 for both width and height. JClic will show a grid of 64 letters, completed with wildcards (*) that will be replaced with random letters when the activity is executed.

11. Click on the **Add a new list element** (+) button under the **Hidden words** list. Enter DOLPHIN and click on **OK**. The new word will appear in this list.

12. Repeat the aforementioned step to add WHALE to the hidden words list.

13. Next, click on the grid and enter each letter in a specific position to display the hidden words in the grid. The next screenshot shows an example of possible locations for these words in the grid:

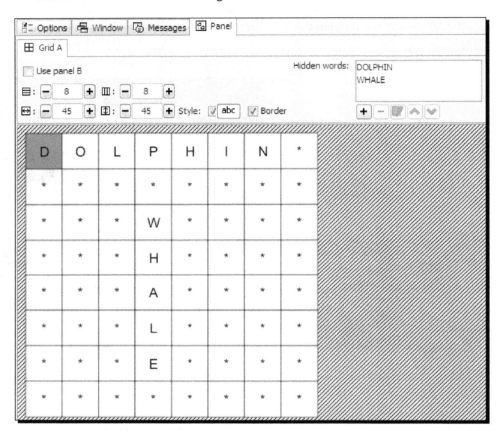

14. Select **File | Save** from JClic's main menu to save the changes made to the project.

15. Click on the **Sequences** tab. Select **Exit JClic** in the **Action** combo box under **Forward arrow** and activate the **Move on automatically** checkbox. This way, JClic will end once the activity is finished. Deactivate the **Show button** checkbox under **Back arrow**.

16. Select **File | Save** from JClic's main menu again.

17. Next, select **View | Preview Activity**. JClic will show a new window with the background photo and 64 letters in a grid, as shown in the next screenshot:

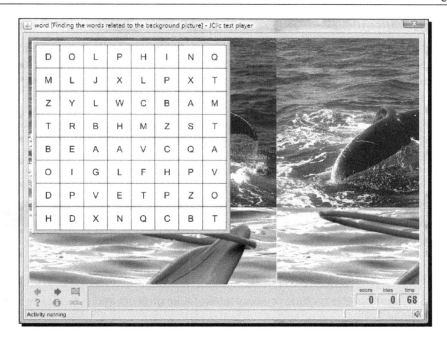

18. Click on the first letter for one of the hidden words, **DOLPHIN** or **WHALE** and then click on the last letter. JClic will invert the colors for the discovered word in the grid, as shown in the next screenshot:

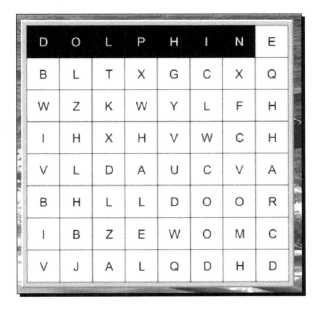

What just happened?

We created a word search puzzle activity using JClic and the previously created background picture with a dolphin and a whale. We used the capabilities offered by JClic to create a grid with 64 letters and 2 hidden words floating over a background. The animals found in the background can be used as a guideline to find the two hidden words in the grid.

We linked the background photo to the window's background, configured the grid, defined the list of hidden words, and entered their corresponding letters in the grid. JClic displayed the changes made in a preview panel. As previously explained, JClic is going to replace the wildcard character (*) with a randomly generated letter each time the students run the exercise.

Time for action – adding the activity to a Moodle course

We now have to add the word search puzzle to an existing Moodle course.

1. Log in to your Moodle server.

2. Make sure that the module to allow adding JClic projects and activities to Moodle is installed.

3. Click on the desired course name (Aquarium). You can create a new course or use an existing one.

4. As we have learned previously, follow the necessary steps to edit the summary for a desired week. Enter Exercise 2 in the **Summary** textbox and save the changes.

5. Click on the **Add an activity** combo box for the selected week and choose **JClic**. A new web page will appear displaying the title **Adding a new JClic to week**.

6. Enter Looking for words in a word search puzzle in the **Name** textbox.

7. Enter Look at the picture at the background and find two animals. Then, find the two words with these animal's names in the grid in the **Description** textbox. Select the desired font and color for this text.

8. Click on the **Choose or upload a file** button and the already well-known pop-up window displaying information about files and folders will appear.

9. Click on the **Upload a file** button and then on **Browse**. Browse to the folder that holds the JClic project (C:\Aquarium\word0602) and select the file to upload, word0602.jclic.zip. Then click on **Open** and then on the **Upload this file** button.

10. Next, position the mouse pointer over the **word0602.jclic.zip** name and move it horizontally to the **Choose** action hyperlink in the same row. Then click on **Choose**, as shown in the next screenshot:

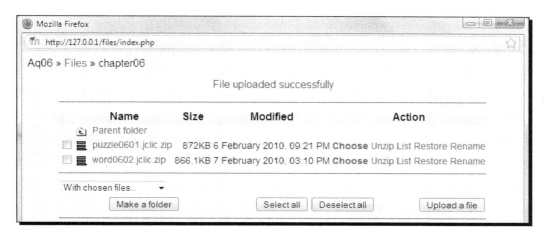

11. Moodle will display `chapter06/word0602.jclic.zip` in the **File name** textbox. This is the ZIP file that contains all the files with the JClic project and its activity, the word search puzzle.

12. Enter `800` in **Width** and `560` in **Height**.

13. Select `1` in **Maximum number of trials**.

14. Scroll down and click on the **Save and return to course** button, located at the bottom of the web page.

What just happened?

We added the word search puzzle exercise to a Moodle course. The students are now going to be able to run the activity by clicking on its hyperlink on the corresponding week.

We used the previously created folder, `chapter06`. We just uploaded one ZIP file that contains many compressed files with the background image and the definitions for the JClic project and single activity.

Time for action – solving the word search puzzle

Let's see what Alice sees when she logs in:

1. Click on the course name (Aquarium) and switch your role to student.

2. Click on the **Looking for words in a word search puzzle** link on the corresponding week. The web browser will show the exercise. The JClic panel that displays the activity can take some time to load.

3. Click on one of the cells. Now when you move the mouse pointer, the JClic application is going to draw a line. Click on another cell. Each time you draw the line over letters that don't represent a hidden word the JClic application will play a sound indicating a mistake.

4. Next, click on the first letter for the WHALE word, written from top to bottom. The JClic application is going to draw a line. Click on the last letter for this word, as shown in the next screenshot. The JClic application will play a sound indicating a successful operation.

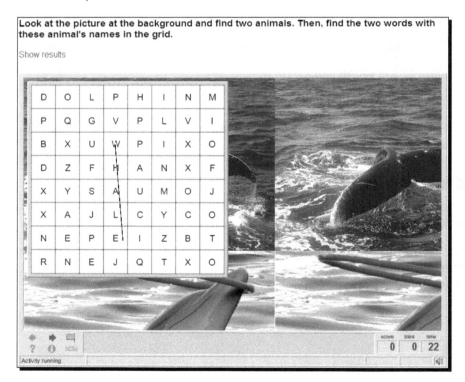

5. After discovering all the hidden words, the activity will finish and you will be able to check your results by clicking on **Show results**.

6. You can return to your normal role and check the number of attempts as done with the previous activities. Remember that they are going to appear grouped in JClic activities.

What just happened?

In this activity, we created a grid with 64 letters that hides two words related to an aquarium. The child has to look at the images and the background of the window and find two animals. The child must then discover the hidden words in the grid.

We applied the following concepts and resources in order to help to reduce attention deficit disorder:

◆ **Reading comprehension**. The child has to find the hidden words according to the background image.

◆ **Photograph**. It offers a perfect representation of a real-life scene, in this case, a dolphin and a whale. The child has to pay attention to the visible parts of a combined photograph to find the words that are related to the animals shown in it.

◆ **Attention stimulation**. The child has to focus on finding the different letters that compose the words.

◆ **Long-term memory**. The child has to recognize what animal appears in the background photograph. He/she has to think about all the animals he/she knows are found in an aquarium, and then associate them with the possible hidden words displayed in the grid.

Have a go hero – adding helping effects and sounds to the word search puzzle

Sometimes, a background photo is not enough to help the student to find the hidden words. Create a new word search puzzle with the following hidden words:

◆ DUCK
◆ PENGUIN
◆ SEAL

Add one video with sound for each hidden word in the JClic activity description. You have already learned to do it for other kinds of activities. This way, the students are going to be able to play the videos and hear the sound for each animal. These clues will offer them a visually rich activity and will help them to relate the videos and the sound with each hidden word.

Pop quiz – working with different kinds of puzzles

1. When you create an exchange puzzle with JClic Author:
   a. You can customize the shape of the virtual pieces
   b. You can only select rectangular virtual pieces
   c. You can only select a jigsaw with curved unions virtual pieces

2. An exchange puzzle created with JClic Author:
   a. Cannot mix text and images in each virtual piece
   b. Can only show text in each virtual piece
   c. Can mix text and images in each virtual piece

3. A word search activity in JClic Author:
   a. Displays a grid with letters that contains hidden words
   b. Displays a video with hidden words in its subtitles
   c. Displays words in a video with a big font

4. The window that displays a word search activity in JClic Author:
   a. Cannot be customized
   b. Cannot display a background image
   c. Can display a background image

5. When you create an exchange puzzle with JClic Author using a jigsaw with curved unions virtual pieces:
   a. You cannot customize the tooth height
   b. You can also customize the tooth height and width
   c. You cannot customize the tooth width

Summary

In this chapter, we have learned how to:

◆ Create visually rich puzzles combining digital photos, virtual pieces, letters, and words

◆ Create virtual pieces with the shape of a jigsaw with curved edges

◆ Design a word search puzzle combining many photos in a single background and adding the letters for each word in a grid

◆ Work with many tools to create realistic activities that can reduce the student's Attention Deficit Disorder and improve their long-term memory management

Now that we have learned how to create exercises to reduce Attention Deficit Disorder, we're ready to prepare exercises to play with mathematics operations, which is the topic of the next chapter.

7
Playing with Mathematical Operations

We can play with mathematical operations by creating different kinds of visually rich activities. It is possible to use many different applications to create exercises that help the students solve simple mathematical operations working with images and symbols instead of numbers and symbols. This way, we can help them to improve their concentration while solving mathematical operations.

In this chapter, Alice goes to a farm. We will learn how to create visually rich activities to play with mathematical operations that are related to her journey. In this chapter we will:

- ◆ Prepare a scene with a background picture and many animals to allow the student to count them
- ◆ Create a multiple choice with a visual description and answers with multiple images
- ◆ Create visual and interactive activities to solve simple mathematical operations
- ◆ Create a complex association activity with visual mathematical operations and their possible results
- ◆ Learn how to combine pictures and symbols to improve the concentration when working with mathematical operations

Solving a multiple choice with multiple images

Alice and her little brother Kevin went to their uncle's farm in Kansas, USA. They were amazed by the barn and they found a lot of animals, hens, cows, pigs, and bees working hard in their beehive.

They spent a lot of time playing and counting the number of each type of animal. Shall we help them?

Time for action – preparing a scene to count elements

We are going to prepare a scene related to the farm by using a background picture and then adding other clipart of animals inside it. We are then going to use this scene to count the number of animals found in it.

1. Create a new folder in Windows Explorer (`C:\Farm`).

2. Start Inkscape and minimize it. You will use it later.

3. Start Word 2007. You will be working in a new blank document.

4. Click on **Insert | Clip Art**. The **Clip Art** panel will appear on the right-hand side of the main window.

5. Click on the **Search in** combo box and activate the **Everywhere** checkbox. This way, Word will search for clipart in all the available collections, including the Web Collections.

6. Click on the **Search for** textbox and enter `Bee`.

7. Click on the **Go** button.

8. Position the mouse pointer over the desired clipart's thumbnail.

9. Right-click on the desired clipart's thumbnail and select **Preview/Properties** in the context menu that appears. Word will display a new dialog box showing a larger preview of the scalable clipart and a temporary file name.

10. Triple-click on the long path and file name shown after **File.** This way, you will be sure that the temporary file's full path is selected. Then right-click on it and select **Copy** in the context menu that appears.

11. Next, activate Inkscape—remember it was running minimized. You can use *Alt + Tab* or *Windows + Tab*. Don't close the clipart's preview window.

12. Select **File | Import** from the main menu. Click on the **Type a file name** button (the pencil with a paper sheet icon) and paste the previously copied temporary file's full path in the **Location:** textbox. The path is going to be similar to `C:\Users\vanesa\AppData\Local\Microsoft\Windows\Temporary Internet Files\Content.IE5\QBDKECTZ\MCj01512070000[1].wmf`.

13. Click on the **Open** button. The previously previewed clipart, a funny bee for our scene, will appear selected in Inkscape's drawing area, as shown in the next image:

14. Select **File | Save As** from Inkscape's main menu. Save the file as `image070101.svg` in the previously created folder, `C:\Farm`.

15. Select **File | Export Bitmap**. A dialog box showing many export options will appear.

16. Click on the **Selection** button, and then on **Export**. Inkscape will export the recently imported clipart in PNG format. The exported bitmap graphics file will be `C:\Farm\image070101.png`.

17. Next, return to Word.

18. Repeat the aforementioned steps (4 to 17) to add each animal to the farm. Save the image files with the names shown in the next table. The next image shows two possible pictures of animals:

Animal	Inkscape file name	Picture file name
Pig	image070102.svg	image070102.png
Hen	image070103.svg	image070103.png

19. Next, return to Word. Search for a clipart image related to the word `barn` and preview it. Since you want to change the picture size without losing quality using Inkscape, remember to make sure it is a **WMF** or an **EMF** file.

20. Next, activate Inkscape and import the previewed clipart following the previously explained steps. The previously previewed clipart, the background for our scene, will appear selected in Inkscape's drawing area.

21. As you want it to be the background for the animals in the farm, select **Object | Lower to bottom** from Inkscape's main menu. This way, the animals will appear on top of the new background picture.

22. Resize the background picture to allow you to use it as a background for all the animals.

23. Click on the bee and select **Edit | Duplicate** from Inkscape's main menu. This way, Inkscape will create a new copy of this element. However, the two bees will appear in the same position, one over the other.

24. Move the selected bee to a different position.

25. Repeat the aforementioned steps (23 and 24) to add a third bee and a second pig, as shown in the next image:

26. Select **File | Save As** from Inkscape's main menu. Save the file as `image070104. svg` in the previously created folder, `C:\Farm`.

27. Select **File | Export Bitmap**. A dialog box showing many export options will appear. Enter `800` in the **Width** textbox under **Bitmap size**. This way, the width for the exported bitmap will be set to 800 pixels.

28. Click on the **Drawing** button, and then on **Export**. Inkscape will export the scene in PNG format. The exported bitmap graphics with the farm scene, three bees, two pigs, and a hen will be saved at `C:\Farm\image070104.png`.

What just happened?

We created a representation of a scene on the farm using Inkscape and scalable vector clipart. We first added each animal and we individually exported them to the PNG format. We now have the following three bitmap images ready to be used in our visual multiple choice exercise:

◆ `image070101.png`: A **bee**

◆ `image070102.png`: A **pig**

◆ `image070103.png`: A **hen**

We then added a background picture, we added copies of some animals, and we distributed them in the farm. Finally, we exported the resulting image to the PNG format.

Time for action – creating a visual multiple choice with many animals

We now have to prepare a visual multiple choice with different numbers of animals as the possible answers, combining text and images.

1. Log in to your Moodle server.

2. Click on the desired course name (`Farm`). You can create a new course or use an existing one.

3. As previously learned, follow the necessary steps to edit the summary for a desired week. Enter `Exercise 1` in the **Summary** textbox and save the changes.

4. Click on the **Add an activity** combo box for the selected week and choose **Quiz**.

5. Enter `Visual multiple choice` in **Quiz name**, then click on the **Save and display** button. Moodle will display the question bank for this quiz.

6. Click on the **Create new question** combo box and choose **Description**. A new page asking for the necessary information to add a multiple choice description will appear.

7. Enter `Look at this picture` in **Question Name**.

8. Click on the big textbox below the **Question text** label. Use different fonts and colors to enter the sentence that defines the goal, `Count the pigs, hens and bees in this farm`.

9. Click on the big textbox below the **Question text** label.

10. Click on the **Insert Image** button (a mountain). A new web page will appear displaying the title **Insert image**.

11. Enter `chapter07` in the textbox located on the left-hand side of the **Create folder** button and then press this button. Then click on the new folder's hyperlink.

12. Follow the necessary steps to upload the file `image070104.png`, the farm scene, in the previously created folder, `chapter07`. Remember to enter an alternate text and the farm with the animals will appear under **Question text**.

13. Scroll down and click on the **Save changes** button, located at the bottom of the web page.

14. Moodle will display a question bank and the questions for the quiz. Now activate the **Action** checkbox corresponding to the row labeled with the previously created description, **Count the pigs, hens and bees in this farm**. Then, click on the **Add to quiz** button. Moodle will add the description to our quiz, as shown in the next screenshot:

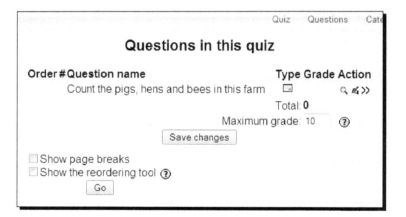

15. Click on the **Create new question** combo box and choose **Multiple choice**. A new page asking for the necessary information to add a multiple choice question will appear.

16. Enter `Counting bees` in **Question Name**.

17. Click on the big textbox below the **Question text** label. Use different fonts and colors to enter the sentence that defines the goal and the question to answer using the visual multiple choice quiz, `How many bees do you see in the farm?`

18. Scroll down and go to the section named **Choice 1** (the first possible answer).

19. Enter `One bee` in the **Answer** textbox inside the **Choice 1** section.

20. Click on the **Insert Image** button (a mountain) under the **Feedback** title inside the **Choice 1** section. A new web page will appear displaying the title **Insert image**.

21. Follow the necessary steps to upload the file `image070101.png`, the bee, in the previously created folder, `chapter07`. Remember to enter an alternate text.

22. The bee will appear in the big **Feedback** textbox. Click on the **Toggle HTML Source** button (the one with the **<>** label) under the **Feedback** title inside the **Choice 1** section. The big textbox will display HTML code, a line similar to the following one:

```
<img hspace="0" height="48" width="46" vspace="0"
    border="0" title="bee" alt="bee" src="http://127.0.0.1/file.
php/10/chapter07/image070101.png" />
<br />
```

23. Select the text from the first < up to the first /> and press *Ctrl + C*. We want to copy the code to display the uploaded image without the `<br />`. Code similar to the following line will be copied:

```
<img hspace="0" height="48" width="46" vspace="0"
    border="0" title="bee" alt="bee"
src="http://127.0.0.1/file.php/10/chapter07/image070101.png" />
```

24. Click on the **Answer** textbox inside the **Choice 1** section. Press *End* and then *Ctrl + V*. The text in this textbox will now be similar to the following:

```
One bee
<img hspace="0" height="48" width="46" vspace="0" border="0"
src="http://127.0.0.1/file.php/10/chapter07/image070101.png"
alt="bee" title="bee" />
```

25. Select **None** in the **Grade** combo box under the section named **Choice 1** because this is a wrong answer.

26. Scroll down and go to the section named **Choice 2** (the second possible answer).

27. Enter `Three bees` in the **Answer** textbox inside the **Choice 2** section and then press *Ctrl + V* three times because in this case three images of the bee must appear. The text in this textbox will be similar to the following:

```
Three bees
<img hspace="0" height="48" width="46" vspace="0" border="0"
src="http://127.0.0.1/file.php/10/chapter07/image070101.png"
alt="bee" title="bee" />
<img hspace="0" height="48" width="46" vspace="0" border="0"
src="http://127.0.0.1/file.php/10/chapter07/image070101.png"
alt="bee" title="bee" />
<img hspace="0" height="48" width="46" vspace="0" border="0"
src="http://127.0.0.1/file.php/10/chapter07/image070101.png"
alt="bee" title="bee" />
```

28. Click on the big textbox under the **Feedback** title inside the **Choice 2** section and then click on the **Toggle HTML Source** button (the one with the **<>** label). Select all the text and press *Ctrl + V* three times. Code similar to the following lines will appear:

```
<img hspace="0" height="48" width="46"
    vspace="0" border="0" title="bee" alt="bee"
src="http://127.0.0.1/file.php/10/chapter07/image070101.png"/>
<img hspace="0" height="48" width="46"
    vspace="0" border="0" title="bee" alt="bee"
src="http://127.0.0.1/file.php/10/chapter07/image070101.png" />
<img hspace="0" height="48" width="46"
    vspace="0" border="0" title="bee" alt="bee"
src="http://127.0.0.1/file.php/10/chapter07/image070101.png" />
```

29. Select **100%** in the **Grade** combo box because this is the correct answer, as shown in the following screenshot:

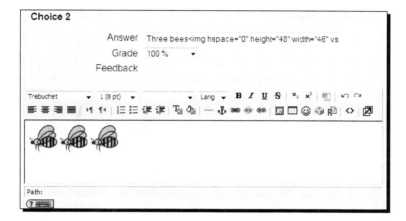

30. Scroll down and go to the section named **Choice 3** (the third possible answer).

31. Enter Two bees in the **Answer** textbox inside the **Choice 3** section and then press *Ctrl + V* two times because in this case two images of the bee must appear. The text in this textbox will be similar to the following:

```
Two bees
<img hspace="0" height="48" width="46" vspace="0" border="0"
src="http://127.0.0.1/file.php/10/chapter07/image070101.png"
alt="bee" title="bee" />
<img hspace="0" height="48" width="46" vspace="0" border="0"
src="http://127.0.0.1/file.php/10/chapter07/image070101.png"
alt="bee" title="bee" />
```

32. Click on the big textbox under the **Feedback** title inside the **Choice 3** section and then click on the **Toggle HTML Source** button (the one with the **<>** label). Select all the text and press *Ctrl + V* two times.

33. Select **None** in the **Grade** combo box under the section named **Choice 3** because this is a wrong answer.

34. Scroll down and click on the **Save changes** button, located at the bottom of the web page.

35. Moodle will display a question bank and the questions for the quiz. Now activate the **Action** checkbox corresponding to the row labeled with the previously created question, **Counting bees**. Then click on the **Add to quiz** button. Moodle will add the description to our quiz.

36. Repeat the aforementioned steps (15 to 35) for the two additional questions about the number of animals seen in the farm. Remember to select the right answer according to the number of animals previously added to the scene, as explained in step 29. The next table shows the animal, the question name, the picture file name, and the correct answer. Finally, Moodle will show the description and the three questions of our quiz, as shown in the next screenshot:

Animal	Question name	Picture file name	Right answer
Pig	Counting pigs	image070102.png	Two pigs
Hen	Counting hens	image070103.png	One hen

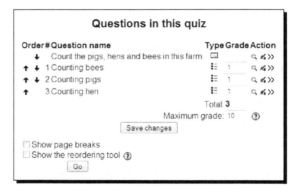

37. Click on the **Save changes** button. The visual multiple choice exercise with images of animals as its possible answers is ready.

What just happened?

We created a visual multiple choice composed of the following elements:

- A description that displays the image of the farm with the animals
- A question about the number of bees
- A question about the number of pigs
- A question about the number of hens

We added the three possible answers to each of the questions. We took advantage of the possibility of adding pictures as feedback for each answer. We then copied the HTML code that displayed a single image and added it after each answer's text as many times as the number of animals that the answer represents.

The students are now going to be able to solve the visual multiple choice that allows them to choose the answer according to the number of animals seen. Inserting HTML code into the answer text allowed us to create a visually rich multiple choice. Therefore, it is possible to play with math.

Time for action – executing the activity

It is time to help Alice to find out how many pigs are there in the farm.

1. Log in to your Moodle server using a user with the student role. If necessary, you can ask your Moodle administrator to create a new user with the student role. You can use this user to test this activity and other activities.

2. Click on the course name (Farm).

3. Click on the **Visual multiple choice** link on the corresponding week.

4. Click on the **Attempt quiz now** button. The description with the farm scene and its animals will appear. Then the three questions with their three radio buttons with text and images will be displayed. The next two screenshots show a reduced view of the description and the visual radio buttons of the possible answers:

Visual multiple choice - Attempt 1

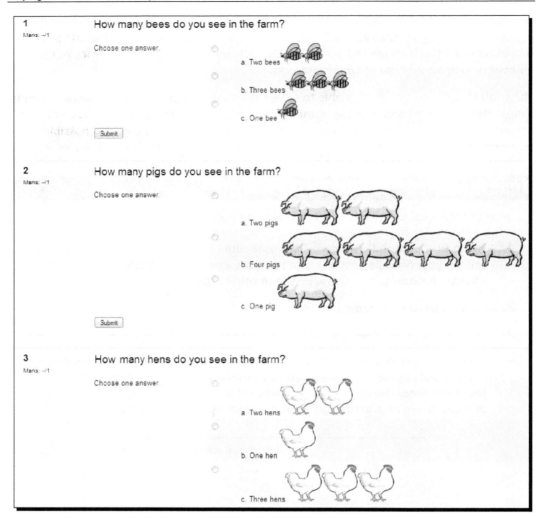

5. Click on the corresponding radio button for a right answer. Then, click on the **Submit** button, located on the lower left-hand side corner of the question section. Moodle will show the feedback, telling you whether the chosen answer was correct or not.

6. Next, click on the corresponding radio button for each correct answer. Then, scroll down and click on the **Submit all and finish** button, located at the bottom of the web page. Moodle will display the review of the results for the activity, as previously learned for our Boolean multiple choice. The next screenshot shows the review of the results with the three correct answers with the green background and their feedback.

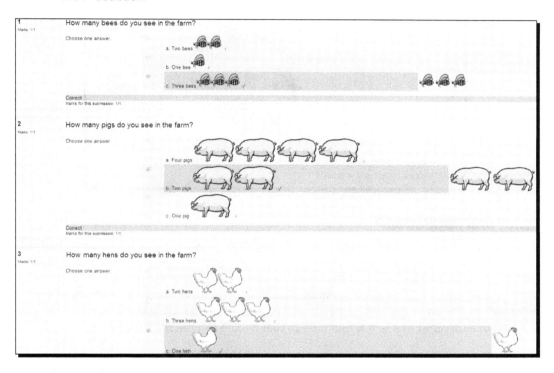

7. Click on the **Finish review** button.

8. Log out and log in with your normal user and role. Go back to the Moodle course.

9. Click on **Quizzes** in the **Activities** panel. The number of attempts will appear in the **Attempts** column.

10. Next, click on the **Attempts** link for the row corresponding to the **Visual multiple choice** activity and Moodle will display details about all the attempts, grouped by user name.

11. Log out and log in using a user with the student role. Re-attempt the visual multiple choice now and select wrong answers to see the visual feedback provided when you don't select the correct answers. The next screenshot shows the feedback provided for the question about the number of bees when the selected answer is wrong.

What just happened?

In this activity, we worked with three questions and three possible answers with radio buttons related to different numbers of images of animals. The objective was to count the quantity of each different animal and to select the correct answer according to the question and the text or the visual representation of the number of animals, located on the right-hand side of each radio button. The child can read, understand, and answer the question by himself/herself, with the help of a therapist or a family member, so that he/she can run the exercise.

The activity consists of clicking each radio button for the correct number of animals according to the related scene with many animals in the farm. We applied the following concepts and resources in order to stimulate the attention, the concentration, and the abstraction capacity:

- **Reading comprehension**. The child has to read and understand the question and the animals' names.

- **Associating concepts**. The child has to associate a question with the possible answers.

- **Short-term memory**. The child has to remember the number of animals seen in the scene when he/she scrolls up and down to choose the right answer. Thus, the child works with his/her short-term memory.

- **Quantity notions**. We worked with composite images, showing one or more animals per answer.

The farm was our main scene for the exercise. It offers a great number of resources and ideas to work with in funny exercises.

 We can create visual multiple choices using the same pattern with different kinds of things. These kinds of visually rich activities are really engaging for children.

Have a go hero – preparing more visual multiple choices

You already know about graphics with animations in animated GIF files. Create a new visual multiple choice with a scene composed of a background scenario and many elements. Then use animated GIF files to combine text in the answers and animated graphics. This way, the student will have to recognize the animated version of the elements found in the scene.

 Combining everything we learned in the previous chapter with the visual multiple choice, you can create more complex exercises to play with mathematical operations.

Completing a grid of visual mathematical operations

It is another great day to spend time on the farm. Alice and her aunt Mary spent an hour picking apples from the apple trees today. They have a lot of apples in their baskets. Can we count the total number of apples?

Time for action – combining pictures with mathematical symbols

We are going to create many visual mathematical operations composed of apples and symbols. We are then going to create possible results with different number of apples. We will then use these composite pictures to fill each cell of a grid.

1. Start Inkscape and minimize it. You will use it later.

2. Start Word 2007. You will be working in a new blank document.

3. Follow the necessary steps to search for a clipart picture of an `apple`.

4. Right-click on the desired clipart's thumbnail and select **Preview/Properties** in the context menu that appears. Word will display a new dialog box showing a larger preview of the scalable clipart and a temporary file name.

5. Triple-click on the long path and file name shown after **File**. This way, you will be sure that the temporary file's full path is selected. Then right-click on it and select **Copy** in the context menu that appears.

6. Next, activate Inkscape—remember it was running minimized. You can use *Alt + Tab* or *Windows + Tab*. Don't close the clipart's preview window.

7. Select **File | Import** from the main menu. Click on the **Type a file name** button (the pencil with a paper sheet icon) and paste the previously copied temporary file's full path in the **Location:** textbox. The path is going to be similar to
`C:\Users\vanesa\AppData\Local\Microsoft\Windows\Temporary`
`Internet Files\Content.IE5\QBDKECTZ\MCj04417080000[1].png`.

8. Click on the **Open** button. The previously previewed clipart, a nice apple for our mathematical operations, will appear selected in Inkscape's drawing area, as shown in the following image:

9. Click on the apple and select **Edit | Duplicate** from Inkscape's main menu. This way, Inkscape will create a new copy of this element. However, the two apples will appear in the same position, one over the other.

10. Move the selected apple to the right-hand side, leaving a space for a big + sign between the two apples.

11. Click on **Create and edit text objects** button (a big **A** with a cursor on the left-hand side) or press *F8*. This function allows you to add text with different fonts and colors in Inkscape's drawing area.

12. Select the desired font and size using the two combo boxes that appear on the upper left-hand side corner of the window, below the main toolbar.

13. Enter the + sign as the new text. This way, you will have the first visual mathematical operation, one apple plus one apple, as shown in the next image:

14. Select **File | Save As** from Inkscape's main menu. Save the file as image070201.svg in the previously created folder, C:\Farm.

15. Select **File | Export Bitmap**. A dialog box showing many export options will appear.

16. Click on the **Drawing** button, and then on **Export**. Inkscape will export the visual mathematical operation in PNG format. The exported bitmap graphics with the two apples and a plus sign will be C:\Farm\image070201.png.

17. Use the created Inkscape drawing as the base for the following.

18. Select **File | New | Default** from Inkscape's main menu. A blank drawing area will appear.

19. Repeat the aforementioned steps (7 to 18) for each of the following visual mathematical operations and possible results to add to the grid. Save the image files with the names shown in the next table. The subsequent image shows all the visual mathematical operations and the possible results:

Visual mathematical operation or result	Inkscape file name	Picture file name
One apple + one apple	image070201.svg	image070201.png
Two apples + one apple	image070202.svg	image070202.png
Two apples (possible result)	image070203.svg	image070203.png
Three apples (possible result)	image070204.svg	image070204.png
One apple (possible result)	image070205.svg	image070205.png
Four apples (possible result)	image070206.svg	image070206.png

What just happened?

We used Inkscape to combine many copies of a bitmap clipart image and a symbol to create two bitmap graphics with two visual mathematical operations:

◆ `image070201.png`: One apple + one apple

◆ `image070202.png`: Two apples + one apple

We then combined many copies of the bitmap clipart image to represent four possible visual results for the aforementioned mathematical operations:

◆ `image070203.png`: Two apples

◆ `image070204.png`: Three apples

◆ `image070205.png`: One apple

◆ `image070206.png`: Four apples

The exercise will look nice using these visual representations of numbers with tasty apples, and it will be more attractive than cells displaying numbers and symbols.

Time for action – generating a grid with images and mathematical symbols

We are now going to generate two grids with a complex association with our two visual mathematical operations, the four possible visual results, and our well-known JClic Author.

1. Run JClic Author 0.2.0.5 from its web page or by clicking on its icon.

2. Select **File | New Project** from JClic's main menu. A new dialog box will appear. Enter the next values for each textbox and then click on **OK**:

   ❑ `complex0702` in **Project name**.

   ❑ `complex0702` in **File name**. JClic will save the complete project in a compressed file, `complex0702.jclic.zip`.

   ❑ A new `complex0702` sub-folder in the previously created folder, `C:\Farm`, in **Folder**, `C:\Farm\complex0702`.

3. Click on the **Project** tab. Enter `Choosing the associated results` in the **Title** textbox.

4. Click on the **Media library** tab.

5. Select **Insert | New media object** from the main menu. Choose one of the previously created bitmap graphics with a visual mathematical operation, `image070201.png` in `C:\Farm` and click on the **Open** button. JClic will ask your confirmation to copy the file to the project's folder; click **Yes**. The `one apple + one apple` operation that will be converted to a visual cell will appear in JClic's media library.

6. Repeat the aforementioned step (5) for each visual mathematical operation and result to add as cells for the complex association. The next screenshot shows the media library with all the images added:

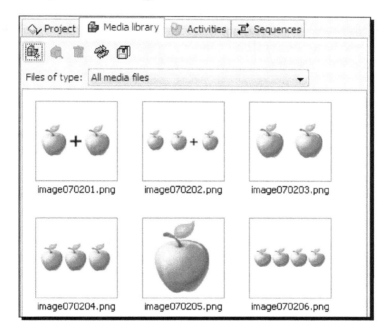

7. Click on the **Activities** tab and select **Insert | New activity** from the main menu. Select **Complex association** in the list shown in the **New activity** dialog box. Enter `Grids` in the **Name of the activity** textbox and click **OK**. JClic will add the new activity to the project and will display new tabs with dozens of options for it.

8. Click on the **Activities** tab and select **Insert | New activity** from the main menu. Select **Exchange puzzle** in the list shown in the **New activity** dialog box. Enter `Puzzle` in the **Name of the activity** textbox and click **OK**. JClic will add the new activity to the project and will display new tabs with dozens of options for it.

9. Next click on the **Panel** tab related to the new activity and then on the **Grid A** panel inside it. This grid will show the two visual mathematical operations.

10. Enter 2 for rows, 1 for columns, 230 for width, and 87 for height. JClic will show a grid at the left with two horizontal cells.

11. Next, click on the first cell on the grid located at the left-hand side. The **Cell contents** dialog box will appear.

12. Click on the button located on the right-hand side of the **Image** label. The **Multimedia object selection** dialog box will appear. Select the bitmap graphics for the first visual mathematical operation, image070201.png, and click on **OK**. Then click **OK** on the **Cell contents** dialog box. The top cell will display the selected bitmap graphics with the visual mathematical operation.

13. Repeat the previous step (12) on the second cell with the bitmap graphics for the second visual mathematical operation, image070202.png. The next screenshot shows the two cells with the visual mathematical operations:

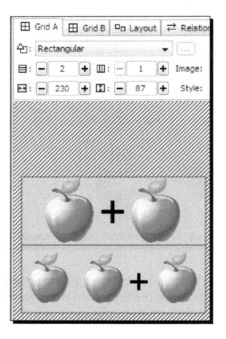

14. Next, click on the **Grid B** panel. This grid will show the four possible visual results for the two visual mathematical operations.

15. Enter 4 for rows, 1 for columns, 230 for width and 87 for height. JClic will show a grid on the right-hand side with four vertical cells.

16. Next, click on the first cell on the grid located on the right-hand side. The **Cell contents** dialog box will appear.

17. Click on the button located on the right-hand side of the **Image** label. The **Multimedia object selection** dialog box will appear. Select the bitmap graphics for the first possible visual result, image070203.png, and click on **OK**. Then, click on **OK** in the **Cell contents** dialog box. The top cell will display the selected bitmap graphics with the visual result.

18. Repeat the previous step (17) on the second, third, and fourth cells with the bitmap graphics for the remaining three visual results, image070204.png, image070205. png, and image070206.png. The next screenshot shows the four cells with the possible visual results:

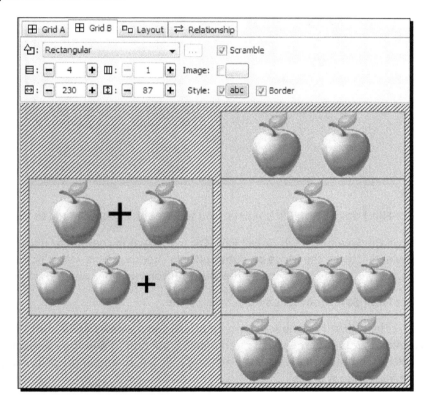

19. It is now necessary to tell JClic the correct answer for each visual mathematical operation. It is possible to do it by establishing a relationship between a cell in the grid on the left and a cell in the grid on the right. Click on the **Relationship** panel.

20. Click on the first cell in the grid on the left-hand side. Next, position the mouse pointer over the cell with the result for this mathematical operation, the first cell in the grid on the right-hand side. Click on it and JClic will show an arrow from the cell on the left to the cell on the right.

21. Repeat the previous step (20) for the second visual mathematical operation and its result. JClic will show two arrows to illustrate the relationships, as shown in the following image:

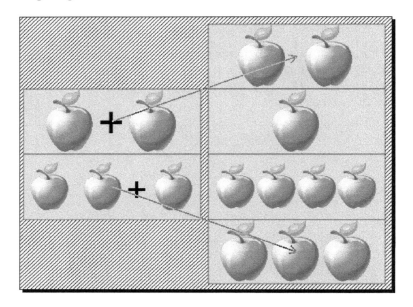

22. Select **File | Save** from JClic's main menu to save the changes made to the project.

23. Click on the **Sequences** tab. Select **Exit JClic** in the **Action** combo box under **Forward arrow** and activate the **Move on automatically** checkbox. This way, JClic will end once the activity is finished. Deactivate the **Show button** checkbox under **Back arrow**.

24. Select **File | Save** from JClic's main menu again.

25. Next, select **View | Preview Activity**. JClic will show a new window with two scrambled grids with the visual mathematical operations and their possible visual results. Each time you preview the activity; JClic will scramble the cells and present them in a random order.

26. Click on each visual mathematical operation and then on its visual result. When the chosen result is the correct one, the visual mathematical operation will disappear from the grid on the left-hand side, as shown in the next screenshot:

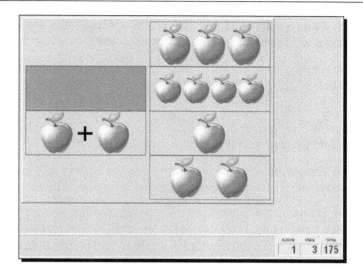

What just happened?

We created a complex association activity using JClic and the previously created bitmap graphics for two visual mathematical operations and four possible visual results. We used the capabilities offered by JClic to create two grids that allow the student to solve visual mathematical operations.

We linked each bitmap to a cell and then we established relationships to indicate the correct result for each mathematical operation. JClic displayed the changes made in each cell in a preview panel. As previously explained, JClic is going to jumble the cells in both grids each time the students run the exercise, using a randomly generated order.

Time for action – adding the activity to a Moodle course

We now have to add the grid with visual mathematical operations to an existing Moodle course.

1. Log in to your Moodle server.

2. Make sure that the module to allow adding JClic projects and activities to Moodle is installed. The necessary steps to perform the installation were explained in previous chapters.

3. Click on the desired course name (Farm). You can create a new course or use an existing one.

4. As previously learned, follow the necessary steps to edit the summary for a desired week. Enter Exercise 2 in the **Summary** textbox and save the changes.

5. Click on the **Add an activity** combo box for the selected week and choose **JClic**. A new web page will appear displaying the title **Adding a new JClic to week**.

6. Enter `Completing a grid of visual mathematical operations` in the **Name** textbox.

7. Enter `Click on each visual mathematical operation at the left and then on its correct result at the right` in the **Description** textbox. Select the desired font and color for this text.

8. Click on the **Choose or upload a file** button and the already well-known pop-up window displaying information about files and folders will appear.

9. Click on the **Upload a file** button and then on **Browse**. Browse to the folder that holds the JClic project (`C:\Farm\ complex0702`) and select the file to upload, `complex0702.jclic.zip`. Then, click on **Open** and on the **Upload this file** button.

10. Next, position the mouse pointer over the **complex0702.jclic.zip** name and move it horizontally to the **Choose** action hyperlink in the same row. Then, click on **Choose**, as shown in the following screenshot:

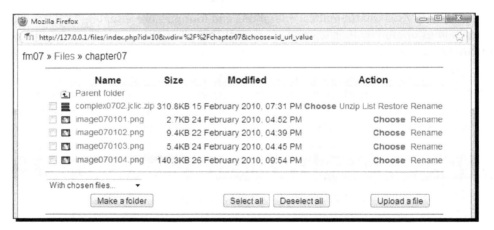

11. Moodle will display `chapter07/complex0702.jclic.zip` in the **File name** textbox. This is the ZIP file that contains all the files with the JClic project and its activity, the complex association.

12. Enter `600` in **Width** and `400` in **Height**.

13. Select `1` in **Maximum number of trials**.

14. Scroll down and click on the **Save and return to course** button, located at the bottom of the web page.

What just happened?

We added the complex association with two grids exercise to a Moodle course. The students are now going to be able to run the activity by clicking on its hyperlink on the corresponding week. We just uploaded one ZIP file that contains many compressed files with the six bitmap graphics and the definitions for the JClic project and single activity.

Time for action – solving the visual mathematical operations

It is time to help Alice to solve visual mathematical operations with apples.

1. Log in to your Moodle server using a user with the student role.

2. Click on the course name (Farm).

3. Click on the **Completing a grid of visual mathematical operations** link on the corresponding week. The web browser will show the exercise. The JClic panel that displays the activity can take some time to load.

4. Click on one of the cells with the visual mathematical operation and try to find its result.

5. Each time you select the wrong result, the JClic application will play a sound indicating a mistake. Each time you select the correct result, it will play a sound indicating a successful operation. When you click on the visual mathematical operation, JClic will draw a line until you click on one of the possible results, as shown in the following screenshot:

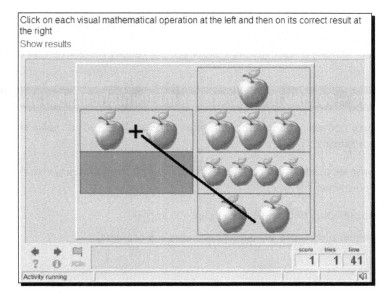

6. After solving all the visual mathematical operations, the activity will finish and you will be able to check your results by clicking on **Show results**.

7. Log out and log in with your normal user and role. You can check the number of attempts as done with the previous activities. Remember that they are going to appear grouped in JClic activities.

What just happened?

In this activity, we created the contents for the cells of a complex association activity using apples and symbols. The child has to solve simple mathematical operations by selecting the correct result in the second grid for the visual operations shown in the first grid.

We applied the following concepts and resources in order to help to reduce Attention Deficit Disorder:

◆ **Quantity notions**. We worked with different numbers of images to represent visual mathematical operations and their possible results. The child has to count apples.

◆ **Pattern recognition**. The child has to recognize the symbols used to display the visual mathematical operations.

◆ **Images**. They offer a visual mechanism to simplify the communication of numbers to guide the child to choose the correct result.

◆ **Long-term memory**. The child has to count the number of apples and has to associate this number with the visual mathematical operation shown in the first grid.

 As previously explained, we can also use the gamepad or a multi-touch screen instead of the mouse to solve the exercise. In this case, the gamepad's usage would make the activity more attractive and require more attention to solve it.

Have a go hero – solving more complex mathematical operations

It is possible to use complex association activities to allow the student solve more complex mathematical operations.

Create a new complex association activity using JClic. Add the following visual mathematical operations:

◆ Three apples plus two apples (3 apples + 2 apples)

◆ Two oranges plus three oranges (2 oranges + 3 oranges)

Then add the following possible results:

- 1 apple
- 2 apples
- 3 apples
- 4 apples
- 5 apples
- 6 apples
- 7 apples
- 1 orange
- 2 oranges
- 3 oranges
- 4 oranges
- 5 oranges
- 6 oranges
- 8 oranges

This way, the student will have to understand the difference between mathematical operations with apples and oranges because in this case, there are results with both fruits.

Pop quiz – working with visual mathematical operations

1. When you need to add a description for a Moodle multiple choice:
    a. You can add a new Multiple choice type question.
    b. You can add a new Description type question.
    c. You can add a new Choice general description type question.

2. In a Moodle multiple choice question, when the user submits a wrong answer:
    a. The feedback for the correct answer will appear on the right-hand side of the correct answer.
    b. The feedback for the correct answer won't appear.
    c. The feedback for the wrong answer will appear.

3. In a Moodle multiple choice question:

   a. You can add graphics with animations by adding HTML code with links to many different WMF files. Moodle will use each WMF as a frame for the animation.

   b. You can add graphics with animations by adding HTML code with links to animated GIF files.

   c. You can add graphics with animations by adding HTML code with links to many different PNG files. Moodle will use each PNG as a frame for the animation.

4. When you create a complex association activity with JClic Author:

   a. You can only specify the number of rows for Grid A.

   b. You can only specify the number of rows and columns for Grid B.

   c. You can customize the number of rows and columns for each of the two grids.

5. A complex association activity in JClic Author:

   a. Displays a grid with letters that contains hidden words.

   b. Displays two grids that hold relationships between some of their cells.

   c. Displays three grids that hold relationships between some of their cells.

Summary

In this chapter, we have learned how to:

- Play with mathematics combining scenes, pictures of animals, images of apples, and symbols

- Create a visual multiple choice that allows students to count the animals in a farm and then select the visual answer by looking at the number of animals shown in each possible one

- Work with many tools to create a complex scene with a farm in the background and many animals on top of it

- Create a pair of grids to let the student associate visual mathematical operations with their visual results

- Use Inkscape to combine pictures with symbols to represent each visual mathematical operation and its possible results, so that students can practice simple mathematical operations by working with visually rich activities

Now that we have learned how to create exercises to play with mathematics operations, we're ready to prepare exercises to perform mental operations with language, which is the topic of the next chapter.

8
Mental Operations with Language

We can practice mental operations with language by creating different kinds of visually rich activities. It is possible to use many different applications to create exercises that help the students understand and organize visual information. This way, we can help them to improve their concentration while performing mental operations with language.

In this chapter, we will:

- Prepare pictures for a visual sequence by using images with multiple elements and layers
- Create visual and interactive activities to understand and arrange a visual sequence
- Work with image manipulation software to adjust color saturation levels
- Prepare images with different color tones to use in a colored sequence
- Learn to create a double puzzle
- Organize a sequence by considering sensory perception resources

In this chapter, Alice goes shopping. We will learn how create visually rich activities to practice mental operations that are related to her journey.

Completing visual sequences

Christmas is coming. Alice and her mother went shopping, as they needed to buy a lot of presents. Alice has always been amazed by the process of preparing the packages, the ribbons, and the bows for all the presents by combining different colors.

She enjoys preparing the packages and this year they bought very big gifts that require extra work. Shall we help her?

Time for action – generating the pictures for a visual sequence

We are going to search for existing 2D vector clipart related to a Christmas package. We are then going to delete parts of this vector clipart to create four parts of the visual sequence of preparing the package with the ribbons and the bows. We will then export each clipart image to a 2D bitmap images by using Inkscape features.

1. Create a new folder in Windows Explorer (`C:\Shopping`).

2. Start Inkscape and minimize it. You will use it later.

3. Start Word 2007. You will be working in a new blank document.

4. Click on **Insert | Clip Art**. The **Clip Art** panel will appear on the right-hand side of the main window.

5. Click on the **Search in** combo box and activate the **Everywhere** checkbox. Click on the **Results should be** combo box and deactivate all the options. Then activate the **Windows Metafile (*.wmf)** checkbox in **All media types | Clipart**. This way, Word will search for scalable vector clipart files in all the available collections, including the Web Collections.

6. Click on the **Search for** textbox and enter `Package`.

7. Click on the **Go** button.

8. Position the mouse pointer over the desired clipart's thumbnail.

9. Right-click on the desired clipart's thumbnail and select **Preview/Properties** in the context menu that appears. Word will display a new dialog box showing a larger preview of the scalable clipart and a temporary file name.

10. Triple-click on the long path and file name shown after **File**. This way, you will be sure that the temporary file's full path is selected. Then right-click on it and select **Copy** in the context menu that appears.

11. Next, activate Inkscape—remember it was running minimized. You can use *Alt + Tab* or *Windows + Tab*. Don't close the clipart's preview window.

12. Select **File | Import** from the main menu. Click on the **Type a file name** button (the pencil with a paper sheet icon) and paste the previously copied temporary file's full path in the **Location:** textbox. The path is going to be similar to `C:\Users\vanesa\AppData\Local\Microsoft\Windows\Temporary Internet Files\Content.IE5\0B6OXKF0\MCj02322010000[1].wmf`.

13. Click on the **Open** button. The previously previewed clipart, a nice package for our sequence, will appear selected in Inkscape's drawing area.

14. Right-click on the recently added picture and select the **Ungroup** option in the context menu. This way, we will be able to manipulate each individual element that composes the picture, as shown in the next screenshot:

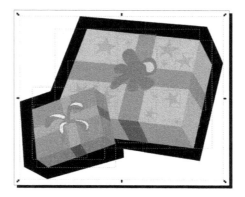

15. Select **File | Save As** from Inkscape's main menu. Save the file as image080104.svg in the previously created folder, C:\Shopping. This picture is going to be the last image for our visual sequence.

16. Select **File | Export Bitmap**. A dialog box showing many export options will appear. Click on the **Drawing** button, enter 200 on the **Width** textbox, and then click on **Export**. Inkscape will export the recently imported clipart in PNG format. The exported bitmap graphics file will be C:\Shopping\image080104.png.

17. Next, select **Edit | Deselect** from Inkscape's main menu. Click on the black shadow behind the two packages and press the *Delete* key on your keyboard. Inkscape will erase the shadow.

18. Then click on one of the dark green stars that appear on the package at the right-hand side. Inkscape will select this individual element, as shown in the following screenshot:

19. Press the *Delete* key and the selected star will be erased. Repeat this procedure to delete all the stars from the package located on the right-hand side.

20. Select **File | Save As** from Inkscape's main menu. Save the file as image080103.svg in the previously created folder, C:\Shopping. This picture is going to be the third image for our visual sequence, as shown in the next image.

21. Select **File | Export Bitmap**. Click on the **Drawing** button, enter 200 on the **Width** textbox, change the **Filename** to image080103.png, and then click on **Export**. Inkscape will export the modified picture in PNG format. The exported bitmap graphics file will be C:\Shopping\image080103.png.

22. Next, repeat the previously explained steps to remove the stars from the drawing, but this time erase all the elements that compose the bows and knots, as shown in the next image:

23. Select **File | Save As** from Inkscape's main menu. Save the file as image080102.svg in the previously created folder, C:\Shopping. This picture is going to be the second image for our visual sequence.

24. Select **File | Export Bitmap**. Click on the **Drawing** button, enter 200 on the **Width** textbox, change the **Filename** to image080102.png, and then click on **Export**. Inkscape will export the modified picture in PNG format. The exported bitmap graphics file will be C:\Shopping\image080102.png.

25. Finally, repeat the previously explained steps to remove the stars from the drawing, but this time, erase all the elements that compose the ribbons, as shown in the following picture:

26. Select **File | Save As** from Inkscape's main menu. Save the file as image080101. svg in the previously created folder, C:\Shopping. This picture is going to be the first image for our visual sequence.

27. Select **File | Export Bitmap**. Click on the **Drawing** button, enter 200 on the **Width** textbox, change the **Filename** to image080101.png, and then click on **Export**. Inkscape will export the modified picture in PNG format. The exported bitmap graphics file will be C:\Shopping\image080101.png. The next screenshot shows the four images that compose the visual sequence with the preparation of the packages:

image080101.png   image080102.png   image080103.png   image080104.png

What just happened?

We chose a scalable vector clipart image to use as a baseline for a visual sequence. We imported the picture into Inkscape and we erased different groups of elements that composed the original clipart to represent different stages of the preparation of the packages. We created several Inkscape files and then we exported them to the PNG format. We now have the following four bitmap graphics ready to be used in our exercise:

◆ image080101: Two boxes

◆ image080102: Two boxes with ribbons

◆ image080103: Two boxes with ribbons, bows, and knots

◆ image080104: Two boxes with ribbons, bows, knots, star stickers, and shadows

Time for action – generating the initial visual sequence

We are now going to generate an exchange puzzle with the different images that compose the previously created visual sequence and our well-known JClic Author.

1. Run JClic Author 0.2.0.5 from its web page or by clicking on its icon.

2. Select **File | New Project** from JClic's main menu. A new dialog box will appear. Enter the next values for each textbox and then click on **OK**:

3. Enter exchange0801 in **Project name**.

4. Enter exchange0801 in **File name**. JClic will save the complete project in a compressed file, exchange0801.jclic.zip.

5. Enter a new exchange0801 sub-folder in the previously created folder, C:\Shopping, in **Folder**, C:\Shopping\exchange0801.

6. Click on the **Project** tab. Enter Arranging the visual sequence in the **Title** textbox.

7. Click on the **Media library** tab.

8. Select **Insert | New media object** from the main menu. Choose the four previously saved images: image080101.png, image080102.png, image080103.png, and image080104.png in C:\Shopping and click on the **Open** button. JClic will ask your confirmation to copy each of the previously selected files to the project's folder; click **Yes** the four times. The four images that compose the sequence will appear in JClic's media library, as shown in the next screenshot.

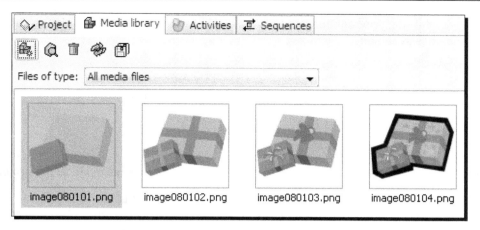

9. Click on the **Activities** tab and select **Insert | New activity** from the main menu. Select **Exchange puzzle** in the list shown in the **New activity** dialog box. Enter Sequence in the **Name of the activity** textbox and click on **OK**. JClic will add the new activity to the project and will display new tabs with dozens of options for it.

10. Click on the **Panel** tab related to the new activity.

11. Select **Rectangular** in the combo box, enter 1 for rows, 4 for columns, 200 for width, and 200 for height. JClic will show a grid with one row and four columns.

12. Next, click on the first square (the first cell). The **Cell contents** dialog box will appear. Click on the button located at the right-hand side of the **Image** label. The **Multimedia object selection** dialog box will appear. Select the first image for the sequence, image080101.png, click on **OK** and then **OK**. The first cell will display the selected bitmap at the center, as shown in the next screenshot:

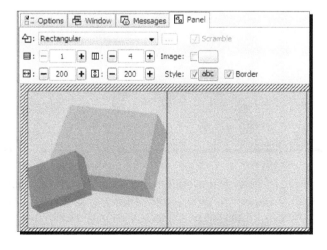

13. Repeat the aforementioned step for the next three cells. Select the picture file names as shown in the following table for each cell:

Column number	Picture file name
2	image080102.png
3	image080103.png
4	image080104.png

14. Select **File | Save** from JClic's main menu to save the changes made to the project.

15. Click on the **Sequences** tab. Select **Exit JClic** in the **Action** combo box under **Forward arrow** and activate the **Move on automatically** checkbox. This way, JClic will end once the activity is finished. Deactivate the **Show button** checkbox under **Back arrow**.

16. Select **File | Save** from JClic's main menu again.

17. Next, select **View | Preview Activity**. JClic will show a new window with the scrambled parts of the visual sequence. Each time you preview the activity, JClic will scramble the images and present them in a random order, as shown in the following screenshot:

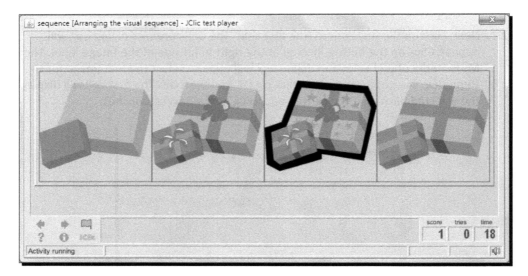

18. Drag-and-drop each part of the sequence to its corresponding position in order to arrange the visual sequence. When a picture is dropped in its correct place, JClic will swap it with the picture in that place, as shown in the following screenshot.

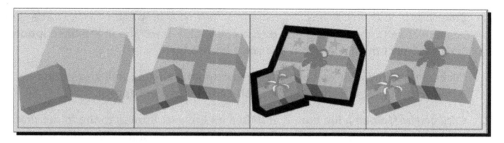

What just happened?

We created an exchange puzzle with rectangular pieces organized in a grid with one row and four columns. We added each of the previously created bitmap graphics for each part to organize a visual sequence as an exchange puzzle. We used the capabilities offered by JClic to create a grid that allows the student to arrange a visual sequence.

We linked each bitmap to a cell in the necessary order to represent the correct sequence. JClic displayed the changes made in each cell in a preview panel. As previously explained, JClic is going to jumble the cells each time the students run the exercise using a randomly generated order.

Time for action – adding the activity to a Moodle course

We now have to add the exchange puzzle with the visual sequence to an existing Moodle course.

1. Log in to your Moodle server.

2. Make sure that the module that allows adding JClic projects and activities to Moodle is installed. The necessary steps to perform the installation were explained in previous chapters.

3. Click on the desired course name (Shopping). You can create a new course or use an existing one.

4. As previously learned, follow the necessary steps to edit the summary for a desired week. Enter Exercise 1 in the **Summary** textbox and save the changes.

5. Click on the **Add an activity** combo box for the selected week and select **JClic**. A new web page will appear displaying the title **Adding a new JClic to week**.

6. Enter Arranging the visual sequence in the **Name** textbox.

7. Enter `Drag and drop each image to its right place to create the right visual sequence of preparing the package` in the **Description** textbox. Select the desired font and color for this text.

8. Click on the **Choose or upload a file** button and the already well-known pop-up window displaying information about files and folders will appear.

9. Click on the **Upload a file** button and then on **Browse**. Browse to the folder that holds the JClic project (`C:\Shopping\exchange0801`) and select the file to upload, `exchange0801.jclic.zip`. Then click on **Open** and on the **Upload this file** button.

10. Next, position the mouse pointer over the **exchange0801.jclic.zip** name and move it horizontally to the **Choose** action hyperlink in the same row. Then, click on **Choose**, as shown in the following picture:

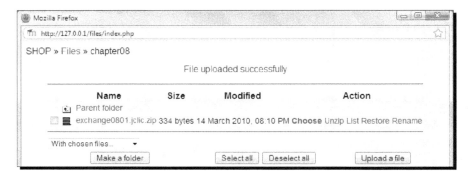

11. Moodle will display `chapter08/exchange0801.jclic.zip` in the **File name** textbox. This is the ZIP file that contains all the files with the JClic project and its activity, the puzzle.

12. Enter `760` in **Width** and `400` in **Height**.

13. Select `1` in **Maximum number of trials**.

14. Scroll down and click on the **Save and return to course** button, located at the bottom of the web page.

What just happened?

We added the arranging the visual sequence exercise to a Moodle course. The students are now going to be able to run the activity by clicking on its hyperlink in the corresponding week.

We created a new folder, `chapter08`. This folder will hold all the necessary files for the activities related to shopping.

We then just uploaded one ZIP file that contains many compressed files with four images that compose the sequence and definitions for the JClic project and single activity.

Time for action – arranging the sequence by dragging and dropping images

It is time to help Alice to drag-and-drop each image to its correct place.

1. Log in to your Moodle server using a user with the student role.

2. Click on the course name (Shopping).

3. Click on the **Arranging the visual sequence** link on the corresponding week. The web browser will show the exercise. The JClic panel that displays the activity can take some time to load.

4. Position the mouse pointer over the desired image that has to be moved to another position in the visual sequence.

5. Click on the image. The image will now change its position according to the mouse movement. Use the mouse to position the image in its correct place, as shown in the following screenshot:

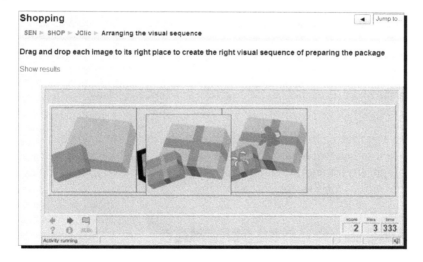

6. Click to leave the image in the selected position. The image that was there will be moved to the original position for the relocated image. Each time you drop an image in its correct place, the JClic application will play a sound indicating a successful operation. Each time you drop an image in the wrong place, the JClic application will play a sound indicating a mistake.

7. After arranging the visual sequence, the activity will finish and you will be able to check your results by clicking on **Show results**.

8. Log out and log in with your normal user and role. You can check the number of attempts as done with the previous activities. Remember that they are going to appear grouped in JClic activities.

What just happened?

In this activity, we created the four parts of the sequence of preparing the packages for two presents. The child has to drag-and-drop the images to arrange the sequence.

We applied the following concepts and resources in order to help to practice mental operations:

◆ **Logical sequence ordering**. The child has to arrange a sequence of images, from left to right, according to the level of completion of the packages.

◆ **Sensory perception resources**. We used images that represent the preparation of packages. The child has to pay attention to the number of elements that appear in each image to understand its correct position in the sequence.

◆ **Images composed of multiple layers**. Many elements compose multiple layers for each picture. The child can identify with the situation of preparing the package and develop his/her imagination whilst solving the exercise.

Arranging the sequence using a netbook's touchpad

New hardware technology such as a netbook and its touchpad usually offers additional motivation to the child. The child can arrange the sequence by using his/her fingers to move the mouse pointer using a touchpad.

In many cases, a netbook's touchpad makes the activity more attractive and it usually requires the child to use two fingers, one finger from one hand to move the mouse pointer and another finger from the other hand to press the touchpad's button. When the child works with the mouse, he/she uses just one hand.

Completing the colored sequence

Two weeks after Christmas, Alice and her mother went shopping again. This time, they were looking for the perfect present for Kevin, Alice's little brother, for his birthday. They spent two hours in a shopping center but they could not find a suitable present.

Finally, Alice stared at a sporting goods shop window because she saw an amazing football, with dazzling colors. It was the perfect gift for Kevin.

Time for action – preparing many images with different colors using GIMP

We are first going to download and install GIMP 2.6.8. We will then search for an existing bitmap image related to a football and prepare five bitmap images with different color saturation levels.

1. If you do not have it yet, download and install GIMP 2.6.8 (`http://www.gimp.org/downloads/`).

2. Start GIMP and minimize its main window. You will use it later.

3. Start Word 2007. You will be working in a new blank document.

4. Click on **Insert | Clip Art**. The **Clip Art** panel will appear on the right-hand side of the main window.

5. Click on the **Search in** combo box and activate the **Everywhere** checkbox. Click on the **Results should be** combo box and deactivate all the options. Then activate the **PNG (Portable Network Graphics) (*.png)** checkbox in **All media types | Photographs**. This way, Word will search for PNG bitmap image files in all the available collections, including the Web Collections.

6. Click on the **Search for** textbox and enter `Football`.

7. Click on the **Go** button.

8. Position the mouse pointer over the desired clipart's thumbnail.

9. Right-click on the desired clipart's thumbnail and select **Preview/Properties** in the context menu that appears. Word will display a new dialog box showing a larger preview of the scalable clipart and a temporary file name.

10. Triple-click on the long path and file name shown after **File**. This way, you will be sure that the temporary file's full path is selected. Then right-click on it and select **Copy** in the context menu that appears.

11. Next, activate GIMP—remember it was running minimized. You can use *Alt + Tab* or *Windows + Tab*. Don't close the clipart's preview window.

12. Select **File | Open Location** from the main menu. Paste the previously copied temporary file's full path in the **Enter location (URI):** textbox. The path is going to be similar to `C:\Users\vanesa\AppData\Local\Microsoft\ Windows\Temporary Internet Files\Content.IE5\0B6OXKF0\ MCj04417880000[1].png`, as shown in the following screenshot:

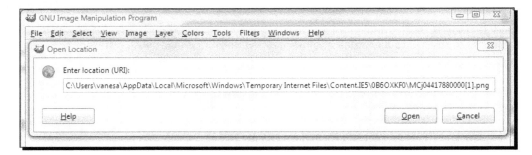

13. Click on the **Open** button. The previously previewed bitmap image, a nice football for our colored sequence, will appear selected in GIMP's image window, as shown in the next screenshot:

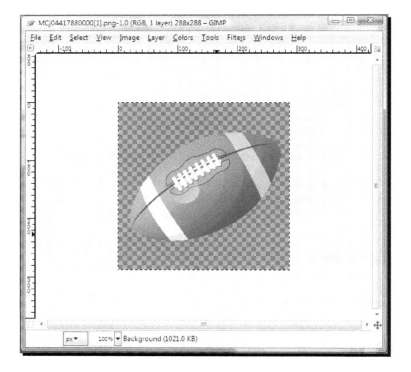

14. Select **File | Save As** from GIMP's main menu. Save the file as `image080205.png` in the previously created folder, `C:\Shopping`. This image is going to be the last image for our colored sequence, the football with the real colors.

15. Next, select **Color | Hue-Saturation** from GIMP's main menu and the **Hue-Saturation** dialog box will appear displaying many sliders. Enter `-30` in **Saturation**. The football shown in GIMP's image window will change its color saturation level and it will appear with darker colors, as shown in the next screenshot:

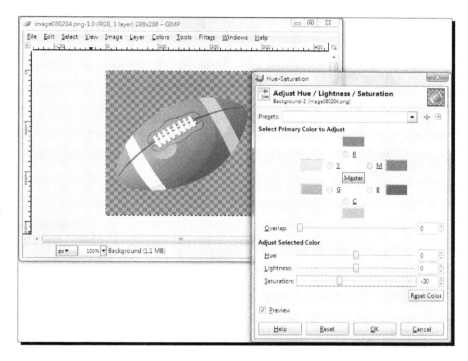

16. Select **File | Save As** from GIMP's main menu. Save the file as `image080204.png` in the previously created folder, `C:\Shopping`. This image is going to be the fourth image for our colored sequence.

17. Repeat the aforementioned steps (15 and 16), reducing the color saturation level to `-30` each time and saving the image files with the names shown in the following table:

Position in the colored sequence	Picture file name
Third	image080203.png
Second	image080202.png

18. Next, select **Color | Hue Saturation** from GIMP's main menu and enter -100 in **Saturation**. The football shown in GIMP's image window will appear in grayscale, as shown in the following image:

19. Select **File | Save As** from GIMP's main menu. Save the file as image080201.png in the previously created folder, C:\Shopping. This image is going to be the first image for our colored sequence. The next image shows the five images that compose the color sequence for the football:

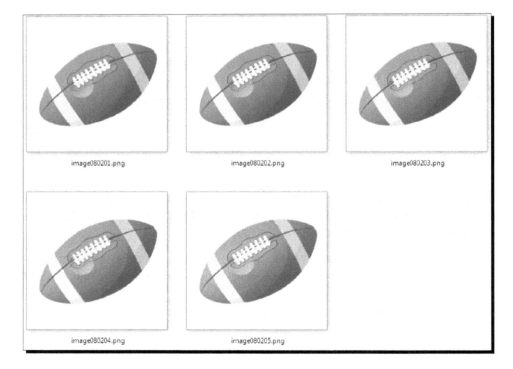

What just happened?

We first installed GIMP, a very powerful open source image manipulation program. We chose a bitmap image to use as a baseline for a color sequence. We imported the picture to GIMP and we modified its color saturation level to generate different stages of the addition of saturation from grayscale to the real colors offered by a football. We created five bitmap graphics ready to be used in our exercise:

◆   image080201: The football in grayscale

◆   image080202: The football with less color saturation than image080203

◆   image080203: The football with less color saturation than image080204

◆   image080204: The football with less color saturation than image080205

◆   image080205: The football with its real colors

Time for action – generating the initial color sequence

We are now going to generate a double puzzle with the different images that compose the previously created color sequence and our well-known JClic Author.

1.   Run JClic Author 0.2.0.5 from its web page or by clicking on its icon.

2.   Select **File | New Project** from JClic's main menu. A new dialog box will appear. Enter the next values for each textbox and then click on **OK**:

❑   double0802 in **Project name**.

❑   double0802 in **File name**. JClic will save the complete project in a compressed file, double0802.jclic.zip.

❑   A new double0802 sub-folder in the previously created folder, C:\Shopping, in **Folder**, C:\Shopping\double0802.

3.   Click on the **Project** tab. Enter Arranging the color sequence in the **Title** textbox.

4.   Click on the **Media library** tab.

5. Select **Insert | New media object** from the main menu. Select the four previously saved images: image080201.png, image080202.png, image080203.png, image080104.png, and image080105.png in C:\Shopping and click on the **Open** button. JClic will ask your confirmation to copy each of the previously selected files to the project's folder; click on **Yes** five times. The five images that compose the sequence will appear in JClic's media library, as shown in the following screenshot:

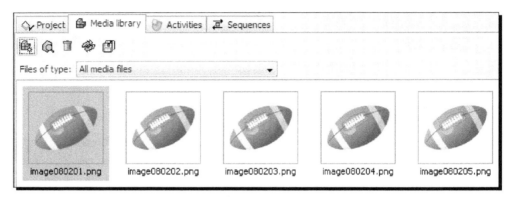

6. Click on the **Activities** tab and select **Insert | New activity** from the main menu. Select **Double puzzle** in the list shown in the **New activity** dialog box. Enter Sequence in the **Name of the activity** textbox and click on **OK**. JClic will add the new activity to the project and will display new tabs with dozens of options for it.

7. Click on the **Panel** tab related to the new activity.

8. Select **Rectangular** in the combo box, enter 1 for rows, 5 for columns, 150 for width, and 150 for height. JClic will show a cell with one row and four columns.

9. Click on the **Style** button and a dialog box will appear. Click on the square that shows the actual **Background color** and a color selection dialog box will appear. Select the white color instead of the default grey background and click **OK**. This way, the white background will make it easier for the student to spot the difference in the color tones.

10. Next, click on the first square (the first cell). The **Cell contents** dialog box will appear. Click on the button located at the right of the **Image** label. The **Multimedia object selection** dialog box will appear. Select the first image for the color sequence, image080201.png, click on **OK**, and then **OK**. The first cell will display the selected bitmap at the center with a white background.

11. Repeat the aforementioned step for the next four cells. Choose the picture file name as shown in the next table for each cell:

Column number	Picture file name
2	image080202.png
3	image080203.png
4	image080204.png
5	image080205.png

12. Click on the **Layout** tab and click on the button with the A over the B, as shown in the next screenshot. This way, the first panel that will show the scrambled images of the colored sequence will appear at the top and the panel that will hold the arranged colored sequence will appear at the bottom.

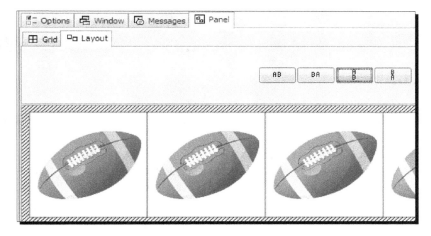

13. Select **File | Save** from JClic's main menu to save the changes made to the project.

14. Click on the **Sequences** tab. Select **Exit JClic** in the **Action** combo box under **Forward arrow** and activate the **Move on automatically** checkbox. This way, JClic will end once the activity is finished. Deactivate the **Show button** checkbox under **Back arrow**.

15. Select **File | Save** from JClic's main menu again.

16. Next, select **View | Preview Activity**. JClic will show a new window with the scrambled parts of the visual sequence at the top of the window. Each time you preview the activity, JClic will scramble the images and present them in a random order, as shown in the next screenshot:

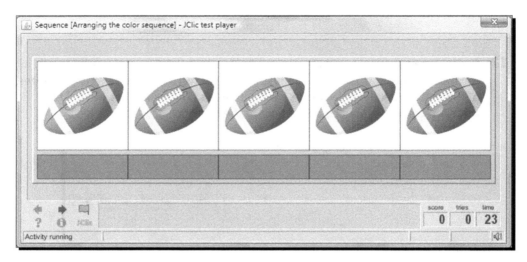

17. Drag-and-drop each part of the sequence to its corresponding empty cell at the bottom panel in order to create the color sequence from grayscale to the real colors. When a picture is dropped in its correct place, JClic will leave it in the cell, as shown in the next screenshot:

What just happened?

We created a double puzzle with five images that have to be ordered according to their color saturation level. We added each of the previously created bitmap graphics to each part to present them scrambled in the panel at the top. We used the capabilities offered by JClic to create two grids that allow the student to arrange a color sequence.

We linked each bitmap to a cell in the necessary order to represent the correct sequence. JClic displayed the changes made in each cell in a preview panel. As previously explained, JClic is going to jumble the cells in the panel displayed at the top each time the students run the exercise using a randomly generated order.

Time for action – adding the activity to a Moodle course

We now have to add the double puzzle with the color sequence to an existing Moodle course.

1. Log in to your Moodle server.

2. Click on the desired course name (Shopping). You can create a new course or use an existing one.

3. As previously learned, follow the necessary steps to edit the summary for a desired week. Enter Exercise 1 in the **Summary** textbox and save the changes.

4. Click on the **Add an activity** combo box for the selected week and choose **JClic**. A new web page will appear displaying the title **Adding a new JClic to week**.

5. Enter Arranging the color sequence in the **Name** textbox.

6. Enter Complete the panel at the bottom with a colored sequence, from black and white to the vivid colors. Drag and drop each image from the top to the corresponding position at the bottom. in the **Description** textbox. Select the desired font and color for this text.

7. Click on the **Choose or upload a file** button and the already well-known pop-up window displaying information about files and folders will appear.

8. Click on the **Upload a file** button and then on **Browse**. Browse to the folder that holds the JClic project (C:\Shopping\double0802) and select the file to upload, double0802.jclic.zip. Then click on **Open** and on the **Upload this file** button.

9. Next, position the mouse pointer over the **double0802.jclic.zip** name and move it horizontally to the **Choose** action hyperlink in the same row. Then click on **Choose**, as shown in the following screenshot:

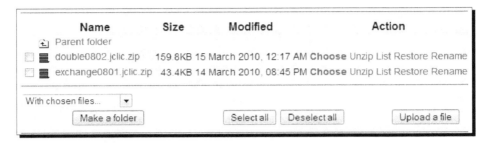

	Name	Size	Modified		Action
	Parent folder				
☐ ▤	double0802.jclic.zip	159.8KB	15 March 2010, 12:17 AM	**Choose**	Unzip List Restore Rename
☐ ▤	exchange0801.jclic.zip	43.4KB	14 March 2010, 08:45 PM	**Choose**	Unzip List Restore Rename

With chosen files... ▼

Make a folder   Select all   Deselect all   Upload a file

10. Moodle will display `chapter08/double0802.jclic.zip` in the **File name** textbox. This is the ZIP file that contains all the files with the JClic project and its activity, the double puzzle.

11. Enter `760` in **Width** and `580` in **Height**.

12. Select `1` in **Maximum number of trials**.

13. Scroll down and click on the **Save and return to course** button, located at the bottom of the web page.

What just happened?

We added the arranging the color sequence exercise to a Moodle course. The students are now going to be able to run the activity by clicking on its hyperlink on the corresponding week.

We uploaded a single ZIP file that contains many compressed files, including the five images that compose the colored sequence, and other files with definitions for the JClic project, as well as the double puzzle as a single activity.

Time for action – arranging the sequence with different color tones by dragging and dropping images

It is time to run the activity as a student and to check the results as a teacher.

1. Log in to your Moodle server using a user with the student role.

2. Click on the course name (`Shopping`).

3. Click on the **Arranging the color sequence** link on the corresponding week. The web browser will show the exercise.

4. Position the mouse pointer over an image on the grid at the top.

5. Click on the image. The image will now change its position according to the mouse pointer's movement. Use the mouse to position the image in its correct place on the panel at the bottom, as shown in the next screenshot:

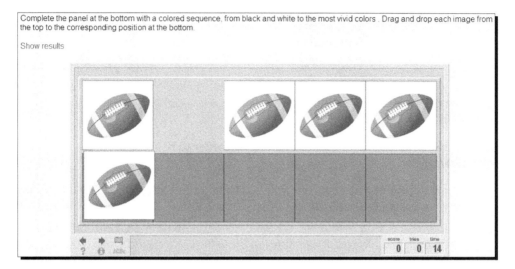

6. Click to leave the image in the selected position on the panel at the bottom. Each time you drop an image in its correct place on the panel at the bottom, the JClic application will play a sound indicating a successful operation. Each time you drop an image on a wrong place, the JClic application will play a sound indicating a mistake and will return the image to its original place in the panel at the top.

7. After arranging the color sequence, the activity will finish as shown in the next screenshot. You will then be able to check your results by clicking on **Show results**.

8. Log out and log in with your normal user and role. You can check the number of attempts as done with the previous activities. Remember that they are going to appear grouped in JClic activities.

What just happened?

In this activity, we created the contents for the cells of a double puzzle activity using a football with different color saturation levels. The child has to create a colored sequence by dragging and dropping each image from the top panel to the bottom panel.

This exercise can be difficult to solve for some children. However, we can create different exercises like this one with diverse number of images. This way, we can create diverse skill levels.

We applied the following concepts and resources in order to help to practice mental operations:

◆ **Logical sequence ordering**. The child has to arrange a sequence of images according to an increasing saturation level.

◆ **Sensory perception resources**. We used images with different color saturation levels. The child has to pay attention to the different tones to create the color sequence.

 As previously explained, we can also use the gamepad or a multi-touch screen instead of the mouse to solve the exercise. In this case, the gamepad's usage would make the activity more attractive and require more attention to solve it.

Have a go hero – working with basic voice recognition

It is possible to use basic voice recognition features instead of dragging and dropping images to solve the color sequence. Windows Vista and Windows 7 offer a voice recognition engine. You can train it to understand basic commands, including the possibility to perform drag-and-drop operations with voice commands.

Work with different alternatives to solve the color sequence exercise by using voice commands. You can create new activities to let the students train their voice recognition engines and solve simpler exercises.

Pop quiz – working with sequences

1. When you ungroup a scalable vector graphic:
   a. You can manipulate each individual element that composes the picture.
   b. You can't manipulate each individual element that composes the picture.
   c. You can only manipulate all the elements that compose the picture at the same time.

2. When you change the color saturation level of a bitmap image to -100:
   a. The image will appear with shinier colors.
   b. The image will appear in grayscale.
   c. The image will disappear because all the colors will be converted to white.

3. When you change the color saturation level of a bitmap image to -30:
   a. The image will appear with shinier colors.
   b. The image will appear with poorer colors.
   c. The image will appear with increased brightness.

4. When you create a double puzzle activity with JClic Author:
   a. The empty panel that will hold the solved sequence will inherit the number of rows for the main grid.
   b. You can specify the number of rows for the empty panel that will hold the solved sequence with a different value than the one specified for the main grid.
   c. You can specify neither the number of rows for the empty panel that will hold the solved sequence nor the number of rows for the main grid.

5. A double puzzle activity in JClic Author:
   a. Displays two grids that hold relationships between some of their cells.
   b. Displays a single grid with scrambled parts.
   c. Displays a grid with scrambled parts and another grid where these parts can be dropped to organize them.

Summary

In this chapter, we have learned how to:

- Practice mental operations with language
- Create a visual sequence by using different images of packages
- Work with many tools to use a vector graphics image as the baseline and then erase elements from its original composition
- Use a single grid to let the students arrange a visual sequence
- Use GIMP to create many different versions of an existing image of a football, modifying its color saturation level to ask the student to arrange a color sequence; this way, students can perform mental operations by working with visually rich activities

Now that we have learned how to create exercises to work with mental operations, we're ready to prepare more advanced exercises to ask the student to write guided sentences and paragraphs, which is the topic of the next chapter.

9

Writing Guided Sentences and Paragraphs

We can guide children to write simple sentences and paragraphs by creating different kinds of activities. Additionally, we can use many different applications to allow the student to record the sentence instead of writing it. This way, it is possible to evaluate their skills and to create motivating exercises to offer them better guidance to write simpler or more complex sentences.

In this chapter, Alice goes to the circus. We will learn how to create simple writing activities that are related to her journey. By reading this chapter and following the exercises we shall:

- ◆ Prepare and record a sentence with many predefined words
- ◆ Record, encode, and upload digitalized voice as a result of a Moodle exercise
- ◆ Prepare images that combine clipart pictures with geometric shapes
- ◆ Learn how to create exercises that allow the student to describe spatial relationships between objects
- ◆ Work with different multimedia resources to motivate students to write guided sentences and paragraphs

Creating a sentence using certain words

Last Saturday, Alice went to the circus with her mother. Today is Priscilla's birthday and Alice cannot wait to tell her friends about the funny and dangerous things she saw in the circus.

She was really scared when she saw the lions jumping through the flaming hoops. She enjoyed the little dogs jumping and twirling, and the big seals spinning balls. However, she has to remember some of the shows. Shall we help her?

Time for action – choosing and preparing the words to be used in a sentence

We are first going to choose the words to be used in a sentence and then add a new advanced uploading of files activity to an existing Moodle course.

1. Log in to your Moodle server.

2. Click on the desired course name (Circus). As previously learned, follow the necessary steps to edit the summary for a desired week. Enter Exercise 1 in the **Summary** textbox and save the changes.

3. Click on the **Add an activity** combo box for the selected week and choose **Advanced uploading of files**.

4. Enter Creating a sentence using certain words in **Assignment name**.

5. Select Verdana in font and 5 (18) in size—the first two combo boxes below **Description**.

6. Click on the **Font Color** button (a **T** with six color boxes) and select your desired color for the text.

7. Click on the big text box below **Description** and enter the following description of the student's goal for this exercise. You can use the enlarged editor window as shown in the next screenshot. Use a different font color for each of the three words: **Lion**, **Hoops**, and **Flaming**.

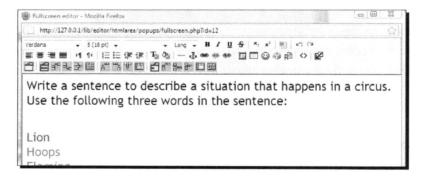

8. Close the enlarged editor's window. Select 10MB in **Maximum size**. This is the maximum size for the file that each student is going to be able to upload as a result for this activity. However, it is very important to check the possibilities offered by your Moodle server with its Moodle administrator.

9. Select 1 in **Maximum number of uploaded files**.

10. Select `Yes` in **Allow notes**. This way, the student will be able to add notes with the sentence.

11. Scroll down and click on the **Save and display** button. The web browser will show the description for the advanced uploading of files activity.

What just happened?

We added an advanced uploading of files activity to a Moodle course that will allow a student to write a sentence that has to include the three words specified in the notes section. The students are now going to be able to read the goals for this activity by clicking on its hyperlink on the corresponding week. They are then going to write the sentence and upload their voices with the description of the situation.

We added the description of the goal and the three words to use in the sentence with customized fonts and colors using the online text activity editor features.

Time for action – writing and recording the sentence

We must first download and install **Audacity** 1.2. We will then help Alice to write a sentence, read it, and record her voice by using Audacity's features.

1. If you do not have it yet, download and install Audacity 1.2 (`http://audacity.sourceforge.net/download/`). This software will allow the student to record his/her voice and save the recording as an MP3 file compatible with the previously explained Moodle multimedia plugins.

> In this case, we are covering a basic installation and usage for Audacity 1.2. The integration of sound and music elements for Moodle, including advanced usages for Audacity, is described in depth in `Moodle 1.9 Multimedia` by *João Pedro Soares Fernandes*, Packt Publishing.

2. Start Audacity.

3. Next, it is necessary to download the LAME MP3 encoder to make it possible for Audacity to export the recorded audio in the MP3 file format. Open your default web browser and go to the Audacity web page that displays the instructions to install the correct version of the LAME MP3 encoder, `http://audacity.sourceforge.net/help/faq?s=install&item=lame-mp3`.

4. Click on the **LAME download page** hyperlink and click on the hyperlink under **For Audacity on Windows**, in this case, Lame_v3.98.2_for_Audacity_on_ Windows.exe. Run the application, read the license carefully, and follow the necessary steps to finish the installation. The default folder for the LAME MP3 encoder is C:\Program Files\Lame for Audacity, as shown in the following screenshot:

5. Minimize Audacity.

6. Log in to your Moodle server using the student role.

7. Click on the course name (Circus).

8. Click on the **Creating a sentence using certain words** link on the corresponding week. The web browser will show the description for the activity and the three words to be used in the sentence.

9. Click on the **Edit** button below **Notes**. Moodle will display a big text area with an HTML editor.

10. Select Verdana in font and 5 (18) in size.

11. Write a sentence, `The lion jumps through the flaming hoops.`, as shown in the next screenshot:

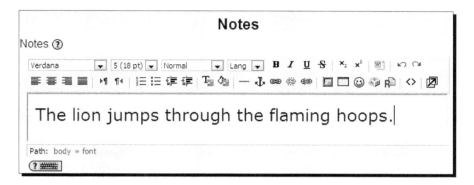

12. Go back to Audacity. Resize and move its window in order to be able to see the sentence you have recently written.

13. Click on the **Record** button (the red circle) and start reading the sentence. Audacity will display the waveform of the audio track being recorded, as shown in the next screenshot:

 You need a microphone connected to the computer in order to record your voice with Audacity.

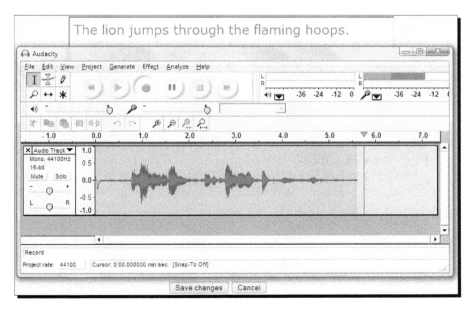

14. Once you finish reading the sentence, click on the **Stop** button (the yellow square). Audacity will stop recording your voice.

15. Select **File | Export As MP3** from Audacity's main menu. Save the MP3 audio file as `mysentence.mp3` in your documents folder.

16. Audacity will display a message indicating that it uses the freely available LAME library to handle MP3 file encoding, as shown in the next screenshot:

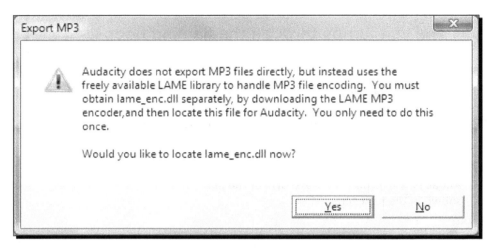

17. Click on **Yes** and browse to the folder where you installed the LAME MP3 encoder, by default, `C:\Program Files\Lame for Audacity`. Click on **Open** and Audacity will display a dialog box to edit some properties for the MP3 file. Click on **OK** and it will save the MP3 file, `mysentence.mp3`, in your documents folder.

18. Next, go back to your web browser with the Moodle activity, scroll down, and click on the **Save changes** button.

19. Click on the **Browse** button below **Submission draft**. Browse to the folder that holds your MP3 audio file with the recorded sentence, your documents folder, select the file to upload, `mysentence.mp3`, and click on **Open**. Then, click on **Upload this file** to upload the MP3 audio file to the Moodle server. The file name, `mysentence.mp3`, will appear below **Submission draft** if the MP3 file could finish the upload process without problems, as shown in the next screenshot. Next, click on **Continue**.

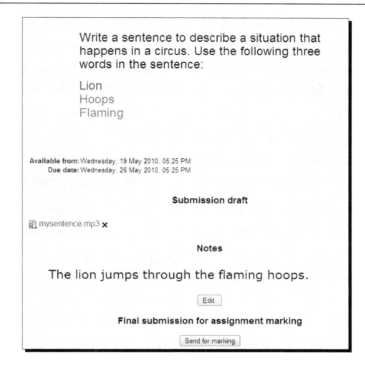

20. Click on **Send for marking** and then on **Yes**. A new message, **Assignment was already submitted for marking and cannot be updated**, will appear below the **Notes** section with the sentence.

21. Log out and log in with your normal user and role. You can check the submitted assignments by clicking on the **Creating a sentence using certain words** link on the corresponding week and then on **View x submitted assignments**. Moodle will display the links for the notes and the uploaded file for each student that submitted this assignment, as shown in the next screenshot.

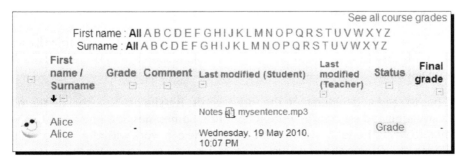

22. You will be able to read the notes and listen to the recorded sentence by clicking on the corresponding links.

23. Once you have checked the results, click on **Grade** in the corresponding row in the grid. A feedback window will appear with a text editor and a drop-down list with the possible grades.

24. Select the grade in the **Grade** drop-down list and write any feedback in the text editor, as shown in the next screenshot. Then click on **Save changes**. The final grade will appear in a corresponding cell in the grid.

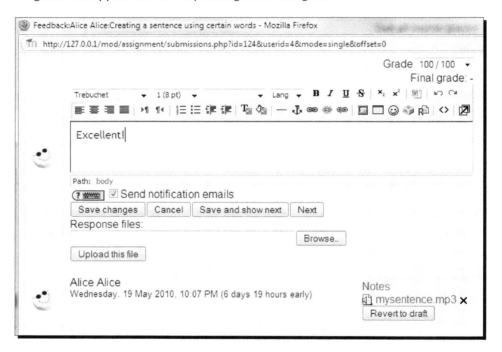

What just happened?

In this activity, we defined a simple list of words and we asked the student to write a simple sentence. In this case, there is no image or multimedia resource, and therefore, they have to use their imagination.

The child has to read and understand the three words. He/she has to associate them, imagine a situation and say and/or write a sentence. Sometimes, it is going to be too difficult for the child to write the sentence. In this case, he/she can work with the help of a therapist or a family member to run the previously explained software and record the sentence. This way, it is going to be possible to evaluate the results of this exercise even if the student cannot write a complete sentence with the words.

Have a go hero – discussing the results in Moodle forums

The usage of additional software to record the voice in order to solve the exercises can be challenging for the students and their parents. Prepare answers of frequently asked questions in the forums offered by Moodle.

This way, you can interact with the students and their parents through other channels in Moodle, with different feedback possibilities.

You can access the forums for each Moodle course by clicking on **Forums** in the **Activities** panel.

Have a go hero – working with images instead of words

Some students have great difficulties reading and understanding written words. Create a new version of the previous exercise by using several images instead of words. By using images, the student will be able to record a sentence by observing the images, and then carrying out the activity with the help of a therapist or a family member.

Create a new activity asking the student to watch a video and record his/her own story about the video.

Time for action – installing a NanoGong assignment to set speaking homework

We can also take advantage of the non-standard module that offers a NanoGong assignment type. This assignment is an excellent way of setting speaking homework without the need to use an additional application as Audacity to perform the digital voice recording process. NanoGong is a voice recording Java applet that offers a new assignment type and was developed by *Dan Poltawski* of **Lancaster University Network Services Ltd. (LUNS)**.

Firstly, it is necessary to install the module that allows us to add NanoGong assignments to Moodle and to analyze the results of their execution. You have to follow these steps with administrator access to your Moodle server.

1. Open your default web browser and go to `http://moodle.org/mod/data/view.php?d=13&rid=2882`. This web page allows us to download the last version of the **Nanogong Assignment Type** module for Moodle.

2. Download the latest version for this module for Moodle by clicking on the **Download the latest version** link, as shown in the next screenshot. In this case, we are going to work with `nanogong.zip`.

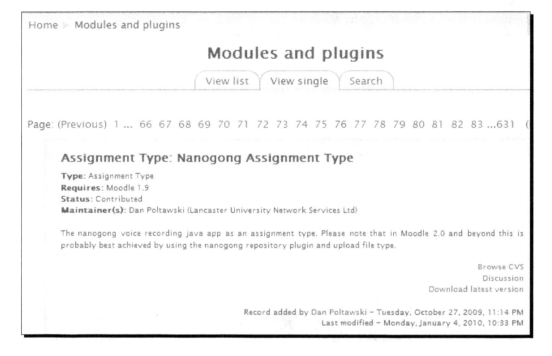

3. Copy the downloaded compressed file to a temporary folder and unzip its contents. Then copy the `nanogong` folder created as a result of uncompressing the zipped file contents.

4. Go to your Moodle server main folder. We will use as an example `C:\Moodle` as the Moodle server folder; replace it with your folder.

5. Next, go to the `server\moodle\mod\assignment\type` folder located in the Moodle server main folder, in our example, `C:\Moodle\server\moodle\mod\assignment\type`.

6. Paste the previously copied `nanogong` folder. As a result, you will see a new `nanogong` folder in the `type` sub-folder, in our example, `C:\Moodle\server\moodle\mod\assignment\type`, as shown in the next screenshot.

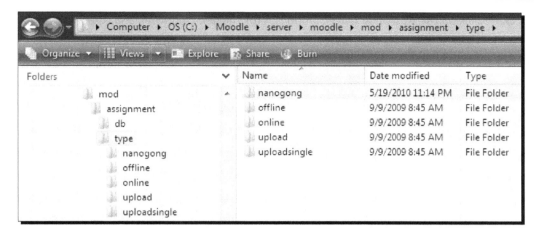

What just happened?

We installed a module to allow Moodle to add NanoGong assignments and to check the results of these exercises. We are now going to be able to add the previously created exercise as a NanoGong assignment to allow the student to record his/her voice without having to work with an additional application.

> The previously explained steps require some knowledge of Moodle administration procedures. NanoGong requires the free Java Runtime Environment (also known as JRE) for both the teacher and the students' computers. You can download and install its latest version from http://java.sun.com. However, if you have already worked with the JClic examples, you already have this pre-requisite installed on your computer.

Time for action – creating a NanoGong assignment to record a sentence

We are now going to add a new NanoGong assignment to an existing Moodle course.

1. Log in to your Moodle server.

2. Click on the desired course name (Circus).

3. Click on the **Add an activity** combo box for the selected week and select **[[typenanogong]]**. The name appears under the **Assignments** category, as shown in the next screenshot.

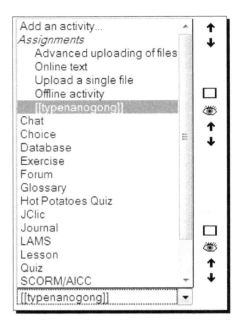

4. Enter `Recording a sentence using certain words` in **Assignment name**.

5. Select `Verdana` in font and `5 (18)` in size—the first two combo boxes below **Description**.

6. Click on the **Font Color** button (a **T** with six color boxes) and select your desired color for the text.

7. Click on the big text box below **Description** and enter the following description of the student's goal for this exercise. You can use the enlarged editor window as shown in the next screenshot:

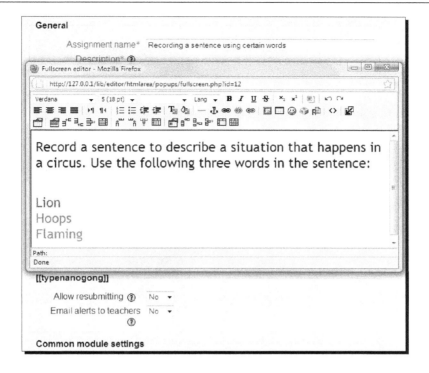

8. Close the enlarged editor's window.

9. Select 100 in **Grade**.

10. Scroll down and click on the **Save and display** button. The web browser will show the description for the NanoGong assignment.

What just happened?

We added a NanoGong assignment to a Moodle course that will allow a student to record his/her voice with a sentence that has to include the three specified words. Now, the students are going to be able to read the goals for this activity by clicking on its hyperlink on the corresponding week and then, they are going to click on the record button in the recorder included at the bottom of the page with the assignment. It is going to be easy for them to upload their recordings.

As NanoGong is an assignment, we were able to add the description of the goal and the three words to use in the sentence with customized fonts and colors using the online text activity editor features.

Time for action – recording the sentence with the NanoGong recorder

We will now help Alice to record her voice by using the NanoGong recorder.

1. Log in to your Moodle server using the student role.

2. Click on the course name (Circus).

3. Click on the **Recording a sentence using certain words** link on the corresponding week. The web browser will show the description for the activity and the three words to be used in the sentence.

4. Click on the **Record** button (the grey circle) on the recorder located at the bottom of the page and start reading the sentence. The recorder will display green bars indicating the input level of the voice being recorded, as shown in the next screenshot:

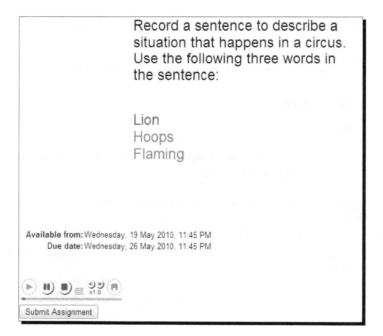

Record a sentence to describe a situation that happens in a circus. Use the following three words in the sentence:

Lion
Hoops
Flaming

Available from: Wednesday, 19 May 2010, 11:45 PM
Due date: Wednesday, 26 May 2010, 11:45 PM

Submit Assignment

 You need a microphone connected to the computer in order to record your voice with the NanoGong recorder.

5. Once you finish reading the sentence, click on the **Stop** button (the grey square). The NanoGong recorder will stop recording your voice.

6. Click on the **Play** button (the grey triangle) on the recorder and check that your voice was recorded as expected.

7. Click on the **Submit Assignment** button below the recorder.

8. Log out and log in with your normal user role. You can check the submitted assignments by clicking on the **Recording a sentence using certain words** link on the corresponding week and then on **View x submitted assignments**. x is the number of assignments submitted so far by the students. Moodle will display the NanoGong recorder for the uploaded recording for each student that submitted this assignment, as shown in the next screenshot:

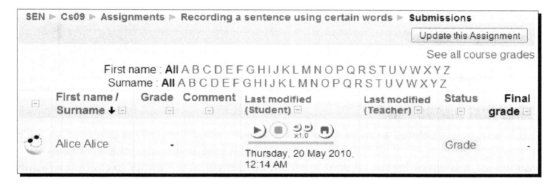

9. You will be able to click on the **Play** button and listen to the recorded sentence without having to leave the web page.

10. Click on **Grade** in the corresponding row on the grid. A feedback window will appear with a text editor, a drop-down list with the possible grades, and the NanoGong recorder. You will be able to click on the **Play** button on this player and listen to the sentence recorded by the student.

11. Select the grade in the **Grade** drop-down list and write any feedback in the text editor, as shown in the next screenshot. Then click on **Save changes**. The final grade will appear in the corresponding cell in the grid.

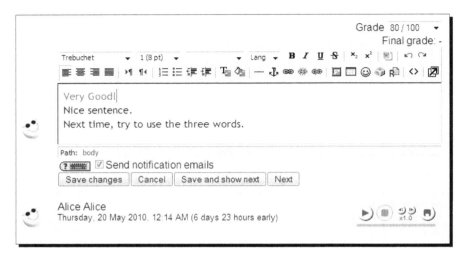

What just happened?

In this activity, we defined a simple list of words and we asked the student to record a simple sentence by using the embedded voice recorder. In this case, as we used the NanoGong assignment, it is easier for the student to record his/her voice. It is easier to check the results for the teacher as well.

Describing spatial relationships between different objects

The circus is a great place to learn about geometry and gravity. A talented juggler was capable of juggling dozens of balls for more than five minutes, a clown on a ball played with an elephant, and an incredible Bengal tiger jumped through a hoop.

Alice wants her father to draw a clown on a ball playing with the elephant. As her father doesn't remember this show, she has to describe the scene to him, including the location of the clown, the ball, and the elephant.

Time for action – creating a scene with a 2D picture related to a geometric shape

We are now going to creating a scene with a clown, an elephant, and a circle.

1. If you haven't already done so, create a new folder in Windows Explorer (C:\Circus).

2. Start Inkscape and minimize it. You will use it later.

3. Start Word 2007. You will be working in a new blank document.

4. Click on **Insert | Clip Art**. The **Clip Art** panel will appear on the right-hand side of the main window.

5. Click on the **Search in** combo box and activate the **Everywhere** checkbox. This way, Word will search for clipart in all the available collections, including the Web Collections.

6. Click on the **Search for** text box and enter Clown.

7. Click on the **Go** button.

8. Position the mouse pointer over the desired clipart's thumbnail. As you want to change the picture size without losing quality using Inkscape, remember to make sure it is a **WMF** or an **EMF** file.

9. Right-click on the desired clipart's thumbnail and select **Preview/Properties** in the context menu that appears. Word will display a new dialog box showing a larger preview of the scalable clipart and a temporary file name.

10. Triple-click on the long path and file name shown after **File**. This way, you will be sure that the temporary file's full path is selected. Then right-click on it and select **Copy** in the context menu that appears.

11. Next, activate Inkscape—remember it was running minimized. You can use *Alt + Tab* or *Windows + Tab*. Don't close the clipart's preview window.

12. Select **File | Import** from the main menu. Click on the **Type a file name button** (the pencil with a paper sheet icon) and paste the previously copied temporary file's full path in the **Location:** text box. The path is going to be similar to C:\Users\vanesa\AppData\Local\Microsoft\Windows\Temporary Internet Files\Content.IE5\R7ZPXDXQ\MCj02792460000[1].wmf.

13. Click on the **Open** button. The previously previewed clipart, the background for our scene, will appear in Inkscape's drawing area.

14. Return to Word 2007, and close the **Preview/Properties** dialog box.

15. Repeat the aforementioned steps (5 to 13) to add an elephant to Inkscape's drawing area. The following screenshot shows possible pictures for a clown and an elephant:

16. Click on the **Create circles, ellipses, and arcs** button (a pink circle) or press *F5*. This function allows you to add circles, ellipses, or arcs with different stroke and fill colors in Inkscape's drawing area.

17. The circle has to be under the clown. Position the mouse pointer on the lower left-hand side corner for the circle and drag the mouse up to the upper right-hand side corner. As we want to create a circle and not an ellipse, hold the *Ctrl* key down in order to maintain a symmetric aspect ratio.

18. Right-click on the desired fill color for the new circle on the colors that appear at the bottom of Inkscape's drawing area and select **Set Fill** from the context menu that appears.

19. Next, click on the **Select and transform objects** button (the first button, a black arrow) or press *F1*. This function allows you to select and move objects.

20. Position the clown on the circle and the elephant on the right-hand side, as shown in the next image:

21. Select **File | Save** from Inkscape's main menu. Save the file as `image090201.svg` in the previously created folder, `C:\Circus`.

22. Select **File | Export Bitmap**. A dialog box showing many export options will appear. Click on the **Drawing** button, enter `780` on the **Width** textbox and then click on **Export**. Inkscape will export the recently imported clipart in PNG format. The exported bitmap graphics file will be `C:\Circus\image090201.png`.

What just happened?

We created a representation of a scene on the circus using Inkscape, scalable vector clipart, and a geometric shape (a circle). We now have a clown on a ball (a circle) and an elephant on the right-hand side. Finally, we exported the resulting image to the PNG format.

Time for action – uploading the scene to Moodle

We now have to upload the previously exported bitmap image to add our exercise to an existing Moodle course.

1. Log in to your Moodle server.

2. Click on the desired course name (`Circus`). You can create a new course or use an existing one.

3. As previously learned, follow the necessary steps to edit the summary for a desired week. Enter `Exercise 2` in the **Summary** textbox and save the changes.

4. Click on the **Add an activity** combo box for the selected week and choose **Journal.**

5. Enter `Describing spatial relationships between objects` in **Journal name**.

6. Select `Verdana` in font and `5 (18)` in size—the first two combo boxes below **Journal question**. Then select your desired color for the text.

7. Click on the big text box below **Journal question** and enter:
   - `Describe the clown's location.`
   - `Describe the elephant's location.`

8. Press *Enter* and click on the **Insert Image** button (a mountain). A new web page will appear displaying the title **Insert image**.

9. Follow the necessary steps to create a new folder, `chapter 09`. Then click on the `chapter09` folder link and then click on the **Browse** button. Browse to the folder that holds the exported drawing and select the file to upload, `image090201.png`. Then click on **Open** and on the **Upload** button. The label **File uploaded successfully** will appear inside the **File browser** box.

10. Next, click on the name of the recently uploaded file, `image090201.png`. The image will appear in the **Preview** box.

11. Enter `clownandelephant` in **Alternate text** and click on **OK**. The image will appear below the previously entered title. Remember that you can click on the **Enlarge editor** button to view more information on the screen, as shown in the next screenshot.

12. Select 100 in the **Grade** combo box.

13. Finally, scroll down and select **Save and return to course**.

What just happened?

We added the describing spatial relationships between objects exercise to a Moodle course. The students are now going to be able to answer the two questions included in the journal entry with the image of the scene.

The journal allowed us to combine an image with two simple questions and it is going to enable the students to write the answers for these questions.

 In this case, the activity includes two simple questions. However, if you wanted the student to record his/her voice with the answer, it would be necessary to write different instructions and to use a NanoGong assignment or an advanced upload of files in combination with Audacity.

Time for action – writing sentences to describe the spatial relationships

Its now time to help Alice write the answers for the two questions.

1. Log in to your Moodle server using a user with the student role.

2. Click on the course name (Circus).

3. Click on the **Describing spatial relationships between objects** link on the corresponding week. The web browser will show the two questions and the scene with the clown, the circle, and the elephant.

4. Click on the **Start or edit my journal entry** button. Moodle will display a big text area with an HTML editor.

5. Select Verdana in font and 5 (18) in size.

6. Write an answer for the first question, describing the spatial relationship between the clown and the blue ball, 1. The clown is on the blue ball.

7. Then write an answer for the second question, describing the spatial relationship between the elephant and the blue ball, `2. The elephant is next to the blue ball.` as shown in the next screenshot:

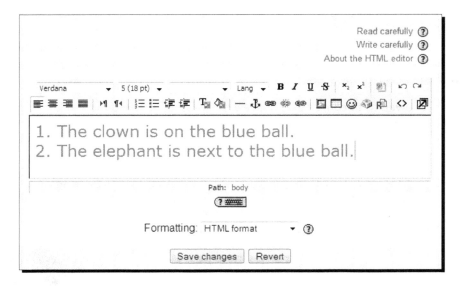

8. Click on the **Save changes** button. This way, Moodle will save the two answers for this exercise.

9. Log out and log in with your normal user and role. Don't forget to check the results for this exercise as previously learned.

What just happened?

In this activity, we mixed scalable vector clipart with a geometric shape. The child has to understand the spatial relationships between different elements and describe them in simple sentences. The child can work alone, with the help of a therapist or a family member, so that he/she can understand and run the exercise.

The child has to describe the relative location of each object. He/She has to focus on understanding the different elements that compose the scene and he/she must use his/her language skills to write each sentence.

We can increase the complexity of this exercise using more elements and many geometric shapes.

Pop quiz – working with audio

1. Audacity allows you to:
    a. Record audio from a microphone connected to the computer
    b. Take rectangular snapshots
    c. Import and manipulate Word scalable vector cliparts

2. Inkscape allows you to:
    a. Import Word scalable vector clipart but you cannot draw geometric shapes
    b. Draw ellipses, but it is really difficult to draw circles
    c. Draw circles, ellipses, and arcs

3. When you upload a scene created with Inkscape to a journal in Moodle:
    a. You can export it to the compatible EMF format
    b. You can export it to the compatible WMF format
    c. You can export it to the compatible PNG format

4. When you create a NanoGong assignment in Moodle:
    a. Students can record videos with their Webcams
    b. Students can record their voice with the answers
    c. Students can record their keystrokes

5. If you want to save recorded audio as an MP3 file with Audacity:
    a. It is necessary to activate the LAME MP3 encoder checkbox in one of the steps of its installation wizard
    b. It is necessary to download the WMF encoder
    c. It is necessary to download the LAME MP3 encoder

Summary

In this chapter, have learned how to:

- Prepare exercises that motivate children to write guided sentences and paragraphs
- Create a list of words related to a scene in a circus and work with specialized software, Audacity, to allow the students to upload an audio file with their sentences
- Create new NanoGong assignments to allow students to record their voice with the answers without requiring the installation of additional software on their computers
- Create a scene and combine it with questions to motivate the students to describe spatial relationships between pictures and geometric shapes

Now that we have learned how to create exercises to write guided sentences and paragraphs, we're ready to use Moodle to run cognitive evaluation tests, which is the topic of the next chapter.

10 Running Cognitive Evaluation Tests

We can use Moodle as a platform to run simple cognitive evaluation tests. We can combine rich activities with additional tools to provide a natural way of solving tests by using video and audio recordings. This way, it is possible to evaluate different aspects of children's comprehension levels and to create exercises to help them improve their skills according to the results.

In this chapter, Alice stays at home. We will learn how to create simple test that are related to activities at home. Reading it and following the exercises we shall:

◆ Prepare exercises to test simple and complex instructions

◆ Learn how to work with a Webcam to record the results of executing an exercise

◆ Organize text and pictures to help the students to understand simple and complex instructions

◆ Prepare exercises to test the comprehension of situations

◆ Learn to use and analyze audio resources to judge causality, functionality, origin, purpose, and creativity with very simple activities

◆ Work with different multimedia resources to motivate students to provide the necessary feedback in tests that are normally boring

Working with simple and complex instructions

Alice loves flowers, and therefore, her father brings her fresh flowers each Friday. She has many nice flower vases and she enjoys taking care of the flowers. She is extremely careful when she changes the water from the flower vases because her little brother Kevin could slip on a wet floor.

Flowers and their related household items are also useful to test the comprehension of simple and complex instructions.

Time for action – generating pictures to prepare the instructions

We are first going to search for existing 2D clipart related to the different elements mentioned in each step. We will then convert them to 2D bitmap images using our well-known Snipping Tool.

1. Create a new folder in Windows Explorer (C:\Home).

2. Open your default web browser and go to http://office.microsoft.com/en-us/clipart/default.aspx. This web page allows us to search for free clipart in **Office Online Clip Art & Media**.

3. Enter vases in the textbox and click on the **Search** button. The available clipart thumbnails related to the entered keyword will appear.

4. Click on the zoom icon located below the desired clipart thumbnail. A new window displaying a small preview of the clipart will appear.

5. Click on **Bigger preview** and this label will change to **Smaller preview**. We want to use the big preview to take snapshots of the clipart images using the same size.

6. Use Snipping Tool to take a snapshot of the clipart preview and save the file as image100101.png in the previously created folder, C:\Home.

7. Next, go back to the web browser and repeat the aforementioned steps (3 to 6) to capture the bitmap images of another clipart. In this case, repeat those steps searching for the following things and saving the image files with the names as shown in the next table. The next screenshot shows four images representing different elements of the simple instructions that we are going to create.

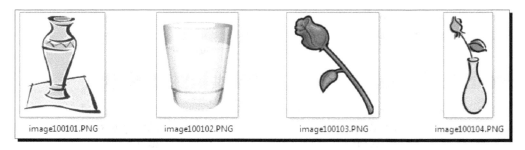

image100101.PNG   image100102.PNG   image100103.PNG   image100104.PNG

Search for	Picture file name
Water	Image100102.png
Rose	Image100103.png
Roses	Image100104.png

What just happened?

We searched for clipart previews in Office Online Clip Art & Media, through our web browser. Instead of working with Inkscape, this time we used the Snipping Tool application to capture the portion of the screen that showed the desired clipart's preview. This way, we could save the necessary images in the PNG format following just a few simple steps.

We now have the following four bitmap graphics ready to be used in our simple and complex instructions exercise:

◆ Image100101.png: A flower vase

◆ Image100102.png: A glass of water

◆ Image100103.png: A rose

◆ Image100104.png: A rose in a flower vase

Time for action – using pictures to prepare the instructions

We are now going to prepare the instructions to test the students' skills in following simple instructions.

1. Log in to your Moodle server.

2. Click on the desired course name (Home). As previously learned, follow the necessary steps to edit the summary for a desired week. Enter Exercise 1 in the **Summary** textbox and save the changes.

3. Click on the **Add an activity** combo box for the selected week and choose **Upload a single file**.

4. Enter Testing simple instructions in **Assignment name**.

5. Select Verdana in font and 4 (14) in size—the first two combo boxes below **Description**.

6. Click on the **Font Color** button (a **T** with six color boxes) and select your desired color for the text.

7. Click on the big text box below **Description** and enter the description of the student's goal for this exercise. Upload and insert the corresponding picture for each of the elements that have a bitmap representation. Include these pictures enclosed in parentheses after their name appears in each sentence. Resize each clipart image as shown in the next screenshot. Remember that you can use the enlarged editor window. Select a bigger font and a different color for each step number.

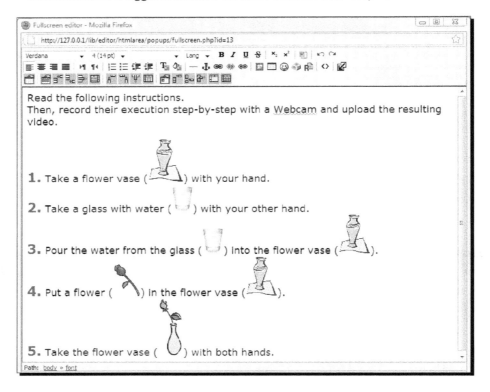

8. Select 10MB in **Maximum size**. This is the maximum size for the video file that each student is going to be able to upload for this activity. However, it is very important to check the possibilities offered by your Moodle server with its Moodle administrator.

9. Close the enlarged editor's window, scroll down, and click on the **Save and display** button. The web browser will show the description for the upload a single file activity.

What just happened?

We added an upload a single file activity to a Moodle course that will allow a student to read, understand, and follow the explained instructions, record the results using a Webcam, and then upload the video to Moodle.

We added pictures of the different elements that appear in each step. This way, it is going to be easier to understand the instructions. Additionally, we used the editor features to resize the uploaded and inserted pictures.

Time for action – using a Webcam to record the results of executing the exercise

It is time to help Alice use a Webcam to solve this exercise.

1. Log in to your Moodle server using a user with the student role.

2. Click on the course name (Home).

3. Click on the **Testing simple instructions** link on the corresponding week. The web browser will show the description for the activity, including the five steps to record with the Webcam. The next screenshot shows the page that appears displaying the text **Upload a file** and two buttons, **Browse** and **Upload this file**, located at the bottom.

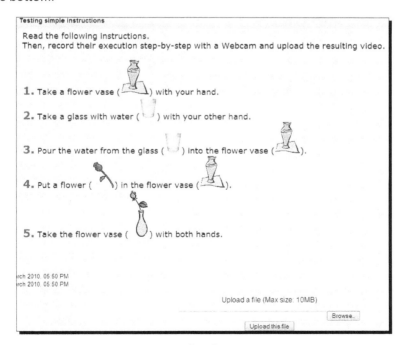

4. Start the software that allows you to record videos with your Webcam. This software could vary according to the Webcam manufacturer.

5. Start recording a video with a 640 x 480 resolution in any of the following video formats supported by Moodle and follow the instructions, as shown in the next screenshot:

   ❑ AVI

   ❑ FLV

   ❑ MPG

   ❑ MOV

   ❑ WMV

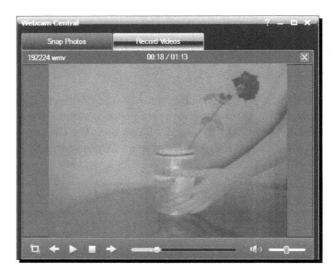

6. Once you finish recording the execution of the instructions, go back to your web browser and click on **Browse**. Browse to the folder where you saved the video file, select it, and click on **Open**. Then click on **Upload this file** to upload the video file to the Moodle server. A **File uploaded successfully** message such as the one shown in the next screenshot will appear if the video file is uploaded without any problems. Then click on **Continue**.

7. Next, the previously uploaded video file will appear below the instructions, as shown in the following screenshot with the name **192224.wmv**:

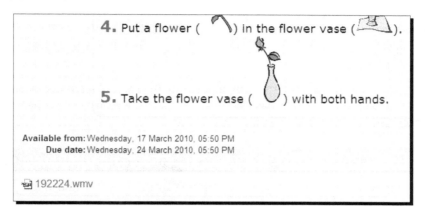

4. Put a flower ( ) in the flower vase ( ).

5. Take the flower vase ( ) with both hands.

Available from: Wednesday, 17 March 2010, 05:50 PM
Due date: Wednesday, 24 March 2010, 05:50 PM

192224.wmv

8. Finally, you will be able to watch the recorded and uploaded video by clicking on the link that appears at the bottom of the page. You are going to be able to download and watch the video with Windows Media Player, VLC Media Player, or any other video player software, as shown in the next screenshot.

What just happened?

In this activity, we defined a simple list of instructions with text and pictures. The child has to read and understand the instructions with the help of a therapist or a family member. Then he/she has to perform the simple instructions and record a video with the results. In this case, each step represents a single instruction, and therefore we are testing the execution of simple instructions.

The Webcam allows us to visualize the time needed to execute the instructions and to determine whether the child can understand each step. This way, we can prepare additional exercises according to the results obtained in this test.

Have a go hero – testing the execution of complex instructions

Create a new upload a single file exercise to test the execution of the following complex instructions:

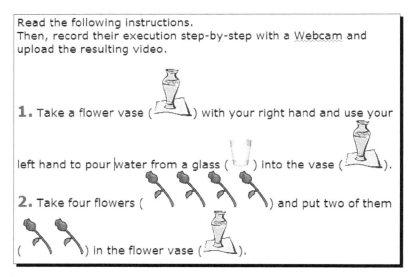

Record an audio file for each step and upload it to allow the student to listen to the instructions instead of reading them.

In this new activity, there is a complex list of instructions with text, pictures, and audio. The child can read or listen to each complex instruction with the help of a therapist or a family member. Then he/she has to perform the complex instructions and record a video with the results. In this case, each step represents a complex instruction because it combines two or more actions, and therefore we are testing the execution of complex instructions.

Testing the comprehension of different situations

Alice likes scrambled eggs for breakfast. However, Kevin doesn't like eggs at all. Children usually find it easy to explain situations that happen in the kitchen. Thus, it is possible to ask them questions about chefs.

Time for action – generating a questionnaire related to a situation

We are first going to search for existing 2D clipart to represent a situation and we are then going to record each query of a questionnaire.

1. Open your default web browser and go to `http://office.microsoft.com/en-us/clipart/default.aspx`. This web page allows us to search for free clipart in **Office Online Clip Art & Media**.

2. Enter `cooker` in the textbox and click on the **Search** button. The available clipart thumbnails related to the entered keyword will appear.

3. Preview the desired clipart of a chef cooking eggs and use Snipping Tool to take a snapshot of the clipart preview and save the file as `image100201.png` in the previously created folder, `C:\Home`. The following image shows an example of one suitable clipart image:

4. Log in to your Moodle server.

5. Click on the desired course name (`Home`). As previously learned, follow the necessary steps to edit the summary for a desired week. Enter `Exercise 2` in the **Summary** textbox and save the changes.

6. Click on the **Add an activity** combo box for the selected week and choose **Upload a single file**.

7. Enter `Testing the comprehension of different situations` in **Assignment name**.

8. Select `Verdana` in font and `4 (14)` in size—the first two combo boxes below **Description**.

9. Click on the **Font Color** button (a **T** with six color boxes) and select your desired color for the text.

10. Click on the big text box below **Description**, insert the previously created bitmap file, `image100201.png`, and enter the questions as seen in the next screenshot. Remember that you can use the enlarged editor window. Select a bigger font and a different color for each step number, as shown in the next screenshot:

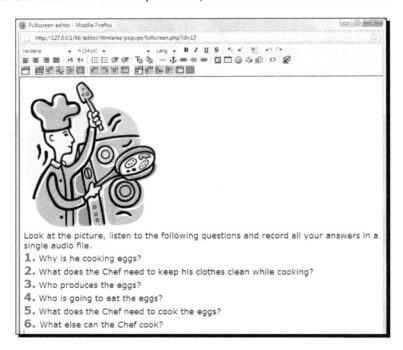

11. Next, use Audacity or any other audio recording software to record each question and save it as an MP3 file, using the file names shown in the next table.

Question #	Audio file name
1	question100201.mp3
2	question100202.mp3
3	question100203.mp3
4	question100204.mp3
5	question100205.mp3
6	question100206.mp3

12. Insert a web link to the appropriate MP3 file for each question. This way, the student is going to be able to reproduce the audio for each question by pressing the play button on each embedded audio player.

13. Select 10MB in **Maximum size**. This is the maximum size for the video file that each student is going to be able to upload as a result for this activity. However, it is very important to check the possibilities offered by your Moodle server with its Moodle administrator.

14. Close the enlarged editor's window, scroll down, and click on the **Save and display** button. The web browser will show the description for the upload a single file activity.

What just happened?

We added an upload a single file activity to a Moodle course that will allow a student to read, understand, and listen to six questions. Then he/she will be able to record the answers for these questions by using a Webcam or a microphone, and upload the resulting video or audio file to Moodle.

We added a picture of a simple situation about a chef cooking eggs and we took advantage of the embedded audio players provided by the Moodle multimedia plugin. This way, it is going to be simple for the students to listen to each question.

Time for action – recording the answers

We already learned about Audacity 1.2 in the previous chapter. We will now help Alice to record her voice with the answers for the six questions by using Audacity features.

1. Log in to your Moodle server with the student role.

2. Click on the course name (Home).

3. Click on the **Testing the comprehension of different situations** link on the corresponding week. The web browser will show the description for the activity and the six questions to be answered, accompanied by the embedded audio player, as shown in the next screenshot:

Look at the picture, listen to the following questions and record all your answers in a single audio file.

1. Why is he cooking eggs?
2. What does the Chef need to keep his clothes clean while cooking?
3. Who produces the eggs?
4. Who is going to eat the eggs?
5. What does the Chef need to cook the eggs?
6. What else can the Chef cook?

4. Start Audacity. Resize and move its window in order to be able to see the questions. You can click on the play button for each question while you are recording your voice with Audacity.

5. Click on the **Record** button (the red circle) and start reading the sentence. Audacity will display the waveform of the audio track being recorded.

6. Listen to the different questions and answer them.

7. Once you finish answering the questions, click on the **Stop** button (the yellow square). Audacity will stop recording your voice.

8. Select **File | Export As MP3** from Audacity's main menu. Save the MP3 audio file as `myanswers.mp3` in your documents folder.

9. Next, go back to your web browser with the Moodle activity. Click on **Browse**. Browse to the folder where you saved the audio file, your documents folder, select it, and click on **Open**. Then click on **Upload this file** and the video file will be uploaded to the Moodle server. A **File uploaded successfully** message will appear if the audio file could finish the upload process without problems. Click on **Continue**.

10. The previously uploaded audio file will now appear below the questions, as shown in the next screenshot with the name **myanswers.mp3**:

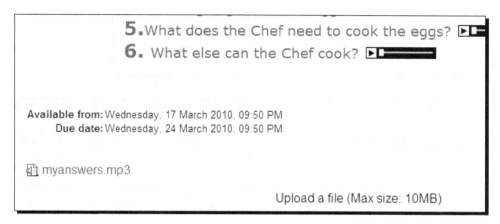

11. Finally, you will be able to listen to the recorded and uploaded audio by clicking on the link that appears at the bottom of the page. You are going to be able to download and listen to the answers with Windows Media Player, VLC Media Player, or any other audio player software, as shown in the next screenshot.

What just happened?

In this activity, we used a picture that represents a specific situation, a chef cooking eggs. The six questions allow us to evaluate the way the child understands a situation. Each question evaluates one aspect, as summarized in the following table:

Question	Aspect being judged
Why is he cooking eggs?	Causality
What does the Chef need to keep his clothes clean while cooking?	Functionality
Who produces the eggs?	Origin
Who is going to eat the eggs?	Purpose
What does the Chef need to cook the eggs?	Functionality
What else can the Chef cook?	Creativity

Pop quiz – uploading files

1. An upload a single file activity in Moodle allows you to:

    a. Define the maximum upload size

    b. Define the maximum number of files to upload

    c. Define the list of the file formats that can be uploaded

2. When you create an upload a single file activity:

    a. You cannot add a description

    b. You can add a description with text and images and other HTML resources

    c. You can add a description with plain text, without HTML resources

3. When you want to record video:

    a. You can use the application provided by the Webcam manufacturer

    b. You can use the special button included in a Moodle upload a single file activity

    c. You can use the embedded recorder included in a Moodle upload a single file activity

Summary

In this chapter, we have learned how to:

- ◆ Prepare exercises to test the comprehension level of simple and complex instructions
- ◆ Create an upload a single file activity with simple instructions by combining text and pictures
- ◆ Test the possibilities offered by a Webcam to generate a natural and appropriate feedback
- ◆ Create a questionnaire related to a typical situation that happens in the kitchen, at home
- ◆ Add audio resources to let the students listen to each question and to record their answers
- ◆ Evaluate many simple cognitive aspects

Now that we have learned how to create dozens of different rich exercises combining many different tools with Moodle, we're ready to use Moodle to help special education children. Their feedback is a great motivation to create the most exciting exercises.

Pop Quiz Answers

Chapter 1—Matching Pictures.

1	a
2	c
3	b
4	a
5	c
6	a
7	c

Chapter 2—Working with Abstraction and Sequencing Disabilities.

1	a
2	c
3	a
4	c
5	b

Chapter 3—Associating Images with Words.

1	a
2	b
3	c
4	c
5	a

Chapter 4—Developing Sorting Activities, Mixing Shapes and Pictures.

1	c
2	a
3	c
4	b
5	b
6	b

Chapter 5—Creating Exercises for Improving Short-term Memory.

1	c
2	a
3	a
4	b
5	a

Chapter 6— Reducing Attention Deficit Disorder Using Great Concentration Exercises.

1	a
2	c
3	a
4	c
5	b

Chapter 7— Playing with Mathematical Operations.

1	b
2	a
3	b
4	c
5	b

Chapter 8—Mental Operations with Language.

1	a
2	b
3	b
4	a
5	c

Chapter 9—Writing Guided Sentences and Paragraphs.

1	a
2	c
3	c
4	b
5	c

Chapter 10— Running Cognitive Evaluation Tests

1	a
2	b
3	a

Index

D

describing spatial relationships between objects exercise
    about 270
    adding, to Moodle course 273, 274
    sentences, writing 275, 276
    stage, mounting with 2D picture 271-273
digital pen
    as classic mouse 58
    used, for solving drawing exercise 58, 59
discovering sentences exercise
    3D models, combining in Inkscape's drawing
        area 35-38
    3D models, creating 35
    3D models, rendering 35
    about 35
    adding, to Moodle course 43, 44
    composite 3D models, organizing into rendered
        2D box 39
    files, organizing 45
    running 45, 46
    solving, gamepad used 47-50
    text block colors, changing 40-42
    text blocks, creating 40-42
drawing exercise
    about 51
    adding, to Moodle course 55-57
    solving, digital pen used 58, 59
    solving, with tracing drawings 61, 62
    speech bubbles, creating 52-54
dynamic HTML color-code chart
    using 22

E

Edraw Max 5.1
    downloading 126
    installing 126
EMF (Enhanced Meta-File) 11
exchange puzzle exercise
    about 174
    adding, to Moodle course 180, 181
    creating, based on vector graphics 187
    exchange puzzle, generating 176-179

high definition photos, selecting 174, 175
    running 182, 183
    solving, gamepad used 182, 183
    solving, multi-touch device used 184-187

F

finding the matching pairs exercise
    about 143
    adding, to Moodle course 156, 157
    animated virtual cards, generating 144-147
    JClic module, installing 154
    running 157, 158
    sounds, adding 159
    virtual cards, organizing 148-153
Flash Video (FLV) 164
Freesound Project website 98

G

gamepad
    about 50
    as input device 50, 51
    discovering sentences exercise, solving 47-49
    using, in matching composite pictures
        exercise 51
gamepad driver
    configuring 47
GIMP 2.6.8
    downloading 241
    installing 241
Google 3D warehouse 35, 38

H

Hot Potatoes 6.3
    download link 19
    installing 19
    JMatch 19
    sentences, preparing for matching
        exercise 19, 20
HTML color picker
    using 22
HTML tags
    using, for background colors 27
    using, for defining colors and fonts 22

I

images
preparing, for Boolean multiple choice exercise 84-86
Inkscape
2D scalable cliparts, combining 10-14
2D scalable cliparts, editing 16-18
download link 8
installing 9
instructions
preparing, for painting exercise 78-80
instructions tests exercise
about 279
complex instructions execution, testing 286
complex instruction test, working with 279
pictures, generating 280, 281
pictures, using 281, 282
results recording, webcam used 283
results recording, webcam used 284, 285
simple instruction test, working with 279

J

JClic
integrating, with Moodle 154
JClic Author 0.2.0.5 234
downloading 144
installing 144
JClic module 154
JCloze 69, 73
JCloze exercise. *See* **rich cloze exercise**
JMatch 19
JMix 132
JQuiz 40

L

LAME MP3 encoder
downloading 257

M

matching composite pictures exercise
adding, to, Moodle course 28-31

composite pictures, adding with different sizes 24-27
running 32, 34
sentences, preparing 19, 20
Microsoft Office 2007
download link 8
installing 9
Microsoft PowerPoint 2007 160
Moodle
JClic, integrating 154
3D scenes related sentences, discovering 35
illustration, drawing according to speech bubbles 51
NanoGong assignment, creating 265-267
Moodle NanoGong assignment, installing 263, 264
Moodle course
finding the matching pairs exercise, adding 156, 157
arranging the color sequence exercise, adding 249
arranging the visual sequence exercise, adding 237, 238
discovering sentences exercise, adding 43, 44
drawing exercise, adding 55-57
exchange puzzle exercise, adding 180, 181
matching composite pictures exercise, adding 28-31
putting words inside an image with structure exercise, adding 111
visual mathematical operations exercise, adding 223
word search puzzle exercise, adding 194, 195
writing sentences using two images exercise, adding 103
ordering the temporary sequence exercise, adding 122, 123
painting exercise, adding 80, 81
rich building a pyramid exercise, adding 134
rich cloze exercise, adding 72, 74
working with a list of words organized in rows exercise, adding 165, 166
multiple files
uploading, in ZIP folder 32
multi-touch screen
using, for executing rich building a pyramid exercise 138

N

NanoGong assignment
creating 265-267
installing 263, 264
NanoGong recorder
sentence, recording 268, 269

O

ordering the temporary sequence exercise
about 118
adding, to Moodle course 122, 123
images, organizing for mixed temporary
  sequence 120, 121
mixed temporary sequence, creating 120, 121
running 124, 125
three bitmap graphics, searching 118, 119

P

Paint 78
painting exercise
about 76
adding, to Moodle course 80, 81
background drawing, digital pen used 76, 77
creating 76
executing 81, 82
instructions, preparing 78-80
silhouettes, painting 83
Tux Paint, using 84
PNG 18
**putting words inside an image with structure
  exercise**
about 105
adding, to Moodle course 111
floating labels, adding to image 108
pictures, dragging and dropping into scene 115
running, netbook touchpad used 112, 113
scene, creating 105, 107
scene, uploading to Moodle 109-111

R

rich building a pyramid exercise
about 126
adding, to Moodle course 134
complex pyramid, creating 139

executing, multi-touch screen used 138
images, organizing 131-133
pyramid, building 126-130
running 135, 136
rich cloze exercise
2D clipart of animals and nature, converting 66
2D clipart of animals and nature, searching
  66-69
adding, to Moodle course 72, 74
creating 66
executing 74
images, organizing 69-72
sentences, preparing 69-72

S

sentence creating exercise
creating 255
images, working with 263
NanoGong assignment, creating 265-267
NanoGong assignment, installing 263
results, discussing in forums 263
sentence, recording 257-262
sentence, recording with NanoGong recorder
  268, 269
sentence, writing 257-262
words, preparing 256
words, selecting 256
sentences
preparing, for matching composite pictures
  exercise 19, 20
silhouettes
painting 83
Snipping Tool 69
about 69
speech bubbles
creating 52-54
text, entering 52-54

T

text blocks
colors, changing 40-42
creating 40-42
tools, for 2D scalable clipart manipulation
Inkscape 8
installing 8-10
Microsoft Office 2007 8

Thank you for buying
Moodle 1.9 for Teaching Special Education Children
(5-10 Year Olds): Beginner's Guide

About Packt Publishing

Packt, pronounced 'packed', published its first book "*Mastering phpMyAdmin for Effective MySQL Management*" in April 2004 and subsequently continued to specialize in publishing highly focused books on specific technologies and solutions.

Our books and publications share the experiences of your fellow IT professionals in adapting and customizing today's systems, applications, and frameworks. Our solution based books give you the knowledge and power to customize the software and technologies you're using to get the job done. Packt books are more specific and less general than the IT books you have seen in the past. Our unique business model allows us to bring you more focused information, giving you more of what you need to know, and less of what you don't.

Packt is a modern, yet unique publishing company, which focuses on producing quality, cutting-edge books for communities of developers, administrators, and newbies alike. For more information, please visit our website: www.packtpub.com.

About Packt Open Source

In 2010, Packt launched two new brands, Packt Open Source and Packt Enterprise, in order to continue its focus on specialization. This book is part of the Packt Open Source brand, home to books published on software built around Open Source licences, and offering information to anybody from advanced developers to budding web designers. The Open Source brand also runs Packt's Open Source Royalty Scheme, by which Packt gives a royalty to each Open Source project about whose software a book is sold.

Writing for Packt

We welcome all inquiries from people who are interested in authoring. Book proposals should be sent to author@packtpub.com. If your book idea is still at an early stage and you would like to discuss it first before writing a formal book proposal, contact us; one of our commissioning editors will get in touch with you.

We're not just looking for published authors; if you have strong technical skills but no writing experience, our experienced editors can help you develop a writing career, or simply get some additional reward for your expertise.

Moodle 1.9 for Teaching 7-14 Year Olds: Beginner's Guide

ISBN: 978-1-847197-14-6   Paperback: 236 pages

Effective e-learning for younger students using Moodle as your Classroom Assistant

1. Focus on the unique needs of young learners to create a fun, interesting, interactive, and informative learning environment your students will want to go on day after day

2. Engage and motivate your students with games, quizzes, movies, and podcasts the whole class can participate in

3. Go paperless! Put your lessons online and grade them anywhere, anytime

Moodle 1.9 Teaching Techniques

ISBN: 978-1-849510-06-6   Paperback: 216 pages

Creative ways to build powerful and effective online courses

1. Motivate students from all backgrounds, generations, and learning styles

2. When and how to apply the different learning solutions with workarounds, providing alternative solutions

3. Easy-to-follow, step-by-step instructions with screenshots and examples for Moodle's powerful features

4. Especially suitable for university and professional teachers

Please check **www.PacktPub.com** for information on our titles

Moodle 1.9 E-Learning Course Development

ISBN: 978-1-847193-53-7   Paperback: 384 pages

A complete guide to successful learning
using Moodle

1. Updated for Moodle version 1.9

2. Straightforward coverage of installing and using the Moodle system

3. Working with Moodle features in all learning environments

4. A unique course-based approach focuses your attention on designing well-structured, interactive, and successful courses

Moodle 1.9 for Second Language Teaching

ISBN: 978-1-847196-24-8   Paperback: 524 pages

Engaging online language learning activities using the Moodle platform

1. A recipe book for creating language activities using Moodle 1.9

2. Get the most out of Moodle 1.9's features to create enjoyable, useful language learning activities

3. Create an online language learning centre that includes reading, writing, speaking, listening, vocabulary, and grammar activities

4. Enhance your activities to make them visually attractive, and make the most of audio and video activities

Please check **www.PacktPub.com** for information on our titles

www.ingramcontent.com/pod-product-compliance
Lightning Source LLC
Chambersburg PA
CBHW062105050326
40690CB00016B/3206